William
Wilberforce

To my mum, another Hull luminary,
because she asked so often

William Wilberforce

a biography

Stephen Tomkins

A Lion Book
an imprint of
Lion Hudson plc
Mayfield House, 256 Banbury Road,
Oxford OX2 7DH, England
www.lionhudson.com
ISBN 978 0 7459 5232 1

First edition 2007
10 9 8 7 6 5 4 3 2

A catalogue record for this book is
available from the British Library

Typeset in 11/14pt Italian Garamond
Printed and bound in Malta
by Gutenberg Press

The text paper used in this book has
been made from wood independently
certified as having come from
sustainable forests

ture Acknowledgments
;e 6: Wilberforce – Anti-Slavery
;rnational

rage 6: Clarkson – Topham/Fotomas
topfoto.co.uk

Page 6: Equiano – HIP/British Library
topfoto.co.uk

The following pictures are located
between pages 119 and 120 in the book:

Page I: John Newton –
TopFoto/Fotomas topfoto.co.uk

Page I: William Pitt – Topham
Picturepoint topfoto.co.uk

Page I: The *Brookes* – Topham
Picturepoint topfoto.co.uk

Page I: Africans in the hold of a slave
ship – Topham Picturepoint
topfoto.co.uk

Page II: The House of Commons – The
National Portrait Gallery, London.

Page II: William Blake engraving –
HIP/British Library topfoto.co.uk

Page II: Medallion – The Trustees of
the British Museum

Contents

Right: William Wilberforce

Bottom left: Thomas Clarkson

Bottom right: Olaudah Equiano

Olaudah Equiano

or

1

The Journey

It is the middle of the eighteenth century and a ten-year-old boy is playing with his sister. Their family is a wealthy and influential one, but the grown-ups are all out on business, and the pair of them are alone in the house.

And then they are not alone. Two men and a woman have climbed over the wall into the yard, and they grab the children, covering their mouths before they can scream, and drag them out into the woods. They are tied up, gagged and carried off, the boy in a bag. Two mornings later the girl is sold, torn from her brother's arms as they sleep. This is the cruellest loss of all for him, and for days he eats nothing but what his captors force into his mouth to keep him in saleable condition. He is sold and continues to change hands over many miles and for many months.

The boy is from what is now Nigeria, and his name is Olaudah Equiano. So far his experiences are little different from those of countless others who have been kidnapped as slaves by raiders or neighbouring tribes. But then he reaches the coast.

Equiano has never seen the sea before, and finds the sight frightening in itself, even before he is taken onto the ship. There he is met by the terrifying scene of countless miserable chained men, a furnace of boiling copper, and long-haired white-skinned spirits – whom he assumes are planning to eat their prey – presiding over the hellish vessel. He is shut up below deck with as many men as can be chained shoulder to shoulder in the space. For all the incomprehensible horror of what is happening, he is curious to know how the ship works and is disappointed not to see it set off. Being a child, he is not shackled with the men, who are allotted around 16 inches' breadth and in many cases lie under shelves 2 feet high.

What strikes him most is the smell. Large conical tubs serve as toilets for those who can reach them – children often fall in – and for those who cannot there is the floor where they lie. In the close quarters and intense heat, the toxic stench is unbearable. Even before they set sail, Equiano falls ill, and many die in the course of the journey. 'The shrieks of the women,' as he recalls in later life, 'and the groans of the dying, rendered the whole a scene of horror almost inconceivable.'[1]

Equiano feels too sick and miserable to eat, but the sailors have the financial sense not to let any slaves starve themselves, and whip him until he eats. Slaves take whatever opportunity arises on the journey to kill themselves. They are allowed on the top deck every day to get air, and though it is sturdily fenced all around for just this reason, three slaves manage to break through. Two of them – being chained together – successfully drown themselves, but the third is retrieved and the sailors flog him severely, 'for thus attempting to prefer death to slavery'.[2]

The journey to Barbados takes a couple of months, and from here Equiano is taken to North America, where he is eventually sold for £30 or £40 to an English naval officer and – having already had his name changed to Michael and then Jacob – renamed, for no obvious reason, Gustavus Vasa.

He survives to publish his autobiography thirty-five years later, thus emerging into history out of a million or two unknown Africans who lost their freedom, their names, their families and, more often than not, their lives to put affordable sugar onto the tables of British homes. *

William Wilberforce was about the same age as Equiano when he was separated from his home and family. In every other way, his privileged life and prospects were immeasurably distant from Equiano's; but it cannot have been a very happy journey, and it was the watershed of his earlier years.

William was born on 24 August 1759 and spent his first ten years in the family home on the high street of Hull, which was also a thriving business premises. His grandfather, also William Wilberforce, had started the trading concern and twice been mayor of the city, and was still an alderman in William's first decade. William's father Robert was a partner in the business.

---

* There are question marks over Equiano's account – there is some evidence he was actually born in North Carolina. If the account is true, it is an invaluable first-hand account of the 'Middle Passage'; if false, it is an imaginative reconstruction of well established facts.

Such trade had made Hull the fourth largest port in England. There were traders there who brought tobacco into the country from the slave farms of North America, but, being on the east coast, most tended to leave that to the larger ports of Liverpool, Bristol and London, cities that had grown fat on the proceeds. Instead Robert Wilberforce and his colleagues imported timber and iron from the Baltic.

Robert and his wife Elizabeth had three children besides William – all daughters – but only one of the girls, Sarah, survived infancy, and William himself was a weak, sickly child, small and with poor eyesight. In later life he often reflected with gratitude that if he had been born in what he was pleased to call 'less civilized times', his parents would not have taken the trouble to keep him alive.

William started at Hull Grammar School at the age of seven, walking three miles there each day with his satchel. The school, which was established in 1330 (and closed in 2005), had once had the poet Andrew Marvell as its headmaster, and was now overseen by Joseph Milner, with his young brother Isaac – later to be a great Cambridge mathematician – teaching the young ones like William. According to Isaac's recollections, they saw William's promise from the start: 'Even then his elocution was so remarkable, that we used to set him upon a table and make him read aloud as an example to the other boys.'[3] How well this endeared him to the other children we are not told. Wilberforce's own recollection was of being forced to stand up on the desk to read because he was so short.

All this changed when William was ten. His father died, and Elizabeth's response was to send William to live with Robert's childless brother – yet another William Wilberforce – and his wife Hannah, 200 miles away in Wimbolton or, as it is now called, Wimbledon. Though today it has long been engulfed within Greater London, Wimbledon in the eighteenth century was a Surrey village, four miles outside the expanding urban sprawl. William's uncle owned a villa beside Wimbledon Common, as well as a Mayfair townhouse. So in addition to the wrench of being taken from his family, friends, school and home, William exchanged being at the centre of a busy city for country life. He went as a boarder to a school in nearby Putney which fell well below the standards of the Milner brothers. 'They taught everything and nothing,' Wilberforce said in retrospect.

Sending a boy off to a surrogate family on the death of his father was so much more common then than now that we cannot know how this lone journey into the unknown would have felt for William, but it is hard to imagine that he was not emotionally delicate, vulnerable to whatever awaited him at the end of it. Fortunately, what awaited him was love. William and Hannah were a kind, warm, attentive and loving evangelical Christian couple, and he was as happy there as he ever had been. The two great characteristics of his new life – the countryside and evangelical Christianity – remained the very heart of his emotional life for the rest of his days.

The greatest change was religious. For William's family in Hull, as for the majority of English people, Christianity was something to take for granted. One attended church, accepted its creeds and expected it to make one a reasonably good person; but being carried away by religion, getting too fervent or overexcited, was dangerous and wicked – and, for the Wilberforces' class, vulgar. Even now, more than a century later, the shadow of the English revolution lay over the land, when religious 'enthusiasts' had executed the king, temporarily dismantled church and state and let loose all manner of sects claiming messages from God. Anything reminiscent of that was deeply suspect, and 'enthusiasm' – mystical fanaticism – was the *bête noire* of the era.

Into this most conservative age, twenty years before William was born, burst the Methodist or evangelical movement. Led by George Whitefield and John Wesley – whose quarrel over the doctrine of predestination quickly split the movement in two – the evangelicals insisted that Christianity was a religion of the heart demanding utter commitment and spiritual fervour. Above all it was about being born again, and they insisted that until that miraculous transformation occurred, the vast mass of English churchgoers were not real Christians at all. They multiplied the offence of this message by preaching it in the fields to vast crowds – Whitefield and Wesley were both ordained by the Church of England, but no longer welcome in many of its pulpits. Whitefield's preaching was notoriously histrionic, and Wesley's, while rather calmer in itself, repeatedly threw his listeners into howling convulsions. There were countless anti-Methodist riots, for which public opinion laid the blame squarely with the Methodists themselves.*

By 1769, evangelicalism had become rather calmer and more accepted, the convulsions and riots having largely died down and some detractors concluding that born-again religion was actually doing some good to 'the common people'. The number of evangelicals was now in the tens of thousands.

William's aunt Hannah was an evangelical convert and a follower of Whitefield, and she raised the boy in the same faith, teaching him daily devotions and taking him to Methodist meetings. Hannah taught William to shun the frivolous diversions and idle conversation of the world in favour of spiritual reading and talk. He was very happy living with his uncle and aunt, finding them a kind, loving family, and he took Hannah's values thoroughly to heart – 'I can taste the sweetness of redeeming love,' he told her. The artist who painted his portrait noted in his diary that William had 'a rare and pleasing character of piety'.[4]

Whitefield shortly left London on his last evangelistic journey to North America, so William may never have met him; but he did get to know John Newton, the former slave trader turned hymn-writing evangelical curate of Olney in Buckinghamshire. Hannah took William to Olney, and Newton returned their visits, lecturing for their edification on *Pilgrim's Progress*. William probably also sang his children's hymns.

Newton's slave-trading, his religious conversion, his writing 'Amazing Grace' and his campaigning against the slave trade are all well-known stories. What is less well known is the timing of it all, which offers a window onto Christian attitudes to slavery at the time of Wilberforce's childhood. When Newton was converted in 1748, he had been a slave trader for three years. He continued for another six. He gave up swearing and drunkenness, he composed prayers and studied theology and each day on board ship he would read the Bible and pray for an hour or two, leading services for the crew on Sunday, while his human cargo lay or sat hunched and chained under their

---

* Today, 'evangelical' and 'Methodist' are quite distinct terms, the first describing a religious tendency across many denominations, the second being the actual name of a denomination. At this point though, the Methodists had not split from the Church of England and so the two terms are interchangeable.

feet. He believed that God had given him his job and granted him success in it, constantly intervening miraculously to deliver the slave captain from unpleasant fates. 'Innumerable changes and difficulties,' he would report to his wife, 'which without superior protection, no man could escape or surmount, are, by the goodness of God, happily over.'[5] When his slaves tried to mutiny, he punished them with thumbscrews and neck-braces (a relatively mild response), praising 'the favour of divine providence' for his deliverance. He had enough sensibility to find it an unpleasant job, but had not the least moral scruple about doing it:

> The office of a gaoler, and the restraints under which I was forced to keep my prisoners, were not suitable to my feelings, but I considered it as the line of life which God, in his providence had allotted to me, and as a cross which I ought to bear with patience and thankfulness.[6]

Whitefield himself, though he had once been critical of slave owners, died owning twenty-five slaves who worked the lands of his orphanage in Georgia, and succeeded in overturning the ban on slavery in order to do so. He believed such work necessary to the prosperity of the orphanage and the state, and thought that only black people could work in that climate, adding, 'I trust many of them will be brought to Jesus.'[7]

Both men treated their slaves better than usual. Newton gave up raping the women after his conversion (a violation that was generally approved of, not just because the women were mere merchandise but because they could fetch a better price when pregnant), and punished his sailors for indulging their brute lusts. For his slaves in general, he resolved: 'I will treat them with humanity while under my power, and not render their confinement unnecessarily grievous.'[8] He took such unusually good care of them that on his last voyage there was not one death. And yet even when he gave up the slave trade, it was for health rather than for moral reasons, and later as a preacher and writer, after fifteen years of landlubbing, he had never spoken out against the trade. Slavery, it was assumed, like poverty, would always be with us. Like war, it was an unpleasant business, but without an alternative.

There were a few voices raised against slavery. The Bishop of Gloucester had preached passionately on the subject in 1766 before the church's missionary arm, the Society for the Propagation of the Gospel in Foreign Parts (SPG). The 'civilised violators of humanity' say that they can do what they will with their own property he said, but:

Gracious God! to talk (as in herds of cattle) of property in rational creatures! Creatures endowed with all our faculties; possessing all our qualities but that of colour; our brethren both by nature and grace, shocks all the feelings of humanity, and the dictates of common sense.[9]

This was far from preaching to the converted. The Society owned nearly 300 slaves on its Codrington Estate sugar plantation in Barbados, allegedly branding them with its own logo, 'Society'. Then in 1769, the clerk and self-taught amateur lawyer and academic Granville Sharp published a tract called *A Representation of the Injustice and Dangerous Tendency of Tolerating Slavery*. He had just successfully gone to court to stop an African, Jonathan Strong, being retaken as a slave in London, having nursed him back to health after he was beaten and left for dead by his owner, and he now printed his arguments against slaveholding. He highlighted the cruel laws of the slave colonies, arguing that either the colonies were guilty of unnecessary barbarity and must be taken in hand or, if the laws were necessary, then slavery itself was an essentially barbarous institution and must be abolished. But these were voices crying in the wilderness.

When William's mother read his letters and realized that he was being turned into a Methodist, she was horrified. In 1771, after he had been with his uncle and aunt for two years, she came and took him home. 'I deeply felt the parting,' said William, 'for I loved them as parents: indeed, I was almost heartbroken at the separation.' Hannah protested that she had 'scarcely ever felt such pain of mind' but Elizabeth tartly turned her own Whitefieldite jargon against her, saying: 'You should not fear; if it is a work of grace, you know it cannot fail.'[10]

Family and friends then set to work to win the twelve-year-old back and deliver his soul from the peril of taking Christianity too seriously. They took him to the theatre, card parties and balls, preaching and practising the gospel of high society. Hull, at this point in the vicissitudes of history, was a hugely fashionable city, 'as gay a place as could be found outside London', reckoned Wilberforce, so time was on their side. The devout and solemn boy sent furtive notes to Wimbledon saying 'they who are in Jesus must suffer persecution', and felt profoundly uncomfortable amid such worldliness, having to be almost dragged into the theatre, 'but by degrees I acquired a relish for it, and became as thoughtless as the rest'. The devotional habits he had been taught slowly slipped away. 'I was everywhere invited and caressed… I might almost say, that no pious parent ever laboured more to impress a beloved child with sentiments of piety, than they did to give me a taste for the world and its diversions.'[11]

Clearly, looking back, Wilberforce felt no great gratitude for these exertions on his behalf, but his attitude to his aunt's religion was not uncritical either: he reflected that if he had stayed there, he 'should probably have become a despised, bigoted Methodist'. Hannah – like most evangelicals outside of Wesley's network, but unlike the later Wilberforce – was a Calvinist, believing that God predestines who will be saved. In this respect, he was glad that his aunt's influence wore off, believing that such fatalism would have persuaded him against taking public office. Then again, he admitted later in life that any kind of true Christianity, as he came to understand it after his adult conversion, would have stopped him entering politics; his backsliding was 'the means of my being connected with political men and becoming useful in life', part of the tactical mystery of God.[12]

To ensure that nothing undermined the rehabilitation of her son, Elizabeth Wilberforce decided not to send him back to Hull Grammar School. It seems she feared the religious influence that the ardent Isaac Milner especially might have had on the boy – and if so, later events were to prove her fears quite prophetic. Precisely what religious convictions Milner had is hard to say: his daughter's biography steers clear of any hint of conversion or evangelicalism, merely portraying him as faultlessly religious from earliest days; but we get a different angle from the biography of Wilberforce written by his sons, who tell us that his grandfather had once said, 'Billy shall travel with Milner, as soon as he is of age; but if Billy turns *Methodist*, he shall not have a penny of mine.'[13] Instead, William went as a boarder to Pocklington Grammar School, a pricey institution run by the happily named Revd K. Basket, whom Wilberforce described as 'an elegant scholar'. Here William proved intelligent and articulate enough to find the work quite undemanding. According to his classmate T. T. Walmsley, 'He greatly excelled all the other boys in his compositions, though he seldom began them till the eleventh hour.'[14] According to Wilberforce himself, the three years he spent in Hull before going to university were 'a life of idleness and pleasure'; his family had ensured that he learnt to enjoy wasting time. He had a taste for literature nevertheless, and spent hours learning poetry by heart. He excelled at singing and toured the houses of the local gentry giving performances. His family said that he suffered from a rather short temper, however, which would still be true when he was an adult.

It is to Walmsley, apparently, that we owe the information that at the age of fourteen William wrote to a newspaper in York condemning the slave trade. Walmsley, as quoted in the earliest biography of Wilberforce, recalled posting the letter for him. If true, this is obviously a remarkable foreshadowing of Wilberforce's later career, and also illustrates the importance of his Yorkshire background. His position and influence in later life would be totally dependent on his family fortune, which in turn was founded on overseas trade. Hull's trade being with the Baltic, it was the largest port in England whose fortune was not based on slave labour, so a Yorkshire lad such as Wilberforce could develop a contempt for the slave trade that was quite unthinkable for a counterpart in Liverpool. He could publish his arguments in the regional press, and do so without offending his family and friends, and without cutting himself off from the inheritance that would as an adult put him in a position of influence.

But the truth of the story has been questioned, and here we run into the fundamental problem of piecing together the facts of Wilberforce's life. The vast majority of information we have comes from the hefty five-volume biography published as was traditional by his sons, Robert and Samuel, five years after his death in 1838. It was widely criticized as being unreadably turgid, full of countless unabridged documents. This is not a great worry for historians and biographers, for whom unabridged documents are an invaluable source of information and who are in their element in the unreadably turgid – though it is clear from other sources that the accuracy of their portrayal is compromised by their own dreariness. More importantly, it was also criticized, justly, as an unedifying and unbalanced polemic against Thomas Clarkson. This must seriously undermine our confidence in it. Clarkson was Wilberforce's friend and a close collaborator in the anti-slave trade campaign, of which he published his own account in 1808. But the Wilberforce brothers felt that Clarkson's book overstated his own importance to the cause at the expense of others. It gave the impression, Robert told Clarkson in 1834, 'that my father was *originally engaged in it by you*, and that he was subsequently a *sort of parliamentary agent, of whom you availed yourself*'. And so the defeat of slavery segued into an ugly squabble about whom the glory belonged to.

The Wilberforce brothers published their book with the express intention, Robert told Clarkson, of proving 'both that Mr Wilberforce did *not originally enter* upon the cause at *your suggestion*, and that when he had taken it up, he was the principal, by whom its operations were directed'.[15] We can try to judge how far this skews their account of the campaign itself in due course. In general, their airbrushing out of Clarkson is positively Stalinist, although Clarkson's own account more than compensates, and they are undeniably selective in presenting information that puts their father in a good light, even if this was normal nineteenth-century editorial policy.

Some of their father's letters and journals which they quote from still exist, and their quotations repeatedly reword them to make them more politically and spiritually correct, from the perspective of nineteenth-century high church rectors. As such, we have to assume flexibility in those quotations we cannot check, especially as many of the quotations in the book are not from documents at all but, like the story about William's letter to the newspaper, from the recollections and comments they remember hearing from their father and his friends. This story is one of several they clearly include in order to show that their father was an enemy of slavery before Clarkson ever came along. There is no other evidence for or against it, and although we do not have sufficient reason to deny it, we probably ought to put a question mark against it.

If the story is true, it makes the fourteen-year-old William part of the first subtle but definite shift of British public opinion against slavery. In 1772, while the unrepentant Newton was writing 'Amazing Grace', the first ripple of a movement began, with the publication in London of *Some Historical Account of Guinea... with an Inquiry into the Rise and Progress of the Slave Trade*. Its author, the Pennsylvania Quaker Anthony Benezet, had already done much to convince his own church that slavery was wrong, and he now began assaulting the consciences of the empire. He described the civilized contentment of life in West Africa, attacking the popular idea that the slave trade did slaves a favour in delivering them from the violent barbarity of life there. He plundered published journals to confront readers with the reality of the trade, the inherent miseries, the cruel punishments and the high death rate. He disproved the argument that Africans' physical fortitude and mental weakness made them ideal for slavery.

The same year, Granville Sharp won a famous legal victory; in defending the right of the escaped slave James Somerset not to be taken back to Jamaica, Sharp forced the lord chief justice against his will to concede, in effect, that slavery was illegal on the British mainland, regardless of what went on in the colonies. This was a staggering achievement for a man with no legal training but what he had given himself for this purpose. The poet William Cowper, Newton's hymn-writing partner, crowed:

Slaves cannot breathe in England; if their lungs
Receive our air, that moment they are free.[16]

In 1773, the evangelical leader the countess of Huntingdon published the poems of Phillis Wheatley, a twenty-year-old slave from Boston. One poem appealed for the abolition of slavery, but their greater impact was to confront readers with the kind of people the British colonies were enslaving. Then in 1774, John Wesley published *Thoughts upon Slavery*. It leaned extremely heavily on Benezet's book, but Wesley's barnstorming appeal to slavers, merchants and plantation owners to quit and save their souls ('Thy hands, thy bed, thy furniture, thy house, thy lands, are at present stained with blood'[17]) was all his own.

In 1775, Benezet helped to found the Pennsylvania Abolition Society, the first anti-slavery organization in British North America, and the following year, at the Philadelphia Yearly Meeting, Quakers in the state were banned from owning slaves. Within five years no American Quakers owned slaves. The Quakers delivered the first petition about the treatment of slaves to the British parliament and, led by Benezet, published a constant stream of free tracts.

The weightiest, though not at first the most widely-read contribution came in Adam Smith's foundational work of economics, *The Wealth of Nations*, in 1776. Smith argued that slavery was fundamentally inefficient: without income, slaves had no proper incentive to work, so paying workers a wage was merely a sensible investment. The number of slave-owners who, in the decades ahead, assured the public that their experience proved the negro to be constitutionally shiftless and therefore incapable of free labour, both confirmed Smith's logic and showed that it took time to get through.

2

Cambridge

To be sold for want of employment... A healthy Negro wench, of about twenty-one years old, is a tolerable cook, and capable of doing all sorts of house-work, can be well recommended for her honesty and sobriety: she has a female child of nigh three years old, which will be sold with the wench if required.

To be sold at the Bull and Gate Inn, Holborn:
A very good Tim Wisky, little the worse for wear...
A Chestnut Gelding...
A very good grey Mare...
A well-made good-tempered black boy, he has lately had the small-pox, and will be sold to any gentleman.
Newspaper advertisements from New York and London, republished by Granville Sharp, 1769[1]

Wilberforce was seventeen when he went to St John's College, Cambridge, in 1776, on the advice of Revd Basket, a fellow of the college. He was a clever, popular and really rather wealthy student. His grandfather had died as had his uncle, so he inherited enough capital – including the house in Wimbledon – to ensure that he would never have to do a day's work. The family business in Hull was being managed by a cousin, so while Wilberforce was entitled to take it on he had no need or inclination to do so. He was a short man, just 5 foot tall, with a big nose and weak eyes but a charming voice; as George Stephen put it eighty years later, 'in personal appearance, he laboured under a positive disadvantage'.[2]

His reconnection to the values of Hull high society remained firm, and William enjoyed a most leisurely three years at Cambridge. He wrote that he fell in from his first night with 'as licentious a set of men as can well be conceived. They were in the habit of drinking hard, and their conversation was in perfect accordance with their principles.' In fact, this kind of lifestyle was not really Wilberforce's cup of tea, and he kept at a distance from their more disreputable behaviour, shaking them off entirely after the first year of college life. A university friend, Lord Clarendon, insists that 'he had never in the smallest degree a dissolute character'. Nevertheless, he spent his time at cards, billiards, dances and what later generations of students would call 'just hanging out'. He skipped lectures and skimped reading. His fortune, his ability, his friends and even his tutors conspired to deter him from exercising his brain. 'Why in the world should a man of your fortune trouble himself with fagging?' his friends would ask when they caught him studying. He was gifted enough to do well without trying, and his tutors, he reports, openly compared him to his classmates saying 'that they were mere saps, but that I did all by talent. This was poison to a mind constituted like mine'.[3]

For the rest of his life, Wilberforce regretted that he had learnt so little in the way of mathematics, having been assured that he was 'too clever to need them'. Worse still, he always felt that he lacked self-discipline, and traced this to the fact that he had never learnt to apply himself to his studies. To the end of his life, friends bewailed his lack of concentration and 'system'; he so bitterly resented it himself that he once visited his old tutor to complain that under his care he had been allowed to inflict 'so irreparable an injury' on himself.

By his second year, Wilberforce was becoming a centre of college life. According to his neighbour Thomas Gisborne, he was the great entertainer, full of witty and interesting conversation:

> There was always a great Yorkshire pie in his room, and all were welcome to partake of it. My rooms and his were back to back, and often when I was raking out my fire at ten o'clock, I heard his melodious voice calling aloud to me to come and sit before I went to bed. It was a dangerous thing to do, for his amusing conversation was sure to keep me up so late, that I was behind-hand the next morning.[4]

Gisborne (writing sixty years later) reckoned him easily the most popular student in Cambridge, his room swarming with visitors throughout the afternoon and night – his waking hours. He continued to sing and was also a good mimic.

During his holidays, Wilberforce went home to Hull and then on through the Yorkshire Dales to the Lake District, indulging his passion for wild natural scenery. He kept a journal describing waterfalls, mountains and sunsets, and used the fashionable if odd-sounding Claude glass, a slightly convex mirror, which allowed one to frame nature like a modern snapshooter.

This love of nature, which seems so natural to us today, was a new development in European life. To earlier generations, nature was a hostile wilderness to be survived, subdued and where possible made fruitful. The Romantic Movement, to put the great cultural shift of the age into a soundbite, was about getting in touch with nature – artistically, spiritually, politically. It can be seen as a reaction to growing urbanization and to the 'dry' rationalism of the Enlightenment. In Britain, the movement would reach full bloom in the poetry of Wordsworth, who was now, at the age of nine, roaming the same lakes as Wilberforce; but its spearhead was the philosopher Jean-Jacques Rousseau. As well as pioneering travel for its own sake, Rousseau insisted that civilization had enslaved and corrupted humanity. Government, he said, was originally appointed by common consent, a social contract to protect our freedom; but kings allowed us no freedom, claiming to have been put there by God to rule in his name. The subversive implications of such ideas could already be glimpsed in the North American revolutionary war that was now underway, and they inspired the radical movements in France and Britain that were to shake the political world in which Wilberforce moved throughout his life. And they were, as his enemies never tired of saying, inextricably linked to the abolitionist movement.

We get a glimpse of Wilberforce's mind at this time from the fact that he was not awarded his BA for two years after his final exams, because he initially refused the unexpected demand to subscribe to the 39 Articles of the Church of England. What his hesitation was we can only guess, but perhaps the most unusual aspect of it was that he took doctrinal signing so seriously. It may or may not be related to this but after moving to London he went to the chapel of Theophilus Lindsey, the founder of the Unitarian denomination; Wilberforce's sons assure us that he was merely there for the quality of Lindsey's preaching, which rarely touched on his unorthodox opinions about the Trinity.

By the time Wilberforce finished at Cambridge in 1779, he had decided what he was going to do with his life: he would become a member of parliament. Business held no appeal, a lifetime of leisure was not enough, so he would serve the public, conscientiously and independently. This was the vocation that would finally animate and focus his life and talents for the first time. A general election was expected soon, and Wilberforce prepared to stand as a parliamentary candidate for Hull.

The British parliament in the eighteenth century was something quite alien to those who know it today, its strangeness masked by the great outward similarity of today – the House of Lords consisting of peers and bishops and the Commons of MPs chosen by local constituencies in the general election. However, it was completely undemocratic, with just 4 per cent of the population entitled to vote. This was not particularly controversial, at least not among the class of people whose opinions survive in writing. Not only were the educated classes expected to have a better understanding of government than illiterate weavers and miners, but the very purpose of elections was not to make government answerable to the whole population, but to give a say in the running of the country to those who had a financial stake in it – to consult the shareholders, as it were. There were reformers, including Wilberforce, who wanted to broaden the franchise somewhat among the growing middle classes, but most of those to whom the present system gave power were happy with it as it was. Certainly any talk of the government of the people, by the people, for the people would merely conjure – for most of the people – the horrid, anarchic spectre of the English revolution. Government of the people, by the king, for God was the eighteenth-century ideal (among those with the privilege of preserving their ideals in writing). The king was still, in principle and in practice, the head of the government. He chose the prime minister, oversaw his policies and, except in extreme cases, could generally depend on the support of a parliamentary majority. The present ill-conceived war with the North American colonies was principally the work of King George III but this was to prove one of those extreme cases, and Wilberforce planned to use his position to oppose the war and the administration of the prime minister Lord North – 'the old fat fellow', as he called him. The level of satisfaction felt by the voiceless majority about all this is, being unvoiced, hard to estimate. But the popularity of radical politics in the 1790s, once voices like Tom Paine's gave the lead, suggests a significant amount of disorganized dissatisfaction already fermenting out of view.

If, by modern standards, the political system seems unjust in principle, in practice it was unbelievably corrupt. Voting was not secret, so votes could be – and had to be – bought. The benefits of office, not least from what we would call bribery, were so rich that it generally cost thousands to out-pay and out-wine-and-dine one's electoral opponents. Wilberforce spent almost £9,000 securing the good will of Hull. In vast numbers of smaller boroughs (i.e. towns), the electorate was so controlled by a landowner or employer (such as the crown) that only its chosen candidate bothered to stand; in the 1761 election, this was the case in more than 90 per cent of the 200 smallest boroughs. It was not unknown for those who controlled a seat to advertise it for sale in a local newspaper. Population shifts meant there were boroughs such as Old Sarum in Wiltshire without a single voter, making them particularly easy to fix. This kind of anomaly was something that Wilberforce among others wanted to amend – not as a 'progressive' measure so much as to restore the system where it had fallen into disrepair.

Each county elected a pair of MPs, as well as those representing its boroughs. County constituencies were far bigger than the boroughs, which made them harder to control, but also too expensive to be worth contesting in many cases (Yorkshire might put you back £100,000, the equivalent of something like £7.5 million today). They were increasingly carved up in back-room deals, and from 1754 to 1790, 30 per cent of them failed to take a single poll.

Parliament did not have political parties of a kind that we would recognize today. In the previous century, it had divided into Whig and

Tory factions, but they were never formal organizations, and by the time Wilberforce entered parliament, labels were rather vague and often contradictory (Wilberforce is often called a Tory today; in fact he seems to have preferred the label 'Whig', but either way he liked, and deserved, the label 'Independent' far better). Instead of official parties, MPs tended to work together as informal interest groups, gravitating around influential or charismatic leaders and following those with deep pockets. In 1780, the main centres of gravity apart from Lord North himself were his opponents Lord Shelburne and Lord Rockingham – whose leading friends in the House of Commons were Edmund Burke and Charles James Fox. Fox was the great liberal voice of the age, who championed the causes of the North Americans and the Commons against the crown. MPs were expected to promote the interests of their constituents, but it was considered dishonourable to commit oneself to any given policy in advance. In the 1807 slave trade debate, the abolitionist William Plumer assured the House that 'if any man had asked me to pledge myself upon that, or any subject, I would have refused to accept of his vote'.[5]

Wilberforce intended to be perfectly independent, to vote as his conscience and good sense dictated, and to take no government office that would tie him to a party line. By standing for Hull, he was choosing an open and expensive contest, but if he could win it he would be answerable to no one. Men stood for parliament for various reasons: to make money, to make a name for themselves or to promote business or family interests. Wilberforce did not need parliament in order to make his fortune and, more unusually, he did not intend to use it to increase his fortune. Later in life, he said the only profit he had ever made from his career was a tea service given him by the King of Prussia. His intention was what we would call public service – as he would put it, 'usefulness'. In this his parliamentary career was remarkable right from the start.

For a year before the 1780 election, Wilberforce lodged in the Adelphi terrace in West London. Having canvassed opinion in Hull itself, he entertained Hull merchants in London pubs, gaining his first experience of public speaking, and promised them the standard 10 guineas each for their vote (local voters got 2 guineas each). The two other candidates for the seat made an equally good impression with their money, but Wilberforce came across as a young man of particular character and principle, and a winning speaker. He was also the local candidate. His contact with voters shows that he was, to put it kindly, not immune from the extreme class-consciousness of his age. Meeting one supporter, Johnny Bell, he shrank from shaking his hand, until persuaded by a campaign manager, because he was a butcher – 'I thought it was going rather too low for votes.' In later years, Wilberforce said that if he had his time again, rather than gain a seat in parliament through such corrupt methods, 'he would have remained always a private man'.[6] Whether right or wrong in his scruples (and whether he knew himself as well as he thought), there is no question that those were the only options open to him at the time.

Wilberforce also prepared for political life by spending time in the public gallery of the House of Commons. It was here that he got to know the man who would become one of his best friends, as well as the greatest politician of the age, William Pitt. Pitt and Wilberforce had been at Cambridge together, but had had little to do with each other, Pitt taking his education rather more seriously than Wilberforce. Pitt's father, also called William, who became the Earl of Chatham, had twice been prime minister himself; he was the man who won the Seven Years' War, and he played a major part in turning Britain into an imperial power. Pitt the Younger was determined to walk in his father's footsteps. Like Wilberforce, he intended to be independent, and had the rhetorical gifts to make an immediate impression – Wilberforce said that 'it was impossible not to be sensible of his extraordinary powers'. Unlike Wilberforce, he was astronomically ambitious, but being a younger son had no independent fortune. He did not have the money to stand for a town such as Hull, but was too honest to take a 'rotten borough' like Old Sarum – though being in the possession of his family it was offered to him. Instead Pitt stood for Cambridge University, which elected two MPs, but was small enough to be affordable.

The general election was called on 1 September 1780. Wilberforce faced fierce competition in Hull – the other two candidates had very influential backers in the parliamentary leader Lord Rockingham and one of the MPs for the county of Yorkshire. Nevertheless, Wilberforce got 1,126 votes, exactly the number of the other two combined. He was just twenty-one years old, having celebrated his coming of age, accompanied by his supporters, with a meal of roast ox in a field, one week before the election was called.

According to Wilberforce's sons, his schoolboy dislike of the slave trade had either been revived, or had continued. There is no corroborating evidence for this, so we must simply trust them or not trust them, but they quote their father as saying:

> As early as the year 1780 I had been strongly interested for the West Indies, and in a letter to my friend Gordon, then going to Antigua, to collect information for me, I expressed my determination, or at least my hope, that some time or other I should redress the wrongs of those wretched and degraded beings.[7]

3

Gambling and Government

The first work I did was fetching water, and carding of cotton; afterwards I was sent into the field to work about the Indian corn and tobacco till I was about nineteen years old...

Our master's name was Chapel – a very bad man to negroes. My oldest sister was called Patty; I have seen her several times so whipped that her back has been all corruption, as though it would rot. My brother Dick ran away, but they caught him, and brought him home; and as they were going to tie him up, he broke away again, and they hunted him with horses and dogs, till they took him; then they hung him up to a cherry tree in the yard, by his two hands, quite naked, except his breeches, with his feet about half a yard from the ground. They tied his legs close together, and put a pole between them, at one end of which one of the owners' sons sat, to keep him down, and another son at the other. After he had received 500 lashes, or more, they washed his back with salt water, and whipped it in, as well as rubbed it in with a rag; and then directly set him to work in pulling off the suckers of tobacco.

I also have been whipped many a time on my naked skin, and sometimes till the blood has run down over my waistband, but the greatest grief I then had was to see them whip my mother, and to hear her on her knees, begging for mercy. She was master's cook, and if they only thought she might do anything better than she did, instead of speaking to her as to a servant, they would strip her directly and cut away. I believe she was on her death bed when I got off, but I have never heard since.

Life in British North America, according to David George, 1793[1]

After his triumph in Hull, Wilberforce returned to Westminster with a ready-made reputation, and he was immediately invited to join the leading St James's Street gentlemen's clubs such as White's and Brooks's. These clubs were not just somewhere to enjoy port and cigars of an evening; as well as being the luxurious centre of fashionable male society, they were crucial parts of the Westminster political machinery. Deals were done there, cabinets chosen, arms twisted and information exchanged. A young politician like Wilberforce could mix on equal terms with leading figures like Charles James Fox, and quickly become known.

And not least, the clubs were gambling houses where, in the words of Horace Walpole, 'a thousand meadows and cornfields were staked at every throw'. Faro, an earlier version of roulette, was the most popular game, at least in Wilberforce's circle, but members would bet on everything from the roll of a dice to the death of a dowager. Lord Arlington once bet £3,000 on a race between two raindrops on a White's window pane. 'If the last trump were to sound,' exclaimed one shocked visitor, 'they would bet puppet-show against judgment.' Whole family fortunes could change hands in an evening. Admiral Harvey, one of Nelson's officers at Trafalgar, had once lost £100,000 (roughly £7.5 million today) in a night at White's, but won back most of it before he was done. Others were less lucky. Sir John Bland and Lord Mountjoy made a bet on which of a pair of old men would die first, and before the bet was decided, both gamblers had killed themselves to escape debt. Fox himself and his brother between them lost £32,000 in one three-day session of dice and drinking, punctuated only by Fox's appearances in parliamentary debates. According to the social historian Venetia Murray, 'This sort of gambling had nothing to do with having fun, or an amusing evening: it was a deadly serious addiction, often conducted in silence apart from the croupier's call.'[2]

Wilberforce knew few people at the clubs at first, and found the faro table the best way to ease himself in. On his first day at Boodle's club, he won twenty-five guineas from the Duke of Norfolk. The first time he went to Brooks's, he played with the notoriously dissolute George Selwyn at the bank. A friend spotted him and, alarmed to see the young ingénue being drawn down this dangerous path, called

'What, Wilberforce, is that you?' The furious Selwyn responded: 'Oh, sir, do not interrupt Mr Wilberforce, he could not be better employed.'

Others saw it differently: 'The strongest and most promising [religious convictions] I ever met with were in the case of Mr Wilberforce when he was a boy,' lamented John Newton to William Cowper. 'But they now seem entirely worn off, not a trace left behind, except a deportment comparatively decent and moral in a young man of a large fortune.'³ Nevertheless, he continued to pray for him daily.

Wilberforce's favourite club became Goostree's, a smaller place in Pall Mall taken over by Pitt and a couple of dozen friends. It was an intimate venue for political discussions, though they also gambled (Wilberforce several times lost £100) and drank liberally. Pitt was reputed to be a six-bottle-a-day man, though taking into account the increase in their size, this would be a mere four bottles today. He had actually come last out of five candidates in the Cambridge election, but a few months later entered parliament as MP for Appleby in Cumbria, a place he had never been to. Instead, a friend of a friend had won two seats and so had one to spare.

Pitt and Wilberforce were becoming close friends. Wilberforce called Pitt 'the wittiest man I ever knew', and after six months in the Commons declared: 'I doubt not that I shall, one day or other, see him the first man in the country.' Pitt returned the compliment, saying: 'Of all the men I ever knew, Wilberforce has the greatest natural eloquence.' After Pitt's apparently impromptu maiden speech, supporting Edmund Burke against the government, Wilberforce reported that Pitt's friends 'had expected much from him, but he surpassed all their expectations'. Nevertheless, Wilberforce was fiercely independent and had no intention of joining Pitt's party. When Pitt used his second speech to attack Lord North's proposed Commission for Public Accounts, Wilberforce felt that North was in the right and voted in favour. 'I remember to this day the great pain I suffered,' he said years later; he was torn 'between my admiration of his powers, my sympathy with his rising reputation, and hopes of his anticipated greatness, while I nevertheless deemed it my duty in this instance to deny him my support'.⁴ At the time he was blunter, saying: 'He did not convince me, and I staid with the old fat fellow.'⁵

Wilberforce himself was in less of a hurry to make an impression, and his first parliamentary session was businesslike. In his first speech, he presented a petition from his Hull constituents against the revenue laws, which he criticized as oppressive, and Pitt told him off for trying to compete in vituperation with Burke.

Thanks to the villa in Wimbledon, Wilberforce was one of just two among the Goostree's crowd who owned his own house, and with its eight or nine bedrooms it became a popular out-of-town haunt. Pitt especially valued the country air, and went there constantly with or without Wilberforce, leaving Westminster as late as midnight to spend the night in the country. One of the notes he sent ahead survives, telling Wilberforce that he and two friends are coming 'and expect an early meal of peas and strawberries'.

In their first summer recess, Wilberforce lived in the Lake District, renting a holiday home at Rayrigg, on the banks of Lake Windermere. His mother visited with his sister Sarah, along with many friends, for 'boating, riding, and continual parties', and many scenic walks. He returned to the same house every summer for seven years.

Two days before parliament reconvened for Wilberforce's second session in November 1781, momentous news reached London. General Cornwallis had surrendered at Yorktown five weeks previously. The war in North America was lost; the social contract had been terminated. The war had been an increasingly unpopular policy of an increasingly unpopular government, and once one was finished the other could not be far behind. And yet the policy was ultimately the king's and he would still not let Lord North admit defeat, militarily or politically.

In the House of Commons, the opposition attacked the government relentlessly. Wilberforce at last took the chance to shine, telling the House that the cabinet were acting more like lunatics than statesmen and that their war strategy had been 'cruel, bloody and impractical'. Pitt's attacks were devastating. North held out for several months, but his majority was approaching vanishing point, and he had to resign. George III was appalled and furious, and understandably so; this was a milestone in British constitutional history. For the first time, a government with royal approval had been brought down merely by its inability to sustain a majority in the House of Commons.

The only man the king could turn to with enough support to form a government was Lord Rockingham, who became prime minister in April 1782. Fox became secretary of state for foreign affairs. Both Pitt and Wilberforce were expected to join the cabinet and tailors tried to sell Wilberforce robes for his imminent rise to the House of Lords. Pitt stunned the House with his arrogance when he publicly announced, one year into his career, that he would refuse any post below that of senior minister. Neither joined the cabinet, however, and within three months Rockingham was dead. Lord Shelburne took over the reins and Pitt became chancellor of the exchequer. Wilberforce was a prominent supporter of the government, but assured friends that 'he would do nothing which obliged him to pledge himself to government'. Pitt and Wilberforce then went to Brighton together for Easter but found the weather unfriendly and did not last a night, enjoying a high-spirited visit to Bath instead.

Throughout the summer, Shelburne's government negotiated a peace treaty to conclude the American War of Independence. Wilberforce's accomplishments, though he worked solidly until the recess, were as much social as political. He sung at the Duchess of Devonshire's house before the Prince of Wales, who, she told him, 'will come at anytime to hear you sing'. George Selwyn came across Wilberforce with his friends on the way out of the House of Commons one night:

> I left in one room a party of young men, who made me, from their life and spirits, wish for one night to be twenty. There was a table full of them drinking – young Pitt, Lord Euston, Berkley, North, etc., etc., singing and laughing *à gorge deployée*; some of them sang very good catches; one Wilberforce, a M. of P., sang the best.[6]

About this time both Pitt and Wilberforce gave up gambling, independently, but for illuminatingly different reasons. Pitt's was the more usual – according to Wilberforce, he found it was becoming an increasingly powerful compulsion, and so quit before it was too late. Wilberforce on the other hand was moved by concern for others. One day at Goostree's, his sons report, there was no one available to be banker at the faro table, so he stood in. 'As the game grew deep he rose the winner of £600. Much of this was lost by those who were only heirs to fortunes, and therefore could not meet such a call without inconvenience. The pain he felt at their *annoyance* cured him of a taste which seemed but too likely to become predominant.'[7]

Shelburne's government was an increasingly weak one, opposed by North and his men on one side, and Fox and his on the other, and failed to secure the support of Independents. So when in February 1783 Pitt tabled a motion declaring that the House was satisfied with the US treaty, his own cousin William Grenville refused to second it, and he turned to Wilberforce instead. Wilberforce agreed, but suffered a sleepless night at the thought of taking on a full, hostile House of Commons. It was a big enough event for his old teacher Isaac Milner, now a tutor at Cambridge, to come and watch from the public gallery. Immediately before the debate, one cabinet member resigned and, worse still, North and Fox – such long-standing personal and political enemies – turned out to have settled their differences and were, incredibly, sitting side by side as leaders of a united opposition. Wilberforce, while defending the peace settlement, took the opportunity to excoriate the 'scandalous intrigue' of the Fox-North alliance as morally bankrupt opportunism. He was mightily impressed by how Pitt fared under trying conditions on the second day of debate. He 'spoke three hours… and actually holding Solomon's porch door open with one hand, while vomiting during Fox's speech to which he was to reply'.[8] Nevertheless, Pitt's motion was defeated by 16 votes, and the government was finished. Wilberforce left the House at 8 a.m., a late night even for him, and headed back to Wimbledon.

George III passed the government on to Fox and North only after he had tried everything else, including asking the 23-year-old Pitt to be prime minister, although he would never have been able to command a majority. The king hated Fox more than anyone in the world, and now regarded North as a traitor. Nevertheless he let the unholy alliance come to power in May, and they became a profoundly uncomfortable *ménage à trois*.

Pitt, ejected from 10 Downing Street,* spent all the more time in Wimbledon. 'Hundreds of times I have roused Pitt out of bed in the morning and conversed with him while he was dressing,' reminisced Wilberforce. 'In fact I was at this time the depository for his most confidential thoughts.' Wilberforce's diary reports: 'Delicious day – lounged morning at Wimbledon with friends, foining [verbal sparring] at night, and run about the garden for an hour or two… Fine hot day, went on water with Pitt and Eliot fishing, came back, dined, walked evening.'[9]

Probably the most consistent passion throughout Wilberforce's life was for the countryside. It was an absolute dependency. In the words of Cowper, his favourite poet, 'God made the country, and man made the town,' and he found the air, pace and spirit of rural life quite essential to his spiritual, emotional and physical health. It allowed quiet reflection away from the seductive flattery of society life. 'I never leave this poor villa without feeling my virtuous affections confirmed and strengthened,' he told his sister Sarah. His career was not a good choice in that respect: after a session in parliament, which got busier and busier over the years, he was always desperate to escape, and 'when I was much confined in later life to London, I could scarce leave the country for a town campaign without being affected even to tears'.[10]

The month that the Fox-North coalition came into office, another slave-trade dispute judged by Lord Mansfield hit the news, the *Zong* trial. From 29 November to 1 December 1781, Captain Luke Collingwood and his crew on a slaver called the *Zong* killed 131 of the 470 West Africans they were carrying to Jamaica. The ship was full of disease, slaves were dying, and Collingwood calculated that under British law, 'if the slaves died a natural death, it would be a loss to the owners of the ship; but if they were thrown alive into the sea, it would be a loss to the underwriters'.[11] So they jettisoned the cargo. The most sickening aspect of the case is that it came to trial not as a murder charge, but as an insurance dispute – were the insurers obliged to pay for the loss of revenue?

---

* 10 Downing Street was, then as now, the official residence of the prime minister, but Pitt had been living there because Shelburne preferred his own house in Berkeley Square.

The case would have passed generally unnoticed if it had not been for Olaudah Equiano whom we previously met being transported as a slave himself. Through some shrewd trading he had amassed the £40 needed to buy back his freedom, and after travels that took in the Arctic, Turkey and Nicaragua, he was back in London. On his tip off, the protester Granville Sharp attended the trial, got reports into the papers and wrote to Lord North about it. He wanted to prosecute the sailors for murder, but was publicly told by the Solicitor-General, 'It is madness: the Blacks were property,' and his plan seems to have got no further.

At the same time, the London Meeting of Quakers, urged by their friends in Philadelphia who were now stout opponents of slavery, started a group to publicize the evils of the slave trade, led by William Dillwyn, a Philadelphian living in London. In May 1783, they presented the first petition against the trade to parliament. They printed 10,000 copies of Benezet's *The Case of our Fellow Creatures* and gave them away, as well as producing their own tracts and lecturing in schools. At the other end of the English religious spectrum, Beilby Porteus, the Bishop of Chester and chaplain to the king, preached the anniversary sermon to the Society for the Propagation of the Gospel, and renewed the Bishop of Gloucester's criticism of their slaveholdings in Barbados, again to no avail.

Wilberforce spent a tranquil summer in the Lake District, and then in September went to France with Pitt and Edward Eliot – a Goostree friend and Pitt's future brother-in-law – to experience the country, learn French, and improve their health, in particular Wilberforce's bad eyes and Pitt's aching teeth. 'We shall agree excellently as invalids,' Pitt said, 'particularly in making the robust Eliot fag for us.' Now Britain and France were at peace, the British were rapidly streaming back.

They visited Rheims for a few weeks *en route* to Paris, meaning to get their French up to speed there. Unfortunately the contact who was supposed to introduce them into society turned out to be a mere grocer, so the tourists spent a week and a half in their hotel, 'without making any progress in the French language,' confessed Wilberforce, 'which could not indeed be expected from us, as we spoke to no human being but each other.' Finally, they managed to make contact, via the police chief, with someone they could allow themselves to talk to, an archbishop. He made a good impression on Wilberforce, who much preferred French archbishops to the English variety – they were 'jolly fellows... who play at billiards etc. like other people'. Being English they were served one night with a huge joint of beef which was somewhere between rare and raw. When they refused to touch it, their host assumed they were naturally embarrassed about eating their horrid national dish in front of foreigners.

They went to Paris and stayed a week, seeing a play every night, though after all their study, 'we were not able to make out a syllable'. Then on to Fontainebleau, where they joined the royal court, hunting for stag and boar and playing billiards. Wilberforce found Louis XVI a 'clumsy, strange figure in immense boots', 'so strange a being (of the hog kind) that it is worth going 100 miles for a sight of him'. In contrast, Queen Marie Antoinette was 'a monarch of most engaging manners and appearance' and quite a wit, asking Wilberforce hilariously 'whether he had heard lately from his friend the grocer'. They also met Benjamin Franklin, there as a United States emissary, and General Lafayette, who had been instrumental in the defeat of Britain, both of whom they got on well with as they had opposed the American war.

The visit was cut slightly short when Pitt was called home before parliament met, to plan with the king the defeat of the Fox-North administration. Wilberforce, a very bad sailor who was always sick on board, was relieved to arrive back at his London lodgings, telling a friend, 'We have with some difficulty escaped with our lives, from the complicated miseries of incessant travelling.' The diary is terser: 'Returned to England in November, and secret plottings.'[12]

4

True Christianity

A woman was one day brought to us to be sold; she came with a child in her arms. The captain refused to purchase her on that account, not wishing to be plagued with a child on board; in consequence of this she was taken back to the shore. On the following morning, however, she was again brought to us, but without the child, and she was apparently in great sorrow. The black trader who brought her on board [said] that the child had been killed to accommodate us in the sale.

James Arnold, slave ship doctor, testifying to the Privy Council, 1789[1]

In November 1759, a slave ship arrived in the Caribbean ravaged by dysentery. Luckily it ran into the British fleet there, and appealed for help. The only doctor willing to go on board was a 26-year-old evangelical Christian called James Ramsay. His first introduction to the slave trade was a hold full of dying prisoners, covered in blood and excrement. Quitting the navy after a leg injury, he became an Anglican minister in St Christopher (now St Kitts) where, as well as his official duties, he enraged the plantation managers by preaching to the slaves and condemning their mistreatment. For fourteen years he faced violent opposition as he tried to teach them prayers and filled their heads with the notion that they were made in the image of God.

Returning to England in 1781, exhausted and disillusioned, Ramsay became the rector of Teston on Kent, appointed by Sir Charles Middleton, Comptroller of the Navy, agriculturalist, evangelical, and Ramsay's erstwhile captain. On Lady Middleton's suggestion apparently, Ramsay reported the treatment of British slaves in the book *Essay on the Treatment and Conversion of African Slaves*. Wilberforce, returning to England from France in November 1783, not long before the book was published, heard about Ramsay's accusations. According to his sons' biography, wanting to gather information about the trade he met Ramsay and asked about his experiences.

The same month, Fox brought before the House of Commons the India bill, designed to bring British rule in India under the control of parliament. Bengal was controlled by the East India Company, a private British corporation, and the bill allowed parliament to appoint its commissioners. It incidentally gave Fox himself permanent control of the vast wealth of that burgeoning empire and made his government unassailable – 'the boldest and most unconstitutional measure ever attempted' as Pitt saw it. George III agreed, and decided to use it to bring down the Fox-North government.

The bill sailed through the House of Commons with a two-to-one majority. 'Fox spoke wonderfully,' admitted Wilberforce, while he himself 'spoke ill – confused'. But when it reached the House of Lords, the king announced that he would regard as an enemy anyone who voted for it. The bill was defeated, the government dismissed, and this time Pitt accepted the king's request that he become prime minister, aged twenty-four. The House of Commons erupted with laughter at the announcement, and Wilberforce's friend Mrs Crewe said to him, 'So your friend Mr Pitt means to come in: well, he may do what he likes during the holidays, but it will only be a mince-pie administration, depend on it.'[2]

Wilberforce did not join Pitt's government; instead he formed a club of about forty independent MPs, who pledged 'to take neither place, pension, nor peerage'. The idea was to ensure that there was a significant minority in the Commons acting on personal principle instead of being steered by the hand that fed them. It did not last long as within a few years Wilberforce was one of only two of the forty who had not succumbed to one of the three Ps. Still, despite his independence, he was an influential young friend of the perilous new government, attacking the Fox-North opposition for undermining the constitution just as dangerously as the king had done, 'prostitut[ing] everything to what they call "the dignity of the house"'. The press predicted Pitt's rapid fall 'in spite of the assistance he receives from the eloquence of Mr Wilberforce'.

This eloquence would soon be instrumental to its triumph. In the meantime, Wilberforce's life was full of business and pleasure. Extracts from his 1784 diary say:

January 20	House – [Fox-Pitt] coalition talked of. Dined independents' – opera – and supped Goostree's.
February 2	House till 12. Then home and dreamed about debate.
February 21	Prince of Wales's Levée – Opera – supped Goostree's – took off people – Bed three.
February 22	Very much fatigued – church – dined G. Hardinge's, Mrs Siddons sang charmingly.
February 24	Lady Howe's ball – danced till half-past four.
March 1	Spoke – at night to Dundas's [Pitt's naval treasurer] – extremely tired.
March 12	House till 11 – parliamentary Reform.[3]

'Took off people' in the entry for February 21 refers to his impersonations of others, which were very popular, especially his Lord North, but he suddenly gave up the habit. Friends asked him to perform for Lord Camden, a wise old man whom Wilberforce often sat with, talking politics and religion, and whose discernment he revered. 'It is but a vulgar accomplishment,' said Camden, and refused to hear his act. With this snub, says Wilberforce, 'he cured me of the dangerous art of mimicry'[4].

Pitt's government limped through its first few months in the bizarre position of hardly being able to win one vote in parliament. But it had the king and the Lords on its side, and growing favour throughout the country; and thanks both to its supporters' eloquence and other more worldly-wise tactics, it gradually clawed away Fox's support in the Commons.

To convert this advantage into a workable majority, a general election would be needed. (Elections never changed governments at the time but instead were tools with which those in power increased their majority.) All sides took to the country to gauge and win round political opinion in the free constituencies. Wilberforce was sent to sound out the county seat of Yorkshire, his home ground, the largest constituency in the country, and a stronghold for the opposition. As the *Public Advertiser* put it: 'Their [Fox's and North's] success in Yorkshire is now the sheet-anchor of the coalition... As some principals of their party have so great an interest in the county, a failure there would entirely blow up their cause; and besides, the example of Yorkshire could not fail to determine other counties.'[5]

Wilberforce approached his weighty task without any great confidence, especially as what opposition there was in Yorkshire to the coalition was deeply divided. The politicians debated before a huge meeting of voters in York Castle Yard on 25 March. The aristocratic big guns of the coalition arrived in full pomp and state, and Pitt's men had nothing with which to compete. It was a six-and-a-half-hour meeting in freezing wind, hail and rain, and by the time Wilberforce stood up to speak the audience had had plenty already. As the little man climbed onto the table to address them, he looked as if he was about to be blown away. James Boswell, the biographer of Dr Johnson, was there, and reported, 'I saw what seemed a mere shrimp mount upon the table; but as I listened, he grew, and grew, until the shrimp became a whale.'[6] More conventional commentators said that he spoke like an angel.

Wilberforce passionately defended Pitt for his talent, his integrity and his loyalty to the king, damning the cynical marriage of Fox and North, and their venal, subversive India bill – 'the offspring of that unnatural conjunction marked with the features of both its parents, bearing token to the violence of the one, and the corruption of the other'. He appealed to the anti-Fox factions to cooperate. While he was speaking, a horseman arrived with a note from Pitt written at noon the previous day, announcing that the king had dissolved parliament and called an election, adding, 'You must take care to keep all our friends together, and to tear *the enemy to pieces.*' Wilberforce incorporated Pitt's announcement – the first part of it – into his speech to dramatic effect, saying that the king had turned to them for a decision and calling on the people of Yorkshire to take their stand. 'There was such an excellent choice of expressions,' reported the *York*

Paper, 'so rapidly pronounced, that we are unable to do it justice.' Wilberforce himself later said, 'I have scarcely ever in my life spoken better than on that occasion.'[7]

That night at the tavern, Wilberforce spoke to a meeting of the government's supporters, having to soothe the conflicts between them again, and making a great impression. Then, as Baron Hawke reports, 'When we broke up at the York Tavern, at twelve o'clock on Thursday night, there was a sudden and spontaneous cry of "Wilberforce and liberty", which was his first nomination for the county.'[8]

They wanted him to stand for election as one of the two MPs for Yorkshire. It was not the most sober proposal. Yorkshire had 20,000 voters, more than any other constituency, making it extremely expensive to contest, and it was firmly under the control of its aristocracy, who had their own pawns to play, and with whom Wilberforce had no connections. Yet even before he was asked, Wilberforce had secretly decided to stand. 'To anyone besides myself I was aware that it must appear so mad a scheme that I never mentioned it at all… My being elected for that great county appears to me, upon the retrospect, so utterly improbable, that I cannot but ascribe it to a providential intimation that the idea of my attaining that high an honour suggested itself to my imagination, and, in fact, fixed itself within my mind.'[9]

As a safety net, Wilberforce stood for Hull again as well. After one more meeting in York to mobilize his county supporters, he rode through the night to Hull and spent a few days meeting voters. 'Canvassed all day – extremely hard work – till night – tired to death.' Naturally the fact that he was not actually planning to be their MP rather dampened his support: he won, but with a much reduced majority, and during his victory parade was pelted with snowballs.

The next day he was back in York, with his running mate and fellow independent, Henry Duncombe. They organized an appeal to help towards their costs and raised £18,670 – four times what they spent on the election as it turned out, so it cost neither of them a penny. In an exhausting four days of canvassing, they covered York, Doncaster, Rotherham, Sheffield, Barnsley, Wakefield, Halifax, Bradford and Leeds. On 7 April, back in York Castle Yard, the votes were counted and Wilberforce and Duncombe were elected MPs for Yorkshire over the heads of the Yorkshire aristocracy.

'My dear Wilberforce,' wrote Pitt the next day, while Wilberforce was celebrating with a hot-air balloon ride (a four-month-old invention), 'I can never enough congratulate you on such a glorious success.' The result in Yorkshire contributed to a substantial majority and a moral victory for Pitt's government. Wilberforce had high hopes for the lesson that Pitt could learn. 'He was then able if he had duly estimated his position, to have cast off the corrupt machinery of influence, and formed his government upon the basis of independent principle'[10] – the words, surely, of a man content to spend his career trying to influence government rather than governing. Pitt confided in him his far-reaching plans to pay off the national debt, which was now eighteen times the annual income of the state, starting with a well-judged raft of new taxes and an efficient crackdown on smuggling. Wilberforce's modest contributions included inserting a clause into the smuggling bill preventing the confiscation of an entire ship for the personal contraband of individual sailors.

Wilberforce's prospects, if he had played the game, were stellar. His rhetorical skills, combined with an utterly beguiling speaking voice, would make him a major figure in the Commons. He had one of the most prestigious seats in the House and was a close friend and invaluable ally of the prime minister. Any MP with such qualifications would be expected to reap sweet recompense from them – a cabinet post, a peerage or a sinecure or two perhaps. But whatever else Wilberforce might prove to be, he was never for sale.

That summer, Ramsay's essay on British slavery was published, and had a huge impact. For the first time, an anti-slavery publication had come from a rector of the Church of England, and one who had lived among the slave plantations for years. Colonists replied with a furious volley of accusations, in print and in parliament. Ramsay had been 'the most harsh, unfeeling surgeon that ever handled an instrument', said a tract written by 'Some gentlemen of St Christopher'. His Caribbean parish had complained about his lax life, they said, and his congregation dwindled because of his invective. He was a money-grubbing pluralist, ever after additional sea-chaplaincies to supplement his parish income. He punished his own slaves more severely than anyone, and never freed them without payment; he once 'had the barbarity to take £90 (her whole substance) for the freedom of a poor woman, whose life could not be valued at four months purchase'.[11] They even suggested that his tales of child prostitution could only have come from personal experience. He replied to their accusations exhaustively but exhaustingly, and fell ill under the stress. Plantation managers also took to sending him packages of Caribbean rock, in the hope, as recipients had to pay postage, of bankrupting him.

When parliament broke up in August 1784, Wilberforce went to Yorkshire to socialize with his new constituents. 'I went to the races and attended the ball. I sang in public, and did everything to please my constituents.'[12] In a little over a year, Wilberforce would renounce such pursuits forever 'for fear of the Lord'; but again providence seems to have bent its own rules for the greater good. At the York races, Wilberforce met an old friend, William Burgh, and they talked of taking a holiday in Europe. Burgh turned down the opportunity, but then while entertaining the voters of Scarborough, Wilberforce met his old teacher Isaac Milner, now a fellow of the Royal Society, moderator of Cambridge University and rector of St Botolph's. Wilberforce enjoyed his erudite conversation and invited him instead, and Milner provisionally agreed.

After this their talk turned to religion, and the name of Stillingfleet, a local evangelical rector, came up. 'A good man, but one who carries things too far,' was Wilberforce's assessment. 'Not a bit too far,' insisted Milner. They began to argue and Milner defended the 'vital Christianity' of such ministers. Wilberforce then started to regret his choice of travelling companion, but Milner got his leave of absence from Cambridge and on 20 October 1784 they left for France. Travelling with them in a separate ladies' carriage were Wilberforce's mother and sister and two young cousins coming south for winter for the sake of their health.

They had a perfectly calm crossing, and Wilberforce was violently sick. On the road, they read, wrote, enjoyed the view and, in Wilberforce's case, caught up on a pile of parliamentary papers. 'At last they are gone, and the devil go with them.' They rode to Lyons, put their carriages on a river boat and sailed in sunlight down to Avignon, finally joining the English crowd in Nice, in a house right on the shore, surrounded by orange trees.

Wilberforce was relieved to find that his 'intelligent and excellent friend' joined in all the entertainments, the balls and concerts, even on Sundays. His sons note with disappointment that 'though a clergyman, he never thought of reading prayers during their whole stay'; none of those present recorded such disappointment. Milner's daughter Mary explains this gap between his devout ideas and relaxed behaviour as a hatred of 'religious affectation' which led him 'to accommodate himself to practices, which his judgment might not entirely approve'. Wilberforce was more severe: 'Milner's religious principles... had at this time little practical effect on his conduct.'[13]

Still, Milner vigorously defended the 'vital Christianity' that he did not practice, though he refused to take Wilberforce on in the verbal jousting he was used to with his political friends. 'I am no match for you, Wilberforce, in this running fire, but if you really wish to discuss these subjects seriously, I will gladly enter on them with you.' And so they spent a warm winter together until, in January 1785, Wilberforce received a message from Pitt asking him to come home and support his parliamentary reform bill. The aim was to abolish thirty-six rotten boroughs, redistributing their seats to counties with more voters. It was the latest in a long line of attempts to reintroduce some common sense into the British constitution, and faced serious opposition in parliament, but Pitt was determined to drive it through.

Following Pitt's call for Wilberforce to come home, he and Milner left the ladies in Nice, planning to return in the summer. They had a rough journey, facing eighteen days of snow. On a steep ascent along a cliff-top road in the hills of Burgundy, Milner got out to walk, but still the horses lost control. A huge strong man, he grabbed hold of the carriage and managed to stop it plunging over the edge. His muscle succeeding where his theology had not, Wilberforce was saved.

On the way, however, at Milner's urging, they read together a book called *The Rise & Progress of Religion in the Soul* by the Dissenting minister and hymn-writer Philip Doddridge. Wilberforce had come across it in Nice, leafed through it and asked Milner what he knew about it. Milner said that it was 'one of the best books ever written' and insisted they take it with them on their journey home. Wilberforce found it uncomfortable reading:

> I beseech you, reader, whoever you are, that you would now look seriously into your own heart, and ask it this one plain question; Am I truly religious? Is the love of God the governing principle of my life? Do I walk under the sense of his presence? Do I converse with him from day to day, in the exercise of prayer and praise? And am I, on the whole, making his service my business and my delight, regarding him as my master and my father?[14]

Doddridge argued from the Bible that readers who answered 'no' were Christians in name only, bound for hell. The only solution was to surrender to Christ, cheerfully, immediately, totally and forever, to turn from one's old life and be born again into a radically new one. Doddridge was advocating the kind of religion Wilberforce remembered all too well from his time under Hannah Wilberforce's wing, and which he despised; but if as Doddridge contended this was the religion of the New Testament, then what kind of Christian was Wilberforce, preferring the religion of English society to the religion of God's word? Then again, could he afford to pursue this line of thinking that, taken to its conclusion, would threaten to shipwreck his career and social life? He and Milner agreed that when they came back in the summer they would study the Greek New Testament and get to the bottom of this.

The Commons voted on Pitt's reform bill in April and Wilberforce, like Pitt, had high hopes for it. But Pitt had failed to rouse enough support throughout the country – not least because his administration offered a new economic and political stability, making change less urgent – and MPs had too much to lose from reform. Lord North protested that 'I never will consent to deface an ancient, venerable, substantial fabric, for the sake of decorating it with modern frippery.' Thomas Powys complimented Pitt 'on the abilities and eloquence he has displayed in the funeral oration he has pronounced on the constitution of his country'. Wilberforce replied to them both robustly and cuttingly, to cries of 'Hear him! Hear him!' and defended Pitt's bill as his greatest service to the country yet: 'I wish to give my vote not with a view to men, but measures,' he said; the bill would 'restore the freedom of opinion', cutting the strings that allowed MPs to be controlled by corrupt interests. Well, quite. It was defeated by 74 votes. 'Terribly disappointed and beat,' says his diary – 'extremely fatigued – spoke extremely ill, but commended.'[15]

His diary during that session is the same mix of politics and society as ever. 'House all night, till eight o'clock in the morning... House – spoke – but... too hot and violent... sitting up all night singing... danced till five in the morning.' There is evidence, however, that some of what Doddridge had written had got through. After talking with an unnamed friend, Wilberforce offered some unusual reflections on what Doddridge would call 'carelessness'. 'Strange that the most generous men and religious, do not see that their duties increase with their fortune, and that they shall be punished for spending it in eating, etc.'[16]

While Wilberforce meditated on his duties to others, the first shift in public opinion against the slave trade continued. The master of Magdalene College, Cambridge, Revd Peter Peckard, apparently read one of Granville Sharp's philippics about the *Zong* massacre, and started preaching against the trade. To some his uninspiring preaching seemed to add insult to injury – 'God Almighty to complete their fate/Chose Peter Peckard for their advocate'[17] – but in 1785 he became vice-chancellor of the university, and chose as a topic for the celebrated Latin essay competition *Anne Liceat Invitos in Servitutem Dare?* (Is it lawful to make slaves of others against their will?) The winner was a young man from the same college as Wilberforce whose dogged, driven campaigning against slavery would eclipse even that of Sharp. His name was Thomas Clarkson. That June, on the road to London, Clarkson tried to forget or dismiss the horrors he had described in his essay, but they continued to fill his head, until he sat down on the roadside near Wade's Mill in Hertfordshire and decided, 'It was time someone should see these calamities to their end.'[18]

5

'O God, Deliver Me from Myself!'

After I was ordered out, the horrors I soon saw and felt, cannot be well described; I saw many of my miserable countrymen chained two and two, some hand-cuffed, and some with their hands tied behind. But when a vessel arrived to conduct us away to the ship, it was a most horrible scene; there was nothing to be heard but rattling of chains, smacking of whips, and the groans and cries of our fellow-men. Some would not stir from the ground, when they were lashed and beat in the most horrible manner. When we were put into the ship, we saw several black merchants coming on board, but we were all drove into our holes, and not suffered to speak to any of them.

And when we found ourselves at last taken away, death was more preferable than life; and a plan was concerted amongst us, that we might burn and blow up the ship, and to perish all together in the flames. But we were betrayed by one of our own countrywomen, who slept with some of the head men of the ship – for it was common for the dirty filthy sailors to take African women and lie upon their bodies, but the men were chained and pent up in holes. It was the women and boys which were to burn the ship, with the approbation and groans of the rest; though that was prevented, the discovery was likewise a cruel bloody scene.

From *Thoughts and Sentiments* by Ottobah Cugoano, 1788, abridged[1]

Parliament dragged on until the end of June 1785, by which time Nice was too hot for the English, so Wilberforce and Milner arranged to meet the ladies in Genoa, from where they travelled to Turin, Geneva, Berne and Interlachen. In Geneva they met a friend from Yorkshire, the leading parliamentary reformer Revd Christopher Wyvill, who was studying the Genevan constitution. Wilberforce was delighted with Switzerland, while his letters contained pessimistic reflections on the state of his homeland; he slipped into prophetic mode against 'the universal corruption and profligacy of our times' – 'I fancy I see storms arising, which already "no bigger than a man's hand", will by and by overspread and blacken the whole face of heaven.'[2] He was not wrong.

As for the state of his own soul, Wilberforce saw little more cause for optimism. He found the New Testament to teach the same Christianity as Doddridge, a conclusion that Milner pressed on him with alacrity. They discussed the matter so intently that the ladies started to complain about the lack of visits to their carriage. Wilberforce was reluctant to change his lifestyle – much like Milner – but increasingly felt its dissonance.

Though Wilberforce's own memoirs of this time dwell on his failure to live out his new beliefs, in fact change began immediately. In September, on the way back to England, the travellers stopped off at Spa in Belgium. Once home, Wilberforce refused to go to the theatre or to a Sunday party, to the surprise of his friends who assumed, ironically, that he was deferring to his mother. In general he joined in with the singing and dancing, games and jokes, but even these started to be invaded, as the thoughts of his quiet hours suddenly caught up with him in public. 'I laughed, I sang, I was apparently gay and happy, but the thought would steal across me, "What madness is this; to continue easy in a state in which a sudden call out of the world would consign me to everlasting misery!"'[3]

It was not thoughts of hell that most plagued him though, but a sense of guilt at a wasted life. In October, he started getting up early to meditate, read and pray, and in 'the solitude and self-reflection of the morning' he was overwhelmed with a sense of his sinfulness and ingratitude, his failure to put what God had given him to any good use. 'For many months I was in a state of deepest depression.'

Wilberforce spent the autumn in seclusion in Wimbledon, immersed in spiritual reading, anxious devotions and bleak self-examination. He declined to visit Pitt and was greatly embarrassed when he called round, though he did not yet feel able to talk about his spiritual changes. He was troubled by the failure of his heart to feel as lost and as bad as his mind knew he was. Sometimes he prayed with fervour, other times he felt dry and cold. He was upset by his mind's tendency to wander when he was in church or listening to readings at home. His greatest stumbling block, he thought, was pride – he felt ashamed to think what the world would make of his new religion, and if he overcame such feelings he felt proud of his achievement.

Eventually, at the end of November, he burned his bridges and wrote to friends, briefly announcing his conversion and a period of contemplative seclusion, while reassuring them that he was not turning 'enthusiast' and did not consider religion to necessitate being gloomy. One threw his letter in the fire; most thought that Wilberforce was down in the dumps and needed to get out a bit more. Wilberforce agreed that society would provide a cure for his unhappy introversion, but did not want to be cured.

His letter to Pitt assured him of continued friendship and support, but warned that 'I could no more be so much a party man as I had been before' – as if any MP had been less of a party man than he had – and suggested that next time they met neither should mention the letter, apparently hoping after this timid announcement to let the subject drop forever. Pitt's reply could not have been more sympathetic. Having no clear indication of what was going on, he vowed that while few things could cause him more pain than a serious disagreement with Wilberforce, and while he did not believe such a thing could happen, if it did, it could not shake their friendship. But he expressed concern about Wilberforce's reclusion. For Pitt, a man of his time, healthy religion was rational and practical, so mystical contemplation and monastic seclusion, even as a preparation for religious life out in the world, seemed morbid, superstitious and un-English. 'Why then this preparation of solitude,' he demanded, 'which can hardly avoid tincturing the mind either with melancholy or superstition?... Surely the principles as well as the practice of Christianity, are simple and lead not to meditation but to action.'[4]

Pitt came to Wimbledon the following day, and for the first time Wilberforce opened his soul to someone. They debated for two hours, but neither orator managed to shift the other's opinions – or, as

Wilberforce put it about his own, Pitt 'soon found himself unable to combat their correctness'.[5] He attributed the prime minister's failure to take Christianity to its logical conclusion to the fact that politics had not given him the time to think things through sufficiently.

The following day Wilberforce found a more like-minded spiritual confidant, John Newton. Newton was now the rector of St Mary Woolnoth in the City of London, and Wilberforce had been thinking for a while that he should visit him, though he fought against it. Sending cryptic notes in private to friends was tough enough, but meeting with Newton would be publicly coming out, turning Methodist by association; and whereas his friends would be only too happy to see the whole thing blow over, evangelicals would attach rather more importance to it. A nagging voice said, 'If ever my sentiments change I shall be ashamed of having done it.'[6]

Wilberforce went to the church on Sunday 4 December with a rather peremptory note for Newton:

Sir,
There is no need of apology for intruding when the subject is religion. I wish to have some serious conversation with you, and will take the liberty of calling on you for that purpose, in half an hour; when, if you cannot receive me, you will have the goodness to let me have a letter put into my hands at the door, naming a time and place for our meeting…

I have had a thousand doubts within myself, whether or not to discover myself to you; but every argument against doing it has its foundation in pride. I am sure you will hold yourself bound to let no one living know of this application, or of my visit, till I release you from the obligation…[7]

Whatever the spiritual hierarchy between the evangelical rector and the anxious new convert, there is no mistaking Wilberforce's tone for one of social equality. Newton was not available that Sunday, but invited Wilberforce back on the Wednesday. When he arrived he had to walk round the square a couple of times before he found the courage to knock. Newton was delighted, of course, to hear that the pious boy he remembered from fifteen years ago had returned to the Lord – though he confessed that he had already heard talk of his reformation – and said that he had never given up hope for him. Newton's advice was not to cut himself off from all his old friends, so that night Wilberforce ventured out to Pitt's, who had several companions round. He had left Newton's feeling spiritually buoyant, but left Pitt's depressed at seeing his zeal so quickly dissipate during an evening in that familiar fashionable society, and that night he found it hard to pray.

It was a dark cold December for his soul. 'I am in a most doubtful state,' cries his diary; 'very wretched – all sense gone'; 'colder than ever – very unhappy'.[8]

Why was spiritual regeneration, instead of making a good man better and happier, such a miserable struggle for Wilberforce? Evangelicals certainly expected Christianity to make a person better and happier, but mere improvement was not what it was about at all. Their spiritual diagnosis was far too dire for that. As Wilberforce put it in his later spiritual writings, every person is 'tainted with sin, not slightly and superficially, but radically and to the very core'.[9] Wilberforce had to learn to see how far his day-to-day conduct fell below God's standard of perfection – his short temper, his flashes of pride, his wounding wit, his willingness to believe gossip – and to see himself as a wretched damned sinner. He had to relearn Newton's lesson: 'Improprieties of conduct, which, though usually considered foibles that hardly deserve a severe censure, are properly sinful.'[10] He had to learn that religion was not what happened when one picked up a Bible or entered church, but was about living every moment of life in the presence and to the glory of God. He had to unlearn the modern gospel that told people like him to repent and do good, by all means, 'but do not make yourselves so uneasy'; true Christians 'prostrate themselves before the cross of Christ with humble penitence and deep self-abhorrence'.[11]

It was hard enough work to maintain such attitudes in his study and in church, where his mind would wander and his heart would tell him that he was not so bad after all. The real battle though was out among his friends. Respectable as they were, their conversation and values were hardly those of Pascal, Butler and the apostle Paul, with whom he spent his reading hours. There was an uncomfortable dissonance between the way he felt among his books, and how he felt among his friends, when he would fall back into old ways and return home feeling far from God.

Another reason for his struggle was that Wilberforce was buying into a strict puritan morality. Evangelicals disapproved of work, play and travel on Sundays. They frowned on dancing and theatre, swearing and wearing decorative buckles or ribbons. John Wesley's Methodist societies (still then a part of the Church of England) forbade, among much else, 'expensiveness or gaiety of apparel', drinking spirits, living beyond one's income, lending with interest, haggling, and receiving money or gifts in exchange for voting. What is perhaps the classic work of evangelical morality was written by John Fletcher, a vicar in Shropshire. Rather than urging readers to turn from sinful pleasures and enjoy the innocent pleasures of life as a gift from God, he saw pleasure itself as the enemy of spiritual life, whether in the form of sweet smells or 'hankerings after news, wit, fine language'. He wrote that if we indulge our tastes, even such apparently harmless ones, they grow and take over our hearts and corrupt us. If we give an inch to our liking for tasty food, we risk dying a glutton and a drunkard. 'Dying to pleasure, we live to God.'[12] Wilberforce did not perhaps go all the way with Fletcher, but still he was starting out on a demanding regime.

More positively, evangelicalism was an activist religion, placing responsibility on every believer to be busy making the world a better place – whether by charity, challenging wickedness, spreading the gospel or just helping people out. Those with the means to do so founded orphanages, labour schemes, free schools and free medical dispensaries. Few people had better opportunities than Wilberforce to make a difference, and yet what did he have to show for the decade since he left home? 'Shapeless idleness,' in a phrase he took from Shakespeare; 'the most valuable years of life wasted and opportunities lost, which can never be recovered.'[13]

And so Wilberforce had to go through the winter of the soul. But as the darkest day of the year passed and Christmas approached, he felt more secure in his new faith, confident enough to resign from all his clubs and to give Newton permission to break the news of his conversion. His aunt Hannah now lived in the village of Clapham, near Wimbledon, with her brother John Thornton, another ardent and wealthy evangelical and a director of the Bank of England. It was Thornton who had appointed Newton to St Mary Woolnoth, and it was to them that Newton brought his glad tidings. Wilberforce started visiting them, and was repeatedly impressed by what a happy man Thornton was, for all his religion. They kept the secret from the wider world until in January Wilberforce was spotted with Newton walking on Wimbledon Common under the cover of darkness. 'Expect to hear myself now universally given out to be a Methodist: may God grant that it may be said with truth.'[14]

As the spring of 1786 passed, Wilberforce continued to mull unhappily over his daily failings, but gradually found 'a more settled peace of conscience' about the state of his soul. In some ways conversion actually eased the burden of conscience – he could spend all day Sunday basking in the sun, enjoying God's creation, without feeling he ought to be working.

In the 1786 parliament, Wilberforce introduced a bill of his own for electoral reform. After the failure of Pitt's efforts, this was a modest attempt to rein in fraud by having a register of voters and requiring different constituencies to vote at the same time. It would only apply to county seats – Wilberforce intended it just for Yorkshire at first, but was persuaded to extend it. It was defeated by the self-interest of the Lords.

In June, Thomas Clarkson's prize essay, translated into English, was published under the title *Essay on the Slavery and Commerce of the Human Species*. Like Ramsay, Clarkson was published by the Quaker James Phillips. He wanted a publisher who saw his essay not as a work of tasteful eloquence, but as an unanswerable demand for justice, and the Quakers were well-established opponents of slavery. What they lacked was the necessary respectability to have an influence; but when they introduced Clarkson to his fellow-Anglicans Ramsay and Sharp (as well as to Equiano), they had the makings of a campaigning group that Britain would listen to. In the meantime, Clarkson devoted himself to gathering intelligence, in which he 'was seldom engaged less than 16 hours a day', he reckoned.

Wilberforce saw his mother and sister for the first time since his conversion, in July 1786 in Yorkshire. He had written before, inviting Sarah 'to participate in the pleasure I am tasting', assuring them that he was not turning into a religious maniac but merely obeying the Bible, nor becoming a hermit but being more 'diligent in the business of life' than ever. His mother, however, had not been reassured, so he did all he could to impress her with the change in his attitudes. He was deferent, patient, mild-tempered and non-judgmental. It worked. 'If this is madness,' said Mrs Sykes, a friend of Elizabeth Wilberforce, as anti-Methodist as Elizabeth herself, 'I hope that he will bite us all.'[15]

Wilberforce gave up his Wimbledon villa in 1786. It was more than a single man needed; its distance from Westminster was a burden on his servants and a waste of time, and the money could be put to better uses. A house in Palace Yard, Westminster, would see him through the parliamentary season, and he had friends throughout the country who were delighted to play host to him in the summer.

As Wilberforce's evangelical faith came through its second winter, he was twenty-seven years old. He felt more secure and confident – although he still had his ups and downs – and no less zealous. He was full of energy, and he also happened to be a prominent, well-respected member of the most powerful political body in the Western world. It was time to move from deploring his failure to do anything to make the world better, to doing something to make the world better. He would use his position to combat the greatest evils of the eighteenth-century world as he saw it: sabbath-breaking, swearing, drunkenness and indecent books.

6

Manacles and Manners

At four o'clock in the morning, the plantation bell rings to call the slaves to the field. Their work is to manure, dig, and hoe, plough the ground, to plant, weed, and cut the cane, to bring it to the mill, to have the juice expressed and boiled into sugar. About nine o'clock, they have half an hour for breakfast, which they take in the field.

Again they fall to the work, and according to the custom of the plantation, continue until eleven o'clock, or noon; the bell rings and the slaves are dispersed in the neighbourhood to pick up... natural grass and weeds for the horses and cattle....

At one, or in some plantations, at two o'clock, the bell summons them to deliver the tale of their grass, and assemble to their field work. If the overseer thinks the bundle too small, or if they come too late with them, they are punished with a number of stripes from four to ten. Some masters under a fit of carefulness for their cattle, have gone as far as fifty stripes, which effectively disable the culprit for weeks.

James Ramsay, *Essay on the Treatment and Conversion of African Slaves*, 1784[1]

What Britain needed, to Wilberforce's mind, was a Society for the Reformation of Manners; and if that sounds somewhat fatuous, this was 'manners' in the sense of behaviour in general, rather than not talking with your mouth full – public morality as we might call it today. He aimed to get the most influential people in the country to join, and to work together against 'the torrent of profaneness that every day makes more rapid advances'. They would get new laws passed, and ensure that existing laws were better enforced by appointing more conscientious men as magistrates and constables, and by prosecuting offenders themselves. And it would be founded by the decree of King George III.

It is not a cause that naturally draws a great deal of sympathy today, and compared to the abolition of slavery it seems especially superfluous. Is this not evangelical morality at its least attractive, poking a holy nose into other people's business? And is it not safe to assume that the supposedly universal clampdown was more rigorously applied on the streets of the mill towns and ports than in White's and Brooks's? Very probably, in both cases – Sydney Smith called it 'the Society for the Suppression of Vice Among Those With Less Than £500 a Year'. But to be fair, Wilberforce's campaign had widespread support from across the religious spectrum, and he was hardly the first person or the last to believe that society was awry, although diagnoses and prescriptions differ. The top-down approach of the Society seems especially unappealing and oppressive today, but eighteenth-century society was thoroughly patriarchal and that is how things got done. There were those like Wesley who appealed directly to men and women to change their ways, but the unruliness of Methodism was more controversial than Wilberforce's approach. His scheme appears at its most sympathetic in a letter to Christopher Wyvill, where he presents it as a replacement for capital punishment: 'The barbarous custom of hanging has been tried too long. The most effective way to prevent the greater crimes is… endeavouring to repress the general spirit of licentiousness.'[2]

The plans for this campaign were at least as important to Wilberforce as his interest in the slave trade. In the autumn of 1786, Sir Charles Middleton, Ramsay's patron, wrote to Wilberforce suggesting he bring the issue of the slave trade before parliament, according to the account of C. I. Latrobe, a Moravian minister and friend of Middleton's. Apparently, Lady Middleton had asked her husband to do the job, but though an MP, he had never made a speech in parliament and did not intend to start. Latrobe tells us that Wilberforce replied 'that he felt the importance of the subject, and thought himself unequal to the task allotted to him, but yet would not positively decline it'.[3]

His sons tell us that he had already been collecting information on the subject, and now stepped up his research, interviewing the traders themselves and finding them happy to talk, their livelihood 'not having yet become the subject of alarming discussion', while also holding meetings in Wimbledon for 'persons who knew anything about the matter', including Ramsay and Middleton.[4]

Clarkson, meanwhile, on behalf of his own group, was visiting all the MPs living in London whom he thought might be sympathetic to the abolition of the slave trade. And so he and Wilberforce met for the first time in the spring of 1787. Clarkson gave Wilberforce a copy of his essay, which Wilberforce read and questioned him on. Clarkson recalls hearing that 'the subject had often employed his thoughts, and that it was near his heart', but Wilberforce divulged no further plans. He was delighted to hear of Clarkson's commitment to the cause, asked to be kept regularly informed, and promised whatever help he could offer.

Clarkson says in his own history of the abolition movement that at one of their talks he suggested to Wilberforce the idea of meeting with his parliamentary friends, and said that the first meeting included the pair of them, Middleton, Ramsay and Sharp among others. Clarkson and the Wilberforce sons are in direct contradiction here over whether these meetings originated with Wilberforce before he met Clarkson, or with Clarkson afterwards. Clarkson is also absolutely emphatic that while he found the slave trade 'deeply impressed on his heart'[5] already, Wilberforce's only information so far was about conditions on the islands, derived from Ramsay and Latrobe, because he had not yet – despite what his sons claim – talked to traders.

It is conceivable that Clarkson is wrong. There is some truth in Robert Wilberforce's remark that Clarkson's recollections, twenty years after the event, offer an 'exaggerated estimate of his own services' to the movement.[6] The Wilberforces' version, on the other hand, fifty years later, is deliberately malicious and possibly unscrupulous in its revision of that estimate. We cannot with any confidence take the word of either over the other, but Robert Wilberforce inspires less confidence than Clarkson.

After these meetings, Wilberforce felt well enough informed to talk about the trade with Pitt. He sat outdoors one day with him and his cousin and minister William Grenville, and laid before them his intelligence. Having been brought up with the values of the British enlightenment, Pitt and Grenville were enthusiastic. 'Why don't you give notice of a motion on the subject of the slave trade?' Pitt says in the Wilberforce brothers' records. 'You have already taken great pains to collect evidence, and are therefore fully entitled to the credit which doing so will ensure you. Do not lose time, or the ground may be occupied by another.'* And so, says Wilberforce, 'in the open air at the root of an old tree in Holwood just above the steep descent into the vale of Keston, I resolved to give notice on a fit occasion in the House of Commons of my intention to bring the subject forward'.[7]

It was shortly after this, apparently, that Clarkson's group approached Wilberforce with the same idea. They had decided to form themselves into an official campaigning organization, but not until they had found someone committed to representing the cause in parliament. Wilberforce was obviously the man although, Clarkson tells us, 'he had never yet dropped the least hint that he would proceed so far'. Clarkson says that he met with him to ask if he would do it, and yet strangely bottled out of putting the great question: 'I seemed unable to inform him of the object of my visit... I had a feeling within me for which I could not account, and which seemed to hinder me from proceeding. And I actually went away without informing him of my errand.'[8]

And so Bennet Langton, the aristocratic dandy of their anti-slavery group, agreed to approach Wilberforce instead. At a dinner party at Langton's in May 1787, Clarkson talked to guests about the horrors of the trade that he had so far unearthed, showing them samples of African cloth to demonstrate that the continent had more to offer Europe in the way of trade than human flesh. The guests were passionately stirred: 'Rather let Liverpool and the Islands be swallowed up in the sea,' said one, 'than this monstrous system of iniquity continue.' Boswell, later an ardent opponent of abolition,

---

* Pitt probably had in mind Fox who, when Wilberforce brought his first slave trade bill, declared: 'I have myself considered the subject very minutely, and it was my intention to bring something forward in this House respecting it.' He added that when he heard that Wilberforce was taking it on, he said: 'I was unaffectedly rejoiced' as he brought to it 'more weight, more authority, and more probability of success' than he himself could.

half-heartedly agreed that, however preferable British slavery was to African savagery, 'we have no right to make people happy against their will'. Langton then suggested to Wilberforce that with his gifts and good name he was the best man to bring a bill to abolish the slave trade before parliament. Wilberforce replied 'that he had no objection to bringing forward the measure in parliament, when he was better prepared for it, and provided no better person could be found'.[9] Other MPs present pledged their support.

There is some contest, then, for who takes the credit for inspiring Wilberforce to take on the slave trade. Latrobe championed the claim of Lady Middleton (it was evidence of the wonderful mystery of God that 'it was the work of a *woman*'[10]); Clarkson championed his own while the Wilberforce brothers championed God's, seconded by the prime minister. It is impossible to adjudicate between their uncorroborated versions of events. Clarkson took the good news to his friends, and on 22 May 1787, they founded the Committee for the Abolition of the African Slave Trade. They formed a management committee of twelve: Sharp was president, being the Anglican with the most longstanding commitment to fighting slavery; Clarkson and one other completed the Anglican contingent; and the other nine were all Quakers, including the printer James Phillips and William Dillwyn.

That year, Pitt translated Porteus, the abolitionist Bishop of Chester, to London, where he had oversight of the colonies as well as the capital. The US Constitutional convention of 1787 discussed the slave trade as an issue dividing the southern plantation states from the north, where some had already abolished slavery. The Constitution debarred Congress from prohibiting slave imports before 1808, as one cost of including the south in the union.

Clarkson and Wilberforce both set off on tours of Britain. Clarkson went principally to Bristol and Liverpool, where he gathered testimony from sailors and doctors among others. He boarded a slaver to see the slave decks, and collected examples of the apparatus of the trade – shackles, thumbscrews and a kind of forceps used to force food into the mouths of the uncooperative. He also collected death threats from traders and sailors, and once narrowly escaped with his life. In Manchester, by contrast, he excited such support for the cause that within a couple of months 20 per cent of the population had signed a petition to parliament protesting against the slave trade. He returned with the stories of 20,000 sailors – more information than the traders themselves had. Wilberforce was touring for his other society, for the reformation of manners. He had won the ear of the Archbishop of Canterbury with his idea, who in turn talked to the king.

The king was most enthusiastic, having issued a proclamation against 'vice, profaneness, and immorality' off his own back twenty-seven years before. He proclaimed again, on 1 June 1787, that wickedness should be dealt with, and the Proclamation Society was founded to do so. With such sponsorship, Wilberforce did not want his humble name too closely connected with the great work, but he quietly toured the country persuading undecided bishops and nobles to give it their active support. He thoroughly succeeded, despite the somewhat misjudged warning from one of the latter – 'So you wish, young man, to be a reformer of men's morals. Look then, and see there what is the end of such reformers'[11] – this said pointing to a picture of the crucifixion of Christ. The Duke of Montagu became the chairman, and under his leadership the dignitaries of the society started to get books censored and moral reforms passed through parliament without needing very much help from Wilberforce. 'God Almighty has set before me two great objects,' he wrote in October, 'the suppression of the slave trade and the reformation of manners.'[12] But whatever their respective merits, it was the former that would now be taking up his time.

By November 1787, both Wilberforce and Clarkson were back in London, procuring the facts and drumming up the support needed to get the slave trade outlawed. They interviewed potential witnesses, and Wilberforce got Clarkson access to valuable documents; he became the first outsider allowed to delve into the Custom House records. Both used whatever contacts they had to organize petitions. According to George Stephen, who was still nine years away from being born but who in time would become a close associate of Wilberforce, Clarkson was his 'abolition walking stick', on whom he leaned too much for information and judgment, rather than making the effort needed to obtain his own. In case it needs saying, nothing in the Wilberforces' biography supports this.

It was forty years after his evangelical conversion and thirty-six after he quit slaving that John Newton was finally stung by the wickedness of the slave trade into campaigning for its abolition, and so he published *Thoughts upon the African Slave Trade*. He would be a major witness for the parliamentary inquiry, and his book not only offered first-hand accounts of the injury the trade did to Africans, but argued that it did immense damage to Britain too: it corrupted and brutalized those who took part, and killed vast numbers – one in five – through storm, disease, liquor, venereal infection and slave insurrection.

Josiah Wedgwood, the celebrated ceramic designer, joined the abolition committee which, showing a genius for publicity that came from the Quakers' years of experience in lobbying and campaigning, commissioned him to produce an engraving 'expressive of an African in chains in a supplicating posture', which they could use as a seal. Wedgwood's design encircled the slave with the words 'Am I Not A Man and A Brother?', and copies were sold throughout the country.

The campaign was now joined by one of the very few African voices to be heard in the debate. Ottobah Cugoano had been taken to the sugar plantations of Grenada from present-day Ghana, but was then brought to England where he was freed and became a servant of the celebrated painter Richard Cosway, and a friend of Equiano. His book, *Thoughts and Sentiments on the Evil and Wicked Traffic of the Commerce of the Human Species*, contained a brief memoir of his experience of slavery, and a much longer Christian political discourse on its iniquity. He went further than most of his white abolitionist brothers, arguing for an immediate abolition of slavery itself rather than just the trade, and he also spoke in defence of Native Americans.

The date set for Wilberforce's Commons motion was 2 February 1788, so the abolitionists hoped that the slave trade would be outlawed by the summer. Wilberforce, like the others, was full of confidence. The prime minister was on their side, as was Fox, the main leader of opposition in the Commons, and Burke, who had planned legislation against slavery in 1780 but dropped it when he realized that the West India party – the largest organized grouping in parliament apart from the main parties – could destroy his career. With the four great orators of British politics for abolition, Wilberforce thought, who could stand against them? Of course the owners of plantations and slave ships had their presence in the House, but not enough to resist the tide of righteous outrage, Wilberforce estimated. 'There is no doubt of the success.'

On 15 January, the London-based abolition committee published a report taking Clarkson's line that abolition was not simply a moral imperative but also made good economic sense: 'The commerce of this kingdom and even the interest of the slave-holders themselves, will be advanced by the success of our endeavours.'[13] Clarkson's researches at the Custom House confirmed Newton's reports that: the disease-ridden slave ships claimed a vast number of sailors' lives as well as slaves'; there were great opportunities for non-human trade with West Africa; and, if decently treated, West Indian slaves would survive and reproduce, without owners having to buy replacements. This last point reflects the committee's tactical decision (opposed by Sharp) to publicly assail only the trade and not slavery itself, despite the fact that they were thoroughly committed, secretly, to the complete emancipation of all slaves. Similarly Wedgwood argued, 'We are already possessed of a stock of negroes fully sufficient... for every purpose of the cultivation and trade of our plantations; and consequently... our West India commerce could not be materially injured by prohibiting further importation.'[14]

Wilberforce got Clarkson an interview with the prime minister to discuss the committee's campaign. There is yet another conflict here between Clarkson's account and the Wilberforces. As far as Clarkson is concerned, his job was 'to try to interest him [the prime minister]' in abolition. 'Mr. Pitt appeared to me to have but little knowledge of it,' he says. 'He had also his doubts, which he expressed openly, on many points.'[15] This account sits poorly with the Holwood story, and with Pitt's later undeniably intimate involvement with the nuts and bolts of abolition; poorly enough, perhaps, to justify the Wilberforces' claim that Clarkson overestimated his importance to the development of the movement, if not their vendetta against him.

Wilberforce was disappointed when Pitt's government failed to engage the French government in a bilateral agreement to abolish the trade. This would have helped allay fears that if Britain renounced it others would simply scoop up their profits, but Wilberforce did not think it essential. All across the country campaigners were drawing up petitions on a scale that had never been known on any issue before. There was clearly a powerful national will for change.

A week before the proposed date for the parliamentary motion, Wilberforce was telling Wyvill: 'The cause of our poor Africans goes on most prosperously. I trust there is little reason to doubt of the motion for the abolition of this horrid traffic in flesh and blood being carried in parliament.'[16] As confident as Wilberforce, Pitt made the arrangements for a Privy Council inquiry into the trade, which would involve interviewing representatives of both sides and producing a report for parliament.

And then disaster struck.

7

The Valley of the Shadow

November 4   One man – inflammation of the liver
November 29   One man – of a dysentery
December 18   One woman – suddenly
January 1   One man – of a dysentery
January 3   One woman – ditto
January 6   One woman – of a lethargy
January 15   One boy – of a dysentery
January 16   One manboy – ditto
January 17   One girl – ditto
January 18   One man – ditto
January 19   One boy – ditto
January 28   One boy – ditto
January 31   One woman – of sulkiness
February 3   One manboy – of a lethargy
February 8   One man – of a dysentery

December 20   Departed this life, Mr Orchard, of a pleurisy

An official list by the ship's surgeon, Joseph Buckham, of deaths on board the ship *James*, 1788–89[1]

Wilberforce had been rather ill in January 1788, and soon worsened. By the end of the month, he was too weak to attend parliament. He was violently sick, feverish and listless. According to a modern diagnosis, he may have been suffering from an ulcerated colon. His sight, as so often, was desperate. A couple of times he seemed to take a turn for the better, but he was confined to bed for most of February and March. Isaac Milner was worried enough to cancel his Cambridge lectures to visit him, and his sister and mother – increasingly frail herself – came down from Yorkshire.

'He cannot last for three weeks,' said a friend. His doctor said he would not last a fortnight. Dr Hey had been prescribing him opium; now all he could do was to send him with his family to Bath, the last resort. His final request to Pitt before he left to take the waters was for Pitt to take over the abolition campaign after Wilberforce's death. The prime minister promised to do so, Wilberforce wrote, 'with a warmth of principle and friendship that have made me love him better than I ever did before'.[2] The difference that Wilberforce's untimely illness made to the cause hardly bears thinking about. An extraordinary surge of public feeling was behind it and there was still no organized opposition to abolition, but there would be no parliamentary bill debated that year.

The day before Wilberforce had been due to announce the motion, Wyvill's first petition from constituents in Yorkshire was presented to parliament. Six days later, on Thursday 7 February, there came one from Ripon and another from Maidstone. On the Friday, Pitt presented the first of two from Cambridge University. On Monday, as the Privy Council inquiry was launched, the Manchester petition inspired by Clarkson's visit arrived, with 10,000 signatures. On Tuesday, there was one from the Dissenting ministers of London, and a second petition from Yorkshire. And they kept coming. By the end of May, more than 100 petitions had been presented. Parliament had never seen anything remotely like it.

The first letters on the subject started appearing in *The Gentleman's Magazine*, the popular pioneering periodical which invented the word 'magazine' in its modern sense. A correspondent from Gloucester protested that British slavery 'was a kind of tyranny hitherto unheard of in the annals of history', but 'a sense of compassion for our West India slaves seems gaining ground in this kingdom'. One correspondent from the Isle of Wight inveighed against 'such frauds and barbarities as are exercised in this man-stealing, man-buying and man-murdering system'; but 'thanks to heaven the morning dawns which brings a brighter prospect'.[3]

Propaganda poured off the abolitionist presses. Clarkson, Ramsay,

Benezet and Peckard all produced new books. James Phillips took the testimonies of Alexander Falconbridge, a slave ship doctor whom Clarkson had met on his travels and who had become a passionate campaigner, and edited them into a book. Others wrote poems, even a play. The abolition committee commissioned Cowper to write a verse for the movement, 'The Negro's Complaint'. This was set to music and the anthem proved as popular and iconic as the civil rights folk songs of the 1960s. Wedgwood's 'Am I Not A Man and A Brother?' was the must-have fashion accessory of the moment, appearing on medallions, snuff boxes, brooches and cufflinks, and printed on posters and in magazines.

Naturally campaigners felt frustrated, having created an unprecedented popular lobbying movement, with no one to bring it to a head in parliament because of Wilberforce's illness. Some of them asked the abolition committee to choose another MP. The committee wrote to Wilberforce in April, asking him what they should do. His doctors would not allow him to read letters about the slave trade, but his mother and friends wrote to Pitt in his name, passing on the baton, and Pitt told Sharp that he would be taking Wilberforce's place.

In May 1788, Pitt formally proposed a parliamentary review of the slave trade to take place after the summer. There was predictable dissent from the MPs most closely concerned with the colonial import of Africans, but a review did not mean a change to the law, and so the motion was carried easily enough. Of its success next year, 'there seems not a shadow of doubt,' he wrote to Wilberforce.[4]

Meanwhile, with all this talk of the inhumanity of the trade, a group of MPs led by Sir William Dolben, an elderly friend of Wilberforce's and a member of his Proclamation Society, visited a slaver moored in the Thames to see for themselves, and the cramped lower decks confirmed the stories they had heard. The appalled Dolben was not satisfied with leaving everything to Pitt's leisurely approach, and wanted a law passed before the end of the parliamentary session that would immediately limit the number of slaves being transported on a ship of any given size. Some abolitionists feared that regulating the trade would seem to legitimize it, making abolishing it all the harder in the long run. But the really worrying sign was how the pro-slavery wing of parliament reared into action against it. They insisted that it was the self-regulation of the industry that brought such great wealth into the country, and that interference could be disastrous. Lord Penrhyn, the Liverpool MP who had built a castle in Bangor on the profits from his plantations, insisted that traders had the sense to do nothing that would endanger the health of their passengers, and assured the House that every slave rescued from the barbarities of African life and given a career in colonial agriculture looked back on that indolent cruise as 'the happiest period of his life'. Pitt was furious, and threatened, if the bill was not passed, to move straight on to 'the utter abolition of a trade which is shocking to humanity, is abominable to be carried on by any country, and reflects the greatest dishonour on the British senate and the British nation'.[5]

This threat carried the bill through the Commons, but not the Lords. There it faced millions of pounds of vested interest, much of which belonged to Pitt's cabinet. The slave trade was vital to the economy, their lordships warned each other. Hampering it would merely hand British trade to the French and would encourage slaves to revolt and massacre their masters. Those stories of the cruelties of the 'Middle Passage' from Africa to the Caribbean were fanatical fantasies, they said. Lord Rodney had spent three years in the West Indies and assured his peers that he never once heard of a slave being abused, 'but had often spoken of their happiness in terms of rapture'. Pitt's Lord Chancellor Thurlow, emboldened by the Lords' coolness, viciously derided the bill: the men behind this 'five days' fit of philanthropy' should learn something from the French, who offered tax breaks for colonial personnel transportation. He spoke, with no little philanthropy himself, of owners coming to London, 'with tears in their eyes and horror in their countenances, to deprecate the ruin of their property, which they had embarked on the faith of parliament'. The king himself, he said, was persuaded that 'it was his royal duty to show humanity to the whites as well as the negroes'.[6]

This time the only threat that could get the bill passed was the ultimate one: Pitt would dissolve the government. This was enough to get the bill through by a slim majority but with sufficient amendments to completely emasculate it. So Pitt introduced a new bill to restore the original regulations, frogmarched it through the Commons in a single day, and again fought his lord chancellor in order to drive it through the Lords, refusing to let parliament break for the summer until it was finally passed, on 11 July, by 2 votes.

And so the first legislation to curtail the slave trade was enacted. It was a small victory, achieving nothing more radical than reducing overcrowding on slave ships. And yet what had it taken? An unprecedented national campaign of 100 petitions, the repeated intervention of the prime minister, the staking of his own government and a second (and in fact a third) bill – and all to haul it through by the narrowest of margins. What hope then for getting parliament to agree to abolishing the slave trade altogether, let alone slavery itself? And the parliamentary leader of the movement was apparently on his deathbed. From that crest of a wave half a year ago, the optimism of the abolitionists was dashed on the rocks.

At the same time, sceptical voices were increasingly being heard, in books, pamphlets, magazines and newspapers, questioning the wisdom of abolition. This reaction is often talked of as a counterattack from the slave-traders and plantation owners, and a large part of it was; but it also came from ordinary educated people with no great financial interest in the trade, who were simply unconvinced by the arguments of the abolition movement. They heard the horror stories of campaigners such as Ramsay and Falconbridge, but then heard them repeatedly denied by many other witnesses, and heard horror stories about the kind of life that slaves left behind in Africa.

Someone calling himself 'Plotinus' wrote to *The Gentleman's Magazine* from Cumberland, with a list of arguments against the abolition campaign – 'one of the most extravagant projects of human folly ever devised'. Abolition would give British commerce to its enemies – we might as well give the French free guns to use against us, he wrote. The movement appealed to gullible consciences with lurid fictions about the 'imaginary anguish' of kidnapped Africans, while more reliable sources assured us that 'the more civilized negroes reflect in horror at their savage condition, and do not easily forgive the reproach of having been born in Africa'. Abolition would also make the British working classes dissatisfied with their own lot, and effectively 'enfranchise' them, till the streets would run with blood. Above all, the abolitionists erred in applying moral judgments to the actions of government, when in reality they only applied to individuals: 'Self-preservation is the primary law of nations.'[7]

'Plotinus' pointed to a travelogue called *A Voyage to the Coast of Guinea*. In this, a naval surgeon assured readers that in his experience most Africans were 'stupid'. They 'would eat all day if victuals were set before them, and, if not, would utter no complaint; part without tears from their wives, their children, and their country'.[8] Similarly, William Beckford, who had spent thirteen years of his childhood in Jamaica, observed of the negro that 'his mind is vacant', not burdened with the power of anticipation, so continual whipping was less unpleasant than one might think. Africans needed slavery to give them something to do – 'They no sooner cease to move, than they cease to think, and four out of five would remain in continual torpor; unless they were roused by the provocatives of thirst or hunger.' Beckford offered these observations 'impartially' and as 'an advocate for humanity', he said; not then, presumably, in his capacity as the owner of twelve plantations which had made him Britain's first millionaire.[9]

In *A Voyage to the River Sierra-Leone*, another traveller John Matthews argued that the people sold to slave traders were convicts who would be executed if the British did not offer them the merciful alternative of transportation to the Caribbean. And while slavery saved their lives, those left behind enjoyed the invaluable goods that the slavers brought in return. It seems the slave trade itself was one sustained fit of philanthropy. The Liverpool trader Robert Norris said that the plantations were 'a land of freedom to them'.[10] The Danish historian Grímr Jónsson Thorkelin went so far as to argue that without this rescue mission the west coast of Africa would be 'reeking with the gore of young and old. Can [Europe] give up, with indifference, those millions whom she might save from brutal tyrants, and place in a state of servitude comparatively happy?'[11]

A army officer by the appropriately memorable name of Philip Thicknesse published a lively volume of memoirs which included some time spent in the Caribbean. From his experience he was able to inform readers that 'the negroes are a species of the human race... but that they are an inferior & a very different order of men, I sincerely believe'. In the most astounding argument of this whole debate, but one quite typical in its own way of the double standards of the slavery lobby, he proved this judgment by referring the reader to the kidnap of Africans by Africans: 'Do the Indians of North America, or any other nation under the sun, beside the negroes, traffic in human flesh?' asked Thicknesse.[12]

One final argument that many defenders of the slave trade reiterated was that even if one could point to certain hardships in the slave lifestyle, their lot was better than that of the working poor in Britain, so why all the fuss? Modern critics of the abolitionists have often made the same point in reverse – why were they so exercised about slavery overseas, and yet blind to the cruel exploitation under their own noses? We shall consider the question later on with respect to Wilberforce himself, but a reader who wrote to *The Gentleman's Magazine* in reply to Thicknesse's memoirs gives us a good provisional answer. He asked 'whether English peasants have their eyes beat out, their bones broken, their flesh furrowed by the whip? Are their wives and children... taken from them, and sold to different parts? Do they cultivate barren spots of ground, on Sundays, for food? Is their daily allowance six ounces of flour?'[13] As long as they were in their homeland, without fear of being sold, and under the full protection of the law, British workers might not be in paradise, but at least they were not in Barbados.

Bath seemed to agree with Wilberforce – medically if not spiritually. His health started slowly to recover, but for all the powers of its waters, he complained that it was 'too dissipated a place', distracting him with leisure and pleasure. He also attributed his recovery to his doctor's daily prescription of opium. He insisted that the dose was so tiny that it had no discernible effect at all, but as he continued to take the same dose every day till he died, he was clearly an addict, if an unusually strong-willed one.

In June, he was well enough to go with his family to convalesce in the Lake District, staying for three months in the old house in Rayrigg. He was not impressed to find that in his absence Windermere had become a tourist attraction, and it crawled with upper class holidaymakers, knocking on his window to waste time with trivial chitchat. He bitterly bewailed his own idleness and self-indulgence throughout the stay as well, though one might have thought a little relaxation was called for, given the circumstances.

George III came to take the Cheltenham waters for his own ills, and though he seemed to recover it turned out he was seriously ill; by November his brain was affected too. Reports circulated of him 'howling like a dog', racing against horses, 'showing his backside to attendants', and shaking hands with the lower branches of an oak tree in Windsor Park under the impression that it was the King of Prussia. This was extremely bad news for Pitt, because the Prince of Wales was a close ally of Fox. He had been hungry for the crown for years, not least because of his vast debts, and it seemed that finally his father was dying and incapable of ruling. Fox's opposition party would waste no time getting the prince declared regent, and he would immediately replace Pitt with Fox, and call an election in which he would spend his new fortune packing the House with Fox's men. All Pitt could do was to stall for time, and hope for a miracle. He was helped by the fact that Fox was currently racing frantically back from Italy, but members of Pitt's cabinet, including Thurlow, started negotiating with Fox's men to save their careers.

Wilberforce came to Westminster twice, just for parliament to be adjourned, and went straight back to Bath each time. In December, however, he returned to full business, examining reports on the king's health and the political precedents for the royal crisis. Then came the great debate in parliament, with Fox arguing that the prince should automatically take the throne as if George III had just died, and Pitt arguing that it was parliament's job to declare Prince George regent and decide the terms of his rule. It was Pitt who was victorious. Fox had devoted his life to promoting the rights of parliament over royal autocracy, and yet he was now demanding that parliament step aside for the prince, simply because it would make him prime minister. Pitt exhibited this hypocrisy to the House unsparingly and won the vote as well as time to negotiate the terms of the regency that would unseat him. 'My friend is every day matter of fresh and growing admiration,' Wilberforce reported to Wyvill. 'I wish you were as constantly as I am witness to that simple and earnest regard for the public welfare, by which he is so uniformly actuated... You would love him more and more.'[14]

By January 1789, Wilberforce, though not entirely well, was strong enough to devote himself to what he called the 'slave business'. His abolition bill was to come before the House of Commons in April and until then, along with Clarkson, he kept himself busy ploughing through the facts, figures and arguments, putting together the case that he was to present to parliament. They spent most of their time in Teston, the home of Middleton and Ramsay. Various visitors joined them in the work, including William Burgh who had declined to join Wilberforce's fateful continental tour, and Edward Eliot, who had accompanied Wilberforce and Pitt to France, later marrying Pitt's sister and being thrown into a religious conversion like Wilberforce's when she died. Wilberforce also paid his only visit to the 85-year-old John Wesley, 'a fine old fellow'. (He later visited Charles Wesley's widow, and, disgusted by how poorly the Methodists had provided for her, arranged a pension.)

Following puritan religious tradition, Wilberforce made new year's resolutions, which included keeping a precise daily log of how he spent his time. So on 26 January, for example, he spent 4 1/2 hours in the Commons, 5 3/4 in his studies, 1 1/2 in spiritual reading and meditation, 1 3/4 in necessary company, 1/4 in necessary relaxation, 1 1/4 getting dressed and undressed and 8 1/2 in bed, which leaves half an hour 'squandered'.

As the weeks passed, George III seemed to recover completely; the regency was avoided and Pitt's administration secured. Wilberforce spent more and more time on the abolition motion but his health suffered, and the work suffered in return. He was repeatedly incapacitated; in February he was out of action for a week. There were other sacrifices too. In April, he heard that Isaac Milner was seriously ill, and badly wanted to visit him, but he decided that it would threaten the abolition bill, and so had to stay in Teston.

The abolition committee stepped up the pressure with the greatest publicity coup of the whole anti-slavery movement: they published a diagram of a slave ship filled with slaves. Specifically it was the *Brookes*, a 300-tonne Liverpool slaver, depicted with the figures of 482 slaves lying shoulder to shoulder, all precisely to scale. They had it printed in posters and magazines, and even had wooden models made, and the image quickly spread through the abolitionist network across Britain. It had a phenomenal impact, making 'an instantaneous impression of horror on all who saw it', in Clarkson's words. It combined the visceral impact of the first visual image that most people had seen of the Middle Passage, with cold, hard facts and figures. The nightmarish claustrophobia of it is all the more powerful for its clinical detachment. And most disturbing of all is the fact, which the posters point out, that this diagram of what one would assume is absolute capacity, is made according to the supposedly ruinous restrictions of Dolben's bill; before then the *Brookes* had carried up to half as many again. Equiano now published his memoirs, *An Interesting Narrative of the Life of Olaudah Equiano*, the compelling story of his kidnap, the Middle Passage, slavery and his travels. It was a huge hit, running to eight editions in the eight remaining years of his life, and he toured the country promoting it 'with his *white* wife', as the papers reported.

By Easter, a week before the motion was due, Wilberforce was spending eight or nine hours every day with Clarkson, Ramsay and others, in preparation. In the seven days around Easter, his daily log records only one quarter of an hour 'squandered'. Even on Easter Sunday, this defender of the Sabbath spent 3½ hours on slave business. When he went to church the following Sunday, it was to hear Clarkson preaching about abolition. In fact, Wilberforce was almost as unhappy about this overwork as he had been previously about his idleness. He felt his spiritual life suffered from his having 'too little leisure for serious thoughts'. And yet to his credit he refused, despite the frowns of friends, to compromise the success of the 'great object' to his private spiritual well-being. On the other hand, his physical well-being suffered too, and once again the motion had to be postponed. Pitt wrote to him on Good Friday telling him to stay in Teston, saying that he was postponing the motion for a month and doing some work with Grenville on the shape of the bill.

The Privy Council's report on the slave trade was finally completed soon after. It was a vast document, 890 large pages long, compiling interviews, tables, letters, reports, accounts, colonial and British laws, surgical journals, muster rolls, land surveys and ship dimensions. It contained the results of fourteen months of interviews with fifty witnesses, detailing – amid a forest of economical and geographical data – the killing of unsaleable slaves, the torture of rebel slaves, the dejection and disease of all slaves, the treatment of 'mistresses', the conning of sailors into the trade and marooning them in the Caribbean when slaves were unloaded. What it did not include, however, except for a short letter from Equiano, was any testimony from a black person. Parliament solicited the opinions and stories of soldiers and doctors, merchants and ministers, colonial governors and even the curator of a museum in Stockholm, but at no point in the course of the investigation was it thought necessary to obtain the information and experiences of slaves themselves, although there were hundreds of former slaves at hand in London. It is not clear whether this is because the prejudice of MPs was so entrenched that abolitionists knew they would not listen to black voices, or whether the prejudice of abolitionists themselves was so entrenched that it simply never occurred to them that the slaves might have something useful to add to their researches into slavery. Either way, the most well-informed witnesses with the greatest right to testify were never heard, depriving us forever of a record of their experiences.

Pitt officially presented the report to the House on 25 April 1789, giving MPs nearly three weeks to digest its contents before the debate on 12 May – including Wilberforce himself, who had to prepare for what would probably be the most important speech of his life.

8

The Greatest Speech in History

Absented himself from the subscriber, the 4th of this instant, negro man, named Limus; he is of a yellow complexion, and has the ends of three of his fingers cut off his left hand; he is well known in Charles-Town from his saucy and impudent tongue, of which I have had many complaints; therefore, I hereby give free liberty, and will be also much obliged to any person to flog him (so as not take his life) in such manner as they shall think proper, whenever he is found out of my habitation without a ticket; for though he is my property, he has the audacity to tell me, he will be free, that he will serve no man, and that he will be conquered or governed by no man.

Appeal for a missing person from Joshua Eden, *South Carolina Gazette*, 7 November 1775[1]

What was the slave trade precisely, and why had such a great and obvious evil ever been permitted?

It was called the 'triangular trade': ships left Britain laden with goods that were in demand from African traders – arms, alcohol, cloth, pots, beads – heading south to the coast of West Africa; there this merchandise was exchanged for slaves, which traders then took west to the Caribbean, the infamous Middle Passage; there they sold them to plantation managers or other traders and with the proceeds the dealers bought sugar, plus perhaps rum, tobacco, or cotton, which they brought back to England. If all had gone well, after about a year, they could perhaps make a 15 per cent profit. This was by no means guaranteed though. Unlucky slavers might face shipwreck, pirates, slave mutiny or disease. The cost of the round trip for a large ship might be £35,000, in which case investors would hope to see a return of £5,000 or more; but fortunes could be lost as well as made. This is why traders had felt genuinely aggrieved by Dolben's law to regulate the traffic – it was perilous enough already.

While all the attention was naturally on the supply of slaves to the British Caribbean, British traders in fact sold up to twice as many to other European powers in the region – to the French, Dutch and Danish islands, to the Spanish and Portuguese colonies on the mainland, and to the United States – a fact that caused widespread consternation when it emerged from the Privy Council investigation that the slave trade was bolstering foreign empires. Available figures are sketchy and contradictory, but throughout the 1780s an estimated total of 794,000 African slaves had been taken across the Atlantic, half of them in British ships. The latter fetched an average of £36 each, a little over £10 profit per head.

Where exactly all these slaves came from is unclear. They were sold to British captains by African slave traders on the west coast, and the buyers had little interest in their provenance. The Privy Council had researched the question, leaving no stone unturned short of actually asking former slaves themselves, but the traders had little more than vague impressions to share. The conclusions from the Privy Council report that Pitt incorporated into Wilberforce's bill were these: the principal source of slaves was from prisoners of war; secondly, there were convicted criminals; thirdly, debtors; and lastly, the victims of kidnap. Anti-abolitionists argued that the first three were entirely legitimate forms of bondage, and even merciful when compared to alternative punishments. Abolitionists replied that wars were waged for the express purpose of taking prisoners to sell – in other words, they were simply mass kidnapping operations. And when there was such a financial incentive for convicting people of crimes, it takes a demanding degree of naivety to assume that hundreds of thousands were sentenced each year to this lucrative trade without any abuse of criminal justice.

The experience of the Middle Passage varied tremendously, without being anything short of horrendous. Some ships were more overcrowded than others; men were shackled together while women and children were not; a man might have the good luck to have standing room, or he might lie in the two-foot space below a shelf, on a platform shorter than himself; he might even spend the journey on his side to fit in more people 'spoonwise'. Some captains and crews were more brutal than others; a slave might or might not catch dysentery; how much choppy seas multiplied the pain and discomfort of the manacles would vary, as would the frequency with which bad weather prevented passengers being allowed up on deck; and the voyage might be over in four weeks, or it could drag on for four months while food and water ran out.

The British slave trade all started in the reign of Queen Elizabeth. Portuguese and Spanish colonists had been taking slaves from Africa to their plantations in the Americas since the start of the sixteenth century, the first generation of explorers having destroyed the indigenous population. Now, in 1562, the 'adventurer' (read 'state-sponsored pirate') John Hawkins took a small fleet of ships including the *Jesus* to Sierra Leone, captured 300 locals, and sold them to the Spanish in Hispaniola. 'If any were carried away without their free consent,' Elizabeth said, 'it would be detestable and call down the vengeance of heaven upon the undertakers'; but then Hawkins came home with five ships full of hides, ginger, sugar and pearls, and she financed his next expedition.

Some British traders refused to take slaves, but the Spanish and Portuguese provided an ever-open market, so as the British navy came to dominate the seas British ships dominated the slave trade. By the time of the Treaty of Utrecht in 1713, Spain agreed to take 4,800 slaves a year off British hands. Early on, traders realized that West Africa already had an established internal slave trade, and it made a lot more sense to buy slaves than to risk their lives taking them for themselves.

Meanwhile, colonists and armed forces had brought parts of North America and the Caribbean under British control, cultivating them to grow new luxuries such as tobacco, cotton, rice, indigo, maize, pimento, fustick and, above all, sugar. The British captured Barbados in the 1620s. They had no great success growing tobacco or cotton, but in 1639 discovered the climate was perfect for sugar, and switched. Six months after the first harvest, land value had increased eighteen-fold and in just five years, the crop covered half the island. But it required intensive labour, and since there was already an international slave trade network it was easy to buy in slaves. By 1650 there were 20,000 slaves on the fourteen-mile-wide island, and Barbados produced two-thirds of the sugar consumed in England. In 1655, Oliver Cromwell's navy completed English domination of the region by seizing Jamaica from the Dutch, and by the 1690s there were 95,000 slaves in the British West Indies. George Downing, of Downing Street fame, reckoned that 'with God's blessing' slaves paid for their own cost in eighteen months.

By 1700, the average Briton consumed 4 lbs of sugar a year. By the time of the abolition campaign, it was 12 lbs, and would increase to 18 lbs by the end of the century. (In 2002, that figure was 65 lbs.) Much of it was for coffee, drinking chocolate and, above all, tea which was becoming ubiquitous; but Britain also became famous for its puddings, pies, tarts, trifles and ices. Even the poorest drank sweetened tea and ate sweetened porridge. What had been an aristocratic luxury only a century before had become an everyday essential. We are told it profits a man nothing if he gains the world and loses his soul, but Britain sold its soul for sweet tea. Luckily, for a century or so the world was thrown in.

Here the ghastly arithmetic comes in. With sugar profitable enough and slaves cheap enough, planters calculated that it was cheaper to flog half-a-dozen years' work out of a malnourished slave and then buy another when he or she died than to provide good enough food and shelter to keep slaves alive for longer. So the squalor and brutality of their conditions reduced life expectancy to seven years. At the same time the total numbers of slaves needed on the plantations to keep British customers sweet continued to grow, the two forces together creating an insatiable demand for new slaves. In the 1770s the slave population of Barbados increased by 700 a year; it took the import of 5,000 slaves a year to achieve this.

Britain took to slavery then rather like an addict getting into drugs: starting slowly, doubtfully following the crowd, the habit growing into an indomitable dependency. And like alcohol, slavery had been more or less ubiquitous throughout the history of the world. It must be far easier for us to see the obvious intolerable evil of an institution that has been officially dead – at least in that form – for over a century than it was for those who had lived with it in one way or another for 3,000 years. All the great civilizations that the West looked back to practised slavery, and were often built on it, including the empires of Greece, Rome, Persia, Egypt and Byzantium; moral authorities from the Greek philosophers to the Hebrew scriptures unequivocally accepted it and it was found everywhere, from China to the pre-colonial Americas, from Egypt to India, throughout Asia, Africa and the entire Muslim world. One of the lesser known chapters in the history of slavery is the kidnapping of something like a million Europeans (including the Cornish) by Islamic raiders to serve in North Africa throughout the seventeenth and eighteenth centuries.

Slavery is a broad term, and few of these examples can compete with the extremity of eighteenth-century European slavery, either in terms of dehumanization or scale. But then, most Europeans had no idea about the realities of slavery until the likes of Ramsay and Clarkson opened their eyes; they just accepted it as a fact of life and assumed it could not be as bad as all that.

But if slavery was so common, this raises the opposite problem of why it should suddenly become so controversial in 1780s Britain. One answer is that it had largely died out in Europe before the era of exploration revived it. It had been generally held throughout the Christian world that it was acceptable to enslave unbelievers, but not Christians. Though this restriction was by no means always respected, it had enough influence to ensure that almost all modern European languages take their word for 'slave' from one of the last pagan peoples left in Europe, the Slavs. The conversion of Europe and the loss of pagan labour coincided with the development of feudal society, in which the ruling classes effectively owned the serfs on their land – even if they could not sell them – so slavery in any other form became largely redundant. And as Europe, led by Britain, rapidly moved from a feudal to a capitalist society, even that kind of ownership was forgotten about and felt alien. Slavery was universal enough to allow Britons to feel complacent about it, but also foreign enough for them to feel bad about it when challenged. The taboo against enslaving Christians, incidentally, was still alive in Wilberforce's time. One of the scandals that exercised abolitionists was the way that plantation managers opposed evangelism like Ramsay's, in case they had to release believing slaves. However, a previous Bishop of London assured them that 'Christianity and the embracing of the gospel does not make the least difference in civil property.'[2]

A second reason why slavery became controversial was the colossal shift in thinking that had swept across the West throughout the previous century, starting from Britain. The Enlightenment was all about remaking the world in accordance with reason, rejecting traditional institutions and ideas. It demanded individual freedoms – of speech, of religion and of the press – and, in Britain at least, it had considerable success. More recently, the Romantic Movement spearheaded by Rousseau rejected the rationalism of the Enlightenment in favour of spirituality and feeling, and yet whatever the differences it only redoubled the demand for freedom, encapsulated in Rousseau's celebrated protest, 'Man is born free; and everywhere he is in chains.' How could a society place such a premium on personal freedoms and universal rights, without having a bad conscience about enslaving 80,000 Africans a year?

One much less widespread school of thought should not be underestimated in its influence on the abolition movement: Quakerism. While the Enlightenment predisposed British society as a whole into renouncing slavery, Quakerism was far more selective and strategic in its influence. It motivated Benezet's pioneering campaign; the first agitation in London was from Quakers and they formed a majority on the abolition committee; and Clarkson, Anglican clergyman that he officially was, was highly sympathetic to their religion. The emphasis of Quaker beliefs was not so much on freedom or rights as on equality. All people are made in the image of God and carry the divine light, so it is blasphemous to elevate one above another they believed. Consequently the Quakers had no ministers or preachers, but let everyone have a go. They refused to raise their hats to their social betters or to call them 'my lord', 'my lady' or even 'you', insisting on the familiar 'thou'.* This, incidentally, meant that the Quakers on the abolition committee could not write the many deferential letters they had to send to noble sponsors and influential dignitaries, though pragmatically they tended to draft them and get Granville Sharp to sign them. Their egalitarianism was still quite scandalous in the eighteenth century, but it made slavery uniquely abhorrent to the Quakers.

One last reason why slavery should suddenly become so controversial is the very fact of the unique horror of the Middle Passage. However conditions in the Caribbean might compare to those on a Roman galley, in an Athenian silver mine or in a Barbary slave pen (not so badly, in each case), no empire before Britain's had ever shipped 40,000 new slaves each year across 4,000 miles of ocean, bound and crammed together like bundles of sugar cane. If a nation was ready to have its conscience stricken, this was the crime to strike it.

When the day finally came, on 12 May 1789, for Wilberforce to present the anti-slave trade bill to the House, he felt very unwell, too ill to prepare precisely what he was going to say. This did not stop him from making the most brilliantly compelling speech of his life, all three-and-a-half hours of it, to ecstatic acclaim. As his diary has it, 'Came to town, sadly unfit for work, but by Divine grace was enabled to make my motion so as to give satisfaction – three hours and a half – I had not prepared my language, or even gone over all my matter, but being well acquainted with the whole subject I got on.'[3]

The point he began with and pressed repeatedly was that 'We are all to blame.' Parliament had permitted human traffic which, whatever the good intentions of the owners of the ships and plantations, was inevitably and unavoidably cruel and destructive. The owners could not be blamed for pursuing their lawful business, it was the nation and its parliament that were to blame for making it lawful. Dubious as this

---

* Ironically and confusingly, considering the later history of 'thou/thee', 'you' was originally the more formal term. The King James Bible calls everyone, including God, 'thou', and reserves 'ye/you' for the plural ('ye are my disciples'), already a slightly antiquated practice even then. As 'you' swallowed up 'thou' in everyday speech, only the Bible and The Book of Common Prayer kept 'thou' alive, and so it became the language of prayer, and English became the first language to have a distinct grammar for the second person deity.

sounds, he was addressing those owners themselves in parliament, and had to do all he could to avoid making them feel attacked. Then he worked gradually through the opposition case. As some of the 'slavery party' (an informal common interest alignment rather than a formal political party) still maintained that the Middle Passage was really a quite pleasant trip, he laid out the evidence of its horrors, concluding, 'So much misery condensed in so little room, is more than the human imagination has ever before conceived.'[4]

Others admitted the trade might not be pretty, but insisted that it was essential to the plantations, which were essential to the British economy. Wilberforce responded to this, first theologically: 'I cannot believe that the same being who forbids rapine and bloodshed, has made rapine and bloodshed necessary to the well-being of any part of his universe.'[5] More practically, he argued that the plantation owners had nothing to fear from abolition. He showed how staggeringly high the death rate was among slaves on the islands, due to abuse, excessive work, paltry food and poor living conditions. No one was to blame for this, he said; it was the inevitable consequence of the slave trade, slaves being so easy to replace. But then by the same token, if the slave trade was abolished, the inevitable outcome would be an improvement in their conditions sufficient to keep the death rate down in balance with the birth rate. The colonies would hardly be ruined just because planters spent on the upkeep of existing slaves what they were currently spending on buying new ones. In a nice rhetorical touch, Wilberforce read from a pamphlet predicting that tens of thousands would be ruined, the economy devastated, industry crippled, taxes multiplied, the navy destroyed and the French strengthened. As the cries of 'Hear, hear' died down, he revealed that the pamphlet was not about abolishing the slave trade, but about the American War of Independence, highlighting how often prophecies of doom prove to be fearful fantasies. In fact, he reminded them that one of the MPs for Liverpool had insisted that Dolben's 1788 bill would mean the instant collapse of the slave trade, but it continued as ever.

The traffic, it was said, was vital to Britain's naval predominance, providing a nursery for seamen. In fact, said Wilberforce, it was increasingly their grave. Paying tribute to 'the indefatigable industry and public spirit of Mr Clarkson', he reported from his research that 'more sailors die in one year in the slave trade, than die in two years in all our other trades put together'.[6] Add to that the revelation made to the Privy Council that captains often abandoned large numbers of sailors in the Caribbean to avoid paying their wages, and the benefits for the navy seemed rather equivocal.

The most popular argument in parliament against abolition was that the trade would simply be taken up by France. Wilberforce not only showed the moral poverty of this justification, but turned it back-to-front:

> Those who argue thus may argue equally, that we may rob, murder, and commit any crime, which anyone else would have committed, if we did not. The truth is, that by our example, we shall produce the contrary effect. If we refuse the abolition, we shall lie, therefore, under the twofold guilt of knowingly persisting in a wicked trade ourselves, and, as far as we can, of inducing France to do the same. Let us, therefore, lead the way.[7]

It was said that Africans were violent and lazy people, better off working for a living in Jamaica than left to their own devices at home. But how can we separate their present behaviour as we see it from the effects of the slave trade, Wilberforce argued? The slave lobby called Africa uncivilized, but it was no worse than the Europe of a few centuries ago, and only the slave trade was now preventing it from following Europe down the path of progress.

Having rebutted the well-known arguments against abolition, Wilberforce went on to offer a positive alternative, a prophetic vision for a new kind of empire:

> Wherever the sun shines, let us go around the world with him, diffusing our beneficence; but let us not traffic, only that we may set kings against their subjects, subjects against their kings... setting millions of our fellow-creatures a hunting each other for slaves, creating fairs and markets for human flesh... concealing from ourselves all the baseness and iniquity of such a traffic.[8]

This is precisely how the British empire came to see itself in the nineteenth century, the empire on which the sun never set, built on commerce instead of conquest, bringing the benefits of trade and civilization to its lucky subjects. We can hardly see it so unequivocally today, but for better and for worse, the colonialism of 'Christianity and commerce', in Dr Livingstone's words, owes some debt to the abolitionists.

Wilberforce's final point was a more personal one. His arguments, he said, had been based on political pragmatism; abolition was sound policy. This was using language that parliament would understand and arguments that it could accept but, he confessed, these were not his own reasons for supporting it. 'Policy, however, sir, is not my principle, and I am not ashamed to say it.' His principle was the command of God, which is above all politics.

Before laying the resolutions for the bill before parliament, he concluded with a challenge:

> Sir, the nature and all the circumstances of this trade are now laid open to us; we can no longer plead ignorance, we cannot evade it, it is now an object placed before us; we may spurn it, we may kick it out of our way, but we cannot turn aside so as to avoid seeing it.[9]

It was a magnificent performance, and the three great speakers, Pitt, Burke and Fox, rose to praise it. 'Principles so admirable, laid down with so much order and force,' declared Burke, 'are equal to anything I have ever heard of in modern oratory; and perhaps are not excelled by anything met with in Demosthenes.'[10] Bishop Porteus called it 'one of the ablest and most eloquent speeches that was ever heard in that or any other place... It was a glorious night for this country'.[11] The *Star* reported that 'the gallery of the House of Commons on Tuesday was crowded with Liverpool Merchants; who hung their heads in sorrow – for the African occupation of bolts and chains is no more'.[12]

The speech as published gives little clue to what all the excitement was about. No speeches were officially recorded and we have to rely on the reports by newspaper men scribbling notes in the gallery (which was technically illegal). These are the sources of all the quotations above, so they are obviously not verbatim – in fact Wilberforce was angry about their inaccuracy. His own notes for the speech tell us little more as they could be read aloud in three minutes. And no great speech can transfer successfully onto paper anyway – even Martin Luther King's makes pretty average reading. Accurate records of Wilberforce's later speeches still contain little hint of what hearers got: 'those tones, so full, liquid and penetrating... the eye sparkling... the fragile form elevating itself into heroic dignity.'[13]

Still, it was all for nothing. As the debate continued into the morning and then the following evening, pro-slavery MPs furiously attacked Wilberforce's facts. Colonel Isaac Gascoyne denied there was one word of truth in his speech and other MPs derided the naivety of imagining the colonies could convert from free to paid labour without economic damage. They said that £70 million of mortgages were at stake, threatening countless British families with ruin through misplaced sensitivity towards Africans, and that 'before [MPs] are humane towards these... they should be tender of their own subjects, whom they have seduced to hazard their property in this trade'. If they passed this law, they 'give up dominion of the sea at a single stroke'.[14] But the fatal blow came when alderman Nathaniel Newnham suggested that before they vote, the House should have the benefit of interviewing witnesses for themselves. The report before them contained a year's worth of interviews and research; but they argued that this only gave one side of the argument – despite the fact that the slavers had provided half of the Privy Council's interviewees. More plausibly, they said that accepting the report would mean sacrificing parliament's historic right to hear witnesses for itself.

This delaying tactic was gladly seized upon by the undecided mass of MPs as well as the slavery party. Few would have got round to studying the report and, although their consciences were wooed by Wilberforce, his opponents had sowed enough doubt about the consequences for them to be glad to postpone the momentous decision. Wilberforce acquiesced. Time was put aside that summer for interviews, but to no one's surprise they dragged on, and had to be carried over to the next session of parliament.

Wilberforce has been criticized as being naively gentlemanly in agreeing to this, acting 'as if his opponents had only the best of intentions'[15]. This may be the case, but it seems just as likely that he was judging the mood of the House correctly. Obviously he had been outmanoeuvred; but if MPs were keen on examining witnesses themselves, then demanding an immediate vote would simply have meant losing it. It was indeed hard on the tens of thousands of slaves that would be taken from Africa over the coming year, but no harder than the defeat of the bill. The attack on Ramsay, meanwhile, had continued relentlessly for years, the stress of it making him constantly ill before finally breaking him. He died in May 1789, and the MP Crisp Molyneux, who had repeatedly libelled him in parliament, wrote to his illegitimate son in St Christopher: 'Ramsay is dead – I have killed him.'

9

The Vote

The legal power of a master over his slave in this island is very extensive: with him lies the right of punishment for all offences committed against himself; and if any slave under punishment by him, or his order, suffers in life or member, no person is liable to any fine... But if any person should wantonly, and without cause, and with any circumstance of cruelty, put an end to his slave's life, he is liable to a penalty of £15.
Governor Parry of Barbados, testifying to the Privy Council, 1789[1]

If any slave having been one whole year in this island, shall run away, and continue absent from his owner's service for the space of thirty days, upon complaint and proof, &c. before any two justices of the peace, and three freeholders, &c. it shall and may be lawful for such justices and freeholders to order such slave to be punished, by cutting off one of the feet of such slave, or inflict such other corporal punishment as they shall think fit.'
Jamaican law quoted by Anthony Benezet, 1772[2]

While the British parliament continued to deliberate over abolition, France – the rival who loomed so large over its debates – was in serious turmoil. In May 1789, economic crisis forced Louis XVI to call a meeting of the Estates General, a three-tier parliament of clergy, lords, and commons, for the first time in 175 years. Dissatisfied with the voting system, the Commons opened a rival parliament, the National Assembly, and persuaded most of the clergy and a good number of lords to join it. Louis XVI was forced to recognize its authority, which was determined to dismantle his absolute power.

Wilberforce decided to visit Paris. 'The present state of politics in that quarter is justly interesting to the highest degree,' he said, but he was not only going for reasons of revolutionary tourism. His secret plan was to make a deal with the French over the slave trade. If they could be persuaded to renounce it in tandem with the British, then the most compelling argument against abolition would be demolished.

Before leaving, he tried to arrange for parliament to agree that a supply of wheat be shipped to France. He was also hard at work managing the abolition cause in parliament, cross-examining opposition witnesses, and helping Clarkson and the others organize publicity. He hoped to persuade the celebrated author Edward Gibbon to contribute, believing that he would write anything for money. He was more successful with Thomas Gisborne, his Cambridge friend so often enticed to chat through the night, whom he now persuaded to give three hours a day to the campaign.

Meanwhile, there were daily meetings and interviews to be held in his Palace Yard house from first thing in the morning, as well as the parliamentary business in the evening. 'House – slave trade – extremely exhausted' is a repeated entry in his diary. His evangelical friend Hannah More compared his house to Noah's ark, 'full of beasts clean and unclean'. His sons give an artists' impression of his entrance hall:

> On one chair sat a Yorkshire constituent, manufacturing or
> agricultural; on another a petitioner for charity, or a House of
> Commons client; on another a Wesleyan preacher: while side by
> side with an African, a foreign missionary, or a Haitian professor,
> sat perhaps some man of rank who sought a private interview, and
> whose name had accidentally escaped pronouncement.[3]

Like all his rooms it was full of books, but he learnt to keep only outsized volumes there 'which could not be carried off by accident in the pocket of a coat'. (Wilberforce himself had his coats made with extra-large pockets and carried a ludicrous number of books wherever he went.)

France was becoming increasingly unstable. While the National Assembly drafted a constitution, the king mobilized troops, but they themselves proved rebellious. Paris was increasingly ruled by the pro-assembly mob. Wilberforce decided it would be improper for a representative of the British parliament to visit in such circumstances.

On 14 July, Parisians seized control of the arsenal, armed themselves against the king and stormed the symbolic Bastille prison. It was just as well Wilberforce had not gone there, said Gisborne: 'The populace might very probably have chaired you round the city, as a patriotic and liberty-loving Englishman; and exposed you on their shoulders to the frowns of the monarch and the bullets of his Swiss guards.'[4]

Instead, when parliament broke up in July, Wilberforce went to Bath with his mother and Sarah, and on his suggestion the abolition committee sent Clarkson to Paris. In popular English mythology, the French Revolution is a terrible, anarchic guillotine-happy massacre, culminating in Napoleon's attempt to conquer the world but foiled by the British (with a little help from the rest of Europe) at the Battle of Waterloo. At the time though, it was hugely popular in Britain in more progressive circles. Wordsworth, Coleridge, Burns, Blake and Southey all wrote poetry in favour of it – 'Bliss was it in that dawn to be alive.' Burns sent guns. The cartoonist James Gillray, an ardent conservative in the 1790s, celebrated the fall of the Bastille. Fox said it was 'the greatest event... that ever happened in the world'. Even Pitt welcomed it, in less superlative terms, as bringing freedom and good government to France, hopefully making it 'a less obnoxious neighbour'; his brother-in-law, the Earl of Stanhope, wrote to congratulate the revolutionaries. The British, as frightened as they habitually were by the thought of repeating the Puritan Revolution of the 1640s, had also had much happier experiences, as the name suggests, of the 'Glorious Revolution' of 1688, when the militant Catholic James II was replaced by William III, by the will of parliament. This in the eyes of many Britons was the foundation of their constitutional monarchy, the envy of the political world, and now it seemed to be happening in France. Burke was the lone prophet who saw the beginning of the end of monarchic Europe, and denounced it from the start.

So Clarkson was delighted to report to the abolition committee that the National Assembly had issued the Declaration of the Rights of Man, recognizing freedom as a universal right, and he had encouraging talks with the Société des Amis des Noirs, the abolition committee recently founded by General Lafayette. 'I should not be surprised', he said, 'if the French were to do themselves the honour of voting away this diabolical traffic in a night.'⁵ But the French were not yet ready for such an honour. Clarkson reported positive noises from leading figures of the assembly, while anti-abolitionists denounced him as a British spy and sent him death threats. Months passed without a debate on slavery, and when black delegates from the French Caribbean turned up requesting seats they were peremptorily refused.

In Bath, Wilberforce found that his best friend there, Hannah More, had moved out of town. She had previously been a very successful playwright and a friend of Johnson and Garrick, but had since renounced the theatre as unchristian and, to Wilberforce's delighted approval, she and her sister Martha had quit the high society of Bath for the serene solitude of country life in Cowslip Green in the Mendips. He and Sarah went to stay there in August.

While there, he started another scheme for improving life spiritually and materially for people in need. He visited the impressive Cheddar Gorge, with a picnic and an edifying book, but found himself too great a celebrity to enjoy this civilized lunch in peace. So instead he talked to the locals and was shocked by their extreme poverty – and their spiritual poverty. Their church had never had a minister, and the area had no cottage industry. He gave them money out of his pocket and doubtless some spiritual spare change too, finding them inordinately grateful.

'Miss Hannah More,' he announced the following day, 'something must be done for Cheddar.' They discussed the possibility of schools, employment and so on, late into the night, and Wilberforce promised, 'If you will be at the trouble I will be at the expense.' At these words, says Martha More, 'something commonly called an impulse crossed my heart, that told me it was God's will and he would do it'.⁶

Eventually, on the strength of Wilberforce's blank cheques, More founded nine schools in the area, and two women's benefit clubs which continued until about 1950. In later life, Wilberforce eulogized the way she 'shut herself up in the country to devote her talents to the instruction of a set of wretched people sunk in heathen darkness, among whom she was spending her time and fortune in schools and institutions for their benefit, going in all weathers a considerable distance to watch over them, until at last she had many villages and some thousands of children under her care. This is truly magnificent.'[7]

While at Cowslip Green, Wilberforce celebrated his thirtieth birthday – if celebrate is the right word. 'What shame ought to cover me when I review my past life in all its circumstances!... How little have I executed the purposes I formed last summer at Rayrigg! Wherein am I improved even in my intellectual powers? My business I pursue but as an amusement, and poor Ramsay (now no more) shames me in the comparison.'[8] He was a man of strong principle, and now had a sense of mission too. But despite the impression given by his son's biography, all those who knew him personally agreed that he was also a man of extraordinary wit and vivacity, with a childlike, impulsive joy, always amusing, always amused. This was said amid strong criticisms – he was infinitely distractible, his benignity outstripped his wisdom and he relied too much on others doing his homework. But little of this comes through in the records of his sons, who seem to have inherited his piety, conservatism and seriousness, but none of his more human qualities, and remade him in their own image.

Wilberforce returned from the revitalizing countryside to his 'amusements' in London when parliament met in January 1790. Before throwing himself back into the slave business, he gave some time to the question of repealing the Test and Corporation Acts, which were designed to keep non-Anglicans out of public life, eventually deciding to vote against their repeal.

Parliamentary hearings on the slave trade resumed, the anti-abolitionists continuing to present their witnesses and Wilberforce cross-examining them. He felt that his total immersion in the subject was increasingly giving him an expertise and a confidence that defeated attempts to pull the wool over his eyes. He put it to one slave captain, for example, that he was reported to have 'held hot coals over the mouth of a slave, in order to compel him to eat'. 'I did not,' replied the captain indignantly, 'and I defy anybody to prove that I did.' 'Did you never order such a thing to be done?' Wilberforce asked. 'I ordered the chief mate or surgeon to present him with a piece of fire in one hand, and a piece of yam in the other, and to let me know what effect it had on him; it was reported to me that he took the yam and ate it.'[9]

His house and his days were as crammed as ever with possible witnesses to be interviewed, papers to be read and colleagues to be consulted. Again he felt the intense business of the campaign conflicted with his own spiritual life – 'Alas, alas, how week passes unimproved after week!' – and sometimes doubted whether it was right. His religious friends were divided in their advice, but the work had become enough of a compulsion to keep him at it anyway.

The pro-slavery case was finally wound up in April 1790, at which point Wilberforce was dismayed to hear Lord Penrhyn move that the evidence the House had heard was so conclusive that the bill should be thrown out without the abolitionists having to waste their time with their own witnesses. Wilberforce rallied Pitt, Fox and Burke and defeated the motion, and he started to bring his own witnesses before the House. Clarkson, who had gone to such lengths to persuade them to testify, complained that they were treated by the other side 'as mercenaries and culprits, or as men of doubtful and suspicious character. They were browbeaten. Unhandsome questions were put to them. Some were kept for four days under examination.'[10] The slave business was then interrupted briefly by a general election in June 1790. Pitt gained an increased majority, and Wilberforce was re-elected after a very short visit to Yorkshire, in which he narrowly escaped death when his carriage was accidentally overturned and dashed to pieces – provoking the now typical damning reflections on the state of his soul.

He took the waters in Buxton again, and then retired until November to Gisborne's Yoxall Lodge in the heart of Needwood Forest in Staffordshire, which became his regular summer retreat after Windermere had become overrun with tourists. His abolition motion was scheduled for December, and he filled every day, alongside Thomas Babington, Gisborne's brother-in-law, 'working like a negro', in his own words, studying and organizing evidence, including 1,400 folio pages from the interviews in the Commons. 'The two friends begin to look very ill,' reported another of Gisborne's guests, 'but they are in excellent spirits, and at this moment I hear them laughing at some absurd question in the examination, proposed by a friend of Wilberforce's.' (Babington was a son of the nobility, a descendant of

Anthony Babington who plotted against Elizabeth I, and his home, Rothley Temple, another haunt of Wilberforce's, was built by the Templars.) Clarkson toured the country once again to find more witnesses, an arduous quest as at one point he covered 2,000 miles without securing one. 'I was almost over the whole island. I intersected it backwards and forwards both in the night and in the day.' Seven thousand miles later, he returned with twenty new contacts.[11] The inquiry heard about slaves being thrown into boiling sugar, ears and limbs being cut off, nursing mothers being beaten for suckling during work (i.e. daylight) hours, and slaves being flogged for ninety minutes or chained for 120 days or beaten to death for making a noise.

They had amassed a formidable body of evidence against the alleged decency of the slave trade and the supposed dangers of abolition. But this itself was a major problem – the documentation was as much as an MP could be expected to lift, let alone read. So a team of about 10 people, including Babington, Gisborne and members of the abolition committee, led by Revd William Dickson – Wilberforce's 'white negroes' as Pitt called them – spent months abridging it all into a single readable book. The Duke of Montagu and Edward Eliot had to work through the book, comparing it to the original, and vouch for its accuracy in parliament. Then the committee printed it and sent copies to every MP.

Come December, the motion was once again put off till April, this time because Pitt wanted to debate taxes. For once Wilberforce was furious with the prime minister – 'too much I fear from wounded pride' – but he used the time to continue wading through the paperwork and to interview Clarkson's new witnesses. Letters of support and encouragement (often more support than encouragement) came from well-wishers. The 86-year-old John Wesley, in his last written words, said:

Unless the divine power has raised you up to be as Athanasius against the world, I see not how you can go through your glorious enterprise in opposing that execrable villainy, which is the scandal of religion, of England, and of human nature. Unless God has raised you up for this very thing, you will be worn out by the opposition of men and devils. But if God be for you, who can be against you? Are all of them together stronger than God? O be not weary of well doing. Go on, in the name of God and in the power of his might, till even American slavery (the vilest that ever saw the sun) shall vanish away before it.

Peckard, who had first set Clarkson on this road, told Wilberforce:

You, sir, will stand in the British parliament as did Episcopius in the famous synod of Dort, with the whole force of truth with every rational argument, and with all the powers of moving eloquence upon your side, and all to no purpose.[12]

The optimism of 1788–89 seems to have been overtaken by experience. The abolitionists felt that their opponents' delaying tactics had worked only too well and that MPs had gradually cooled towards the cause.

Just weeks before the debate, two events happened that made them considerably cooler. Tom Paine published *The Rights of Man*, defending the French Revolution against Burke's condemnations. He went further than most English admirers, arguing against monarchy and for universal male suffrage. Paine was, naturally, an abolitionist and it was easy enough for the slavery lobby to show that this was where their cause led: they were closet revolutionaries, fomenting unrest with their talk of rights, justice and equality. 'The very book of the abridgment of the evidence', said Clarkson 'was considered by many members as poisonous as that of *The Rights of Man*.'[13]

And then, as if to prove the point, there was a slave revolt in Dominica. This was a constant hazard for the colonists, who were outnumbered ten to one by their slaves (thirty to one in Grenada), their inhumanity driven as much as anything by fear. But managers reported that for the first time the slaves were not demanding better food or clothes but 'what they term their "rights"'. And yet, far from welcoming slaves' attempts to gain their own freedom, abolitionists knew that an insurrection would damage the campaign in Britain.

So when after three years of exhausting preparation Wilberforce finally got the House of Commons to vote on abolishing the slave trade, the mood seemed less propitious than ever. A few days before the debate, he prayed:

> May I look to him for wisdom and strength and the power of persuasion, and may I surrender myself to him as to the event with perfect submission, and ascribe to him all the praise if I succeed, and if I fail say from the heart thy will be done.[14]

He presented the bill on Monday 18 April, 1791. This time his speech, as well as refreshing arguments that the slave trade was 'contrary to every principle of religion, morality, and sound policy', also included what had emerged from the inquiry. After two years of further research, his attitude to the trade seems, so far as one can judge from the reports, considerably harsher than in 1789 – but he had since learnt his lesson and this time dictated his speech to a reporter afterwards, instead of relying on journalistic shorthand.

It was now incontestable, he insisted, that slaves came into British hands through the most lawless violence, which was devastating African society, and that the trade was responsible for this – quite apart from the murder, rape and robbery committed directly by the British in Africa. Yes, he admitted, this had been denied by some witnesses, but with astonishingly gross and inconsistent prejudice. He enjoyed telling the House about reading one witness' own testimony back to him, which the witness – before realizing whose it was – denounced as 'the merest burlesque in the world'.

Arguing against the case that Africans did not have the capacity for anything better than slavery, he told the House about their genius for commerce, their gold craftwork, their excellent cloth making and production of dyes. The idea that Europeans were God's instrument for punishing the sins of Africa was a 'gross and impious blasphemy', which merely used God as a front for godless greed.

Wilberforce took great pains to disprove calculations that abolition would ruin the colonies. Everything had been stacked against the survival of the 'imported Africans': they were cruelly treated; they had less food than British convicts; they had negligible protection from the law; there was one doctor for every 4,000–9,000 slaves; well-meaning owners in Britain were completely ignorant of conditions on their plantations, and the lack of moral teaching meant that 'promiscuous intercourse, early prostitution, and excessive indulgence in spirituous liquors are material causes of their decrease'. The causes of decline in the numbers of slaves were so great – and the actual decline so relatively small – that managers would find it very easy to keep their numbers stable.

As for the devastation of the navy and the economies of Liverpool and Bristol, Wilberforce bombarded his audience with new figures that seemed irresistible. But he insisted that financial worries were no excuse anyway: 'The principle argument rested on in support of this wicked trade, is gain; but will the House agree to give their consent to plunder, rapine, and murder, even was that gain, which I dispute, fully proved? I am confident that they will not, for gain is not to be their God.'[15]

Against the old patriotic sticking point about France taking up the trade, he presented abolition as the true patriotism: surely our 'superior power' and 'superior light' could be put to nobler uses than slavery. And to allegations that the abolition campaign was inciting slave rebellion, he responded that abolition was the only way to prevent it.

While Wilberforce spoke, Clarkson up in the public gallery counted their supporters and opponents in the House and knew that they would lose the vote. Wilberforce probably got a similar impression and his conclusion was defiant rather than confident:

> Interested as I might be supposed to be in the final event of the question, I am comparatively indifferent as to the present decision of the House. Whatever they might do, the people of Great Britain, I am confident, will abolish the slave trade… For myself, I am engaged in a work I will never abandon… Let us persevere, and our triumph will be complete. Never, never will we desist, until we have wiped away this scandal from the Christian name, released ourselves from the load of guilt, under which we at present labour, and extinguished every trace of this bloody traffic, of which our posterity, looking back to the history of these enlightened times, will scarce believe that it has been suffered to exist so long a disgrace and dishonour to this country.[16]

The response from pro-slavery MPs was led by Banastre Tarleton, the new MP for Liverpool, a commanding figure in his military uniform and proudly exhibiting his mutilated hand, an injury that he had suffered fighting for king and country in North America. His very public affair with the poet Mary Robinson – who wrote his speeches, as well as anti-slavery verse in which there was now good money – only made him more of a celebrity. He and others rehearsed the familiar arguments – parliamentary precedent for the trade, its commercial necessity, the kind treatment of slaves. The most gloriously insane response came from Thomas Grosvenor who said that the very amount of evidence presented by Wilberforce disproved his cause – 'for, if it was so clear a point as he declared it to be, it could not have needed… so much evidence'. As for the horrors of kidnapping and transport that Wilberforce had mentioned, Grosvenor conceded that 'it is not an amiable trade, but neither is the trade of a butcher an amiable trade, and yet a mutton chop is, nevertheless, a very good thing'.[17]

On the following evening after Wilberforce's speech, Sir William Young, who would go on to become the Governor of Tobago, opened with the first great speech of the pro-slavery campaign. He insisted that he devoutly wished to see the trade finished, but it was impossible for practical reasons. He offered concrete evidence, for once, that the French and Dutch were trying to expand their own slave trafficking, which meant that 'Great Britain may abandon her part of the trade, but cannot abolish it.' Moreover, he offered evidence that the colonial economy would indeed suffer from abolition, a fact that could only bring misery to the slaves there. Abolitionists asked Britons 'to pay the price of our virtue', he said: 'I am ready to pay my share of this, or any price; but the object of purchase must be ascertained. Is it the happiness, or is it the wretchedness of thousands?'[18]

Burke and Pitt each spoke at length, but it was Fox who shone. In a much repeated analogy, he compared the argument about France taking over the trade to a highwayman excusing his own trade, saying: 'I know that if I should not rob him, there is another highwayman, half a mile farther on the road who certainly will, and thus he will get the man's purse instead of myself.' He argued that Christianity forbade slavery by teaching that 'in the sight of heaven all men are equal', listing the great men of the ancient world who had praised liberty while keeping slaves, and arguing that it was Christianity that had overturned that attitude, and modern Europe that had revived it.[19]

The debate ploughed on through the early hours, as one MP after another rose to have his say. John Stanley confessed that he had come to vote against abolition, but was entirely won over by Wilberforce's speech. Many more said that they were not. The House finally divided to vote at 3.30 on Wednesday morning, and the abolitionists were in Wilberforce's words 'sadly beat', and resoundingly, by 163 votes to 88.

10

Fighting Back

If me want to go in a Ebo
Me can't go there!
Since dem tief me from a Guinea,
Me can't go there!
Caribbean slave song, reported by William Moreton, 1790[1]

How to respond to this defeat for the abolition movement? Above all, to carry on as ever. Wilberforce planned to introduce another motion to outlaw the slave trade immediately after the summer recess. 'Consider yourselves not as having concluded,' he told Hey, the doctor who had steered him through his illness and become a campaigner, 'but only as beginning your work.'[2]

There was another powerful if somewhat controversial way for ordinary people to be involved in the campaign, and that was by boycotting West Indian sugar. This was a new idea that had little precedent – the word 'boycott' would not be coined for another ninety years. But as soon as Wilberforce's bill was defeated in parliament, tracts started appearing throughout the country arguing for abstention, and many abolitionists either switched to Indian sugar, or gave up sugar entirely – and therefore tea, cake and puddings.

He and the abolition committee also had two new tactics to try. The first, as the conclusion of his speech suggested, was to mobilize the British people. Parliament had 'proved above all things the extremely low ebb of real principle there', he told his team, and so 'it is on the general impression and feeling of the nation that we must rely, rather than on the political conscience of the House of Commons'.[3] There was considerable support for abolition among ordinary people, and the petitions that they had bombarded the

House with in 1788 showed they were willing and able to put pressure on the government. This is why Wilberforce dictated his speech for publication. Clarkson got to work on the abridged version of the evidence, abridging it further for the committee to publish. He then hit the road once again, distributing the *Reader's Digest* version throughout Britain. It had a huge impact, presenting an impressive body of damning facts, on the authority of parliament, and thus enraging their opponents: 'Parts of the flimsy hearsay evidence, which for a length of time oppressed and disgraced the table of this House,' protested Tarleton in the Commons, 'are mutilated, distorted, and reduced to the size of pamphlets, in order to promote their circulation throughout all the alehouses and excise-offices in this kingdom, where the unwary and uninformed are tricked out of their humanity, by inflammatory extracts.'[4] The miles, meanwhile, were wearing away Clarkson's health, and he had to turn back home before he reached Scotland, handing the baton on to Revd Dickson.

There can be no better demonstration of the patriarchy of eighteenth-century Britain than the misgivings some leading abolitionists had about the sugar boycott. It was the role of crown and parliament to exercise power, it was the role of the people to make their requests known to them; that was what was meant by mobilizing the nation against the slave trade. A boycott would mean people taking power into their own hands, which might seem to smell of sedition and *The Rights of Man*. Would it not risk making the cause seem even more unruly? Wilberforce was all in favour at first, but on reflection thought it should be postponed until everyone was behind it. The committee did not officially encourage it, but Clarkson did on his travels, and calculated joyfully that 300,000 people had joined the boycott.

People also tried to drive on the campaign by forming local groups to liaise with the London-based abolition committee, but Wilberforce again queried this as counterproductive. The slave trade could only be outlawed by parliament, and anything that made MPs feel that the cause was giving the masses political ambitions above their station in life would only make that harder to achieve. So Wilberforce was setting himself the tricky task of mobilizing the people against parliament, without appearing to encourage democracy.

The other tactic that the committee turned to after their defeat was colonialism. This story dates back to the American War of Independence, when the British, already it seems attached to the idea that treating slaves decently would mean devastation to the colonies, declared them free for exactly that reason. They promised that any slave escaping a rebel owner and coming over to the British would be released. Several thousand duly came and the loss seriously hampered the efforts of the American slave owners fighting for universal freedom and equality. Once the war was lost and emancipation had outlived its usefulness, the British government decided to give the slaves back to their owners; but General Guy Carleton regarded the promise as a promise and, saying 'The national honour... must be kept with all colours,' shipped the remaining 3,000 freed slaves to British Nova Scotia. There they eked out a ragged, cold and hungry existence. Now, in 1791, Washington was still demanding their return to slavery.

Some of the freed slaves travelled to England with the defeated army, joining the black population of London, which was several thousand strong and lived almost entirely in extreme poverty. Granville Sharp, like other philanthropic Londoners, provided food for them, but he also took the lead in a more ambitious scheme – to set up a colony for them in Sierra Leone, so they could be free and prosper in their native continent. He insisted that it should be run according to an Anglo-Saxon local government system called Frankpledge, an eccentric obsession of his, but considerably more democratic than anything currently existing in Britain. The expedition set off in 1787 in naval ships and was financed by Pitt's government, which was more than happy to be rid of several hundred destitute Londoners. Abolitionists were excited by the scheme, hoping that by establishing profitable trading links with free African farmers they would prove that the continent had more to offer British commerce than slaves, and that the well-run Christian settlement would show that Africa was capable of what the British saw as progress. In fact, the settlers struggled desperately to raise a bare living out of the unwelcoming Sierra Leone soil. Half of them died in the first year, most of the survivors ended up having to take jobs at local slave-trading stations, and they only survived the second year thanks to supplies sent by Sharp. Then in 1789 a local chief, seeing the township as British, burnt it to the ground.

But the following year, the former slaves in Nova Scotia heard about the Sierra Leone colony, and sent Thomas Peters – who had fought for the British in North America on another foresworn promise of land and provisions – to London to ask the government to take the lot of them to Sierra Leone. The abolitionists leapt at the prospect of salvaging 'the province of Freedom', and set up the Sierra Leone Company to finance and oversee the project. The president was Sharp, and the chairman was Wilberforce's cousin Henry Thornton, the son of Hannah Wilberforce's brother John. Henry was an MP, a successful merchant banker whom even Wilberforce called 'my wealthy friend', and a major figure in monetary theory. After the deaths of Hannah and John, he had moved to Clapham, buying a house called Battersea Rise, which became Wilberforce's base for London, being close to the city while still feeling like the countryside. Wilberforce was a director of the Sierra Leone Company along with Thomas Babington. He was warned against the venture as a bad investment, but said he was not particularly concerned about that: 'I considered its principal object to be the abolition of the slave trade.' Clarkson was involved for the same reason, expecting it to be 'one of the greatest wounds the slave trade ever received'. 'Sierra Leone business' now became as familiar a refrain in Wilberforce's diary as 'slave business'.

He took time off in June, going to Bath with Thornton, where they rented a house in the nearby countryside, just close enough for Wilberforce to take the waters daily and wash off the effects of London and Westminster; he spent his days reading theology, poetry and the classics. In July he visited Cheddar to inspect Hannah More's work, and was then called back to London by Clarkson on Sierra Leone business. The government was persuaded to support Thomas Peters's exodus, and the company asked Clarkson's brother John, a naval officer, to organize it. They were expecting him to conduct a couple of hundred former slaves from Canada to Africa, but by January 1792 he had gathered 1,196 migrants in fifteen ships, including four who had walked 340 miles through snow to join the expedition. They also included the great preacher David George, who had been one of the first black pastors in North America.

The French Revolution, meanwhile, had become more controversial in Britain over the past two years. The assembly had abolished hereditary nobility, and all bishops and priests were now elected by the people. All the king's powers were suspended after he tried to escape, and a further levelling of society was planned. In such an atmosphere, it caused rather a scandal when Clarkson attended a dinner at the Crown and Anchor Inn in London to celebrate the second anniversary of the storming of the Bastille. One of Pitt's closest cabinet colleagues Henry Dundas protested to Wilberforce, who agreed that if Clarkson carried on that way 'it will be ruin to our cause'. The pair had a long talk, and Clarkson accepted Wilberforce's caution about displaying radical tendencies.

While a gathering of 3,000 slaves celebrated Wilberforce's thirty-second birthday in Jamaica in 1791, the man himself toured the great houses of friends throughout Britain, continued to catch up on his reading and busied himself with Sierra Leone paperwork. He kept in touch with what was being said and written about abolition throughout the country, and by the time he returned to London for parliament in December he was excited. Defeat had not dampened popular determination to end the traffic – quite the opposite. It was intense enough, in fact, for him to postpone his next abolition motion. He had planned to table it as soon as parliament sat, as a gesture of defiance, 'that we may then, being defeated, sound the alarm throughout the land'. But he realized that there was such a will spreading across the nation that if it was channelled into another petitionary assault on parliament, as in 1788, they might just win. So Wilberforce planned an underground campaign. He gave no notice to parliament, but secretly sent messages to his friends throughout Britain to draw up local petitions.

Just as he was preparing the motion, news came of a slave revolt in the French Caribbean colony of San Domingo, modern-day Haiti. After long and careful planning, which culminated in the leaders killing a pig among voodoo incantations and drinking its blood in pledge, they rose against their masters with all the furious vengeance sowed over 200 years of persecution. All the most brutal executions, dismemberings and sadistic rapes that had been meted out to slaves were repaid in full measure. The 'standard' of one army was a white child on a spike. They burned all the sugar fields and wrecked the machinery, and several hundred thousand slaves gained their freedom. With British help, the armies of revolutionary France were sent over, under the banner of liberty, equality and fraternity, to return the slaves to the plantations, and a slave war was soon under way.

Naturally in Britain as in France, people reacted with utter horror to these stories; and naturally it was generally quite out of proportion to the horror they felt at the same stories about the treatment of slaves. 'People here are panic-struck,' reported Wilberforce. British slaves reportedly told their owners, 'Slap me again if you please, 'tis your time now, but we shall drink wine before Christmas.'[5]

'It is to be hoped, for heaven's sake,' said *The Gentleman's Magazine*, 'we shall hear no more of abolishing the slave trade.'[6] And indeed Wilberforce was pressed to postpone the motion; but he insisted that an end to the trade was the best way to bring peace to the colonies, and that Africans deserved as much protection from violence as colonists. Pitt disagreed and threw the motion out. It occurred to Wilberforce for the first time that his commitment to this cause might end up wrecking his friendship with the prime minister, and he was desolated by the thought. 'I could hardly bring myself to resolve to do my duty and please God at the expense (as I suspect it will turn out) of my cordiality with Pitt, or rather his with me.' But resolve he did. 'Do not be afraid lest I should give ground,' he told Babington. 'This is a matter wherein all personal, much more ministerial, attachments must be as dust in the balance.' And he expected his friends to be as resolute: 'Exert yourselves with tenfold earnestness,' he told Gisborne; 'petition, resolve, etc.; if it was before important, it is now indispensable.'[7]

On 16 March 1792, the Prince Regent of Denmark signed a law prohibiting the export of slaves from its three Caribbean islands. It was a small abolition: Denmark was a minor slave power, having taken 5,000 slaves there from Africa over the last decade, in comparison to the British Caribbean's 200,000; it did not effect the import of slaves to the islands and it gave traders eleven years before coming into effect. Still, it was something.

Pitt's opposition to the abolition bill did not last, and Wilberforce brought it before the House for the third time on 2 April 1792, and this time it was Pitt's turn to stun lovers of rhetoric with the brilliance of his speech. Wilberforce, as ever, outlined the evidence and arguments against the slave trade, explaining on the one hand why abolition was good economic policy, and on the other hand that the only motive he personally cared about was the rights of Africans. He insisted that the slavery party was losing the argument and increasingly resorting to blind prejudice.

The greatest impact of his speech came from two new stories. In August 1791, he said, six slavers were anchored at Calabar (now in Nigeria) and the captains tried to buy slaves; but the sellers would not take what they offered, so they bombarded the town for three hours – killing twenty people – until they did. The House was shocked, but incredulous anti-abolitionists shouted 'Names! Names!' Wilberforce was reluctant to get personal, but eventually named the six captains and their ships. The second account was of a fifteen-year-old girl on a ship who tried to conceal her pregnancy, so the captain tied her up in such a way as to make it more obvious. When this entertainment palled, he hung her up by one foot for a while. She died three days later. 'Name! Name!' MPs shouted again. This time Wilberforce did not have the least compunction about getting personal: 'Captain Kimber is the man.'[8]

He ended by presenting the petitions his underground network had been arranging. The 1788 campaign had been utterly without precedent in sending 100 petitions to parliament; today there were 517. The Lord Mayor and aldermen of London had managed to delay their council's petition meeting until that very day, and it was signed just over half an hour before Wilberforce's speech, but somehow got there in time. The anti-abolitionists managed five.

Led by Tarleton, they replied with customary vigour; but while they happily assured the House that Wilberforce's petitions were an obvious scam and insisted as ever that abolition would be ruinous, they seemed less willing than they had been to insist that there was nothing wrong with the slave trade. The relentlessness of the abolitionists' disclosures seemed now to be forcing them to argue for slavery as a necessary evil rather than the opportunity of a lifetime. And then the home secretary, Henry Dundas, rose. He had always opposed abolition privately, on economic grounds, but being Pitt's closest political ally and knowing his opinions on the subject he had so far kept his views to himself. Now he professed to approve of abolition if it could be made practicable. He proposed a solution to the impasse between the two sides: amend the motion by inserting the word 'gradually'. Gradual abolition, he argued, would give Wilberforce and friends what they wanted eventually, while allowing their opponents to wind down the trade without financial distress.

Wilberforce was appalled. The amendment would actually allow the trade to continue indefinitely, and under the cover of abolition make it harder than ever to abolish; and yet it was just the kind of offer of compromise and procrastination to appeal to MPs, as Alderman Newnham's motion did in 1789. Several, especially the speaker of the House Henry Addington, expressed their delight.

Then Pitt replied. It was about four o'clock in the morning and, apparently impromptu, he gave perhaps the most acclaimed speech of his life. He vigorously and comprehensively contested Dundas's proposal. He showed that every argument for gradual abolition applied better to immediate abolition. As for France, he argued that when one added war in San Domingo to the tally of the troubles caused by their slave trade, for them to take up what Britain might abandon would simply be feeding a monster that threatened to destroy them. But the main thrust of his speech was the 'irreparable mischief' that British depredation was doing to Africa, a theme suggested to him by Wilberforce that morning. 'Africa is known to you only in its skirts; yet even there you are able to inject a poison which penetrates to its very centre.' 'For the last twenty minutes,' said Wilberforce, 'he really seemed to be inspired.' The colonists declared that Africa could never be civilized, said Pitt, but had not that other great empire, Rome, enslaved the British as barbarians, saying '*There* is a people that will never rise to civilization – *There* is a people destined never to be free?' As first light broke through the high, arched windows of St Stephen's

Chapel, he spoke glowingly of the day when modern civilization and peaceful commerce would dawn upon Africa, 'the beams of science and philosophy breaking in upon their land'.[9] Fox confessed that it was one of the most extraordinary displays of eloquence he had ever heard; but it was no match for the forces of compromise. Dundas's proposal to insert the word 'gradually' was carried by 193 votes to 125; and then Wilberforce's emasculated motion romped home by 230 votes to 85.

'I am congratulated on all hands,' sighed Wilberforce, 'yet I cannot but feel hurt and humiliated.' It is generally assumed, naturally, that Pitt and Dundas were in conflict with each other here, but William Hague, writing in his biography of Pitt, argues that they may have actually been collaborating. Dundas is unlikely to have proposed his amendment without consulting Pitt, who may have felt that, politically, it offered Wilberforce's bill its only chance of being passed, while, personally, it allowed Pitt himself to speak out for the immediate abolition he fervently believed in.

Wilberforce disowned the bill – 'for I will never myself bring forward a parliamentary licence to rob and murder' – and his tactic now was to 'endeavour to force the gradual Abolitionists in *their* bill... to allow as short a term as possible, and under as many limitations.'[10] So two evenings later, in the Commons, he asked Dundas what he was doing about his gradual abolition bill. Dundas answered that it was Wilberforce's bill, and he did not see why he should be expected to do anything about it at all.

Fox responded that the abolitionists had voted against gradual abolition as wrong and impracticable. If Dundas could make his scheme work, he should do so. If he declined, Wilberforce should be allowed to pursue his original proposals. The upshot was that Dundas brought more detailed proposals before the House on 24 April. The slave trade would be abolished on 1 January 1800 – in eight years time – whereupon traders would be compensated. Until then, no new slave ships should be made; no slaves should be sold to foreign nations; slaves should receive moral and religious teaching to improve their chances of staying alive; negotiations should be reopened with France and others; and only young slaves should be taken from Africa to increase longevity and avoid filling the plantations with convicted criminals. He appealed to both sides to accept these compromises, as otherwise the abolitionists would never give up, and the anti-abolitionists would never give in.

The slavery party offered little opposition to Dundas's proposals, but Fox tore them to shreds. The 'total inconsistency and impracticability' of his propositions powerfully proved the case for immediate abolition. His disgusting proposal to fill slave ships with children to avoid importing criminals was an admission that the trade was not about removing convicts, and dismantled its only claim to justice. If it was merely about child-stealing then what ground was there for continuing it for another eight years? How were the children to be obtained by the British if they had not been arrested? How were they to judge their age? In order to keep up the numbers of slaves being imported, Dundas had had to raise the age limit to twenty-five for men – as if that would exclude convicts! Laughing, Fox said that Dundas had warned abolitionists that the trade would continue indefinitely if his bill failed, while warning anti-abolitionists that if it failed the trade would be abolished immediately; he should have threatened them separately, Fox suggested.

Pitt then asked why, since Dundas's proposal admitted that abolition was right, it should not be done immediately. Dundas replied that it was because gradual abolition would actually get quicker results than hastier attempts, by allowing planters time to be reconciled to it. In that case, said Fox, the whole debate was changed. 'All defence of the trade itself is given up. It is universally condemned to abolition at some period or other, as inhuman, and repugnant to the first principles of justice.'[11]

The abolitionist Earl of Mornington tried his luck proposing a change to Dundas's wording, from '1 January 1800' to '1 January 1793' – gradual abolition over nine months instead of eight years. The amendment was defeated by 49 votes, the narrowest margin of defeat for the abolitionists yet. Mornington said that if he could do so, he was tempted to follow it up the next day by proposing an amendment of 2 January 1793.

One of the few protests from slave-owners came from Lord Carhampton, a ferocious Irish military lord, who entertained his friends with a hilarious skit on Pitt's speech: 'In favour of those delightful people of Africa, described by the hon. gentleman as the prettiest men and women on the face of the globe.' He caricatured Wilberforce as a member of one of the extreme religious sects of the Puritan Revolution, 'one of your Fifth Monarchy men and representative of the New Jerusalem; full of Methodism and full of enthusiasm'; while Fox 'lifts up his hands to the skies, and then points them to the floor, his eyes rolling all the time as in a frenzy, seems as if he were grasping both Heaven and earth at once'. These men were not content to govern Britain – 'they undertake the care and protection of all the world; but not without squinting a little at the world to come'. It was an ill-timed diversion. Wilberforce replied with controlled anger: 'I feel myself much obliged to the noble lord, for having, in his facetious speech, contrived to relieve the dullness of a debate, which certainly, from its nature, gives rise to other passions than that of laughter'; and Carhampton's speech only seems to have further alienated wavering voters.[12]

The abolitionists continued to insist on a shorter term, until the only debate left was between choosing 1795 or 1796 or, as Fox put it, 'whether they choose… to condemn 14,000 human beings to death, and sacrifice them to the West India planters'. He proposed an amendment for 1795, but was beaten by 40 votes. He then went for 1796, and the amendment was carried by 19 – 151 votes to 132.

It was then Dundas's turn to disown the bill, so Pitt steered his amended proposals through the House, minus the age limit that Fox had spectacularly demolished. On 1 May 1792, the House of Commons finally passed the bill that would make the slave trade illegal within the British colonies in three and a half years.

But it still had to pass the House of Lords, and when the bill came before them on 3 May, the Duke of Clarence – the third son of George III who would become King William IV – chose the occasion to make his maiden speech. The royal family had always been cool towards abolition – the king had teased Wilberforce about his 'negro clients' – but after the French revolution and San Domingo they had turned violently against it. Clarence now, rather than haggling over the terms of abolition, insisted 'it ought not to be abolished at all'. He called on the peers to have no qualms about overturning the decision of the lower chamber – what else was the House of Lords for? Viscount Stormont asked why they should be satisfied with four years of investigation into the slave trade when they had not heard their own witnesses, and demanded further examinations at their own bar. The Bishops of London and St Davids protested that there was already enough evidence to prove that the slave trade was 'essentially and radically vicious', but the Lords voted to hold their own inquiry. They heard seven witnesses before the summer recess, and then carried the business over till the following session. And by then the political world would have a lot more on its mind than slavery.

11

Collapse

We had not been a fortnight at sea, before the fatal consequence of this despair appeared; they formed a design of recovering their natural right, liberty, by rising and murdering every man on board; but the goodness of the Almighty rendered their scheme abortive, and his mercy spared us to have time to repent.

The plot was discovered; the ring-leader, tied by the two thumbs over the barricade door, at sun-rise received a number of lashes: in this situation he remained till sun-set, exposed to the insults and barbarity of the brutal crew of sailors, with full leave to exercise their cruelty at pleasure. The consequence of this was, that next morning the miserable sufferer was found dead, flayed from the shoulders to the waist. The next victim was a youth, who, from too strong a sense of his misery, refused nourishment, and died disregarded and unnoticed, till the hogs had fed on part of his flesh.

A repentant Captain Thomas Philips recounts a slave-trading trip to Guinea, 1746[1]

In the summer of 1792, with the amended bill stranded in the House of Lords, the abolition movement was at a low ebb. At first Wilberforce planned to bring in some other bills to limit the slave trade in the meantime, but Grenville – now made a lord by Pitt, and replacing Dundas as home secretary – warned Wilberforce that the Lords would never pass them while their own inquiry was under way, and even he would have to oppose them as 'an excess of zeal'. Without the support of ministers such as Grenville the plan was hopeless, and Wilberforce could do nothing but wait. Donations to the abolition committee largely dried up, and it started meeting less frequently.

A number of people who had given evidence on the slave trade to parliament had lost their jobs as a result and came to Wilberforce for help. His contacts in Liverpool and the Caribbean had papers seized, so he had to start sending letters without franking them to avoid anyone being connected with his name. In Bath, he was repeatedly challenged by a slave captain to a duel which, he insisted, he refused on grounds of morality, not fear.

Captain Kimber, whom Wilberforce had accused of such atrocity, was tried for murder; but thanks to the impressive presence in the courtroom of the Duke of Clarence 'identif[ying] himself with the prisoner's cause', and what Wilberforce saw as 'the shameful remissness of the crown lawyers', not only was Kimber acquitted, but one of the witnesses was convicted of perjury, though never punished. 'After their fate,' said the disgusted Wilberforce, 'he will be a bold man who shall venture to step forth to bring an African captain to justice.' It was then Kimber's turn to get personal with him. As an MP, Wilberforce was immune from prosecution, but Kimber demanded: 'A public apology, £5,000 in money, and such a place under government as would make me comfortable.' When Wilberforce refused to give him anything at all, he took to stalking him – threateningly enough that when Wilberforce went to Yorkshire his friend Lord Rokeby insisted on accompanying him with a gun – until Lord Sheffield called Kimber off. Wilberforce was phlegmatic about the adventure: 'If he were to commit any act of violence it would be beneficial rather than injurious to the cause.'[2]

The cause was certainly injured in the minds of many of the people to whom Wilberforce was trying to sell it by the fact that the French revolution, with which it seemed to be linked in all kinds of ways, was becoming ever more radical. After Prussia declared war on France with the express intention of restoring Louis XVI to the throne and punishing the rebels, the rebels stormed the palace. In a purge of suspected political enemies, between 1,100 and 1,400 prisoners were killed in one night. The monarchy was abolished by a convention elected by universal adult male suffrage. The Prussians, who expected more or less instant victory over a lawless mob, were driven out of France. Excited by this unforeseen victory, the French invaded the Austrian Netherlands, and published an offer of military help to any nation that wanted to overthrow its monarchy. Wilberforce was declared an honorary French citizen for his services to liberty, equality and fraternity, but had little enough taste for such honour that his reply was to join Burke's committee in support of the dispossessed French clergy. The eccentric anti-abolitionist Thicknesse then died, bequeathing his hand to his estranged son, 'that such a sight may remind him of his duty to God'.

Meanwhile, the British harvest of 1792 was bad, provoking serious unrest. Revolutionary societies and pro-French meetings sprang up around the country as a result. There were riots throughout Scotland and Ireland and slogans like 'No King' appeared on public monuments. The second part of Tom Paine's *The Rights of Man* was now on sale, alarming Wilberforce's class not only by calling for revolution in Britain but also by selling for a fraction of the price of the first book. It was cheap and readable enough to come into the rough hands of cutlers and shoemakers. It sold 200,000 copies in the first few weeks and, despite being banned, there was eventually one copy in circulation for every twenty literate people in the country. Wilberforce heard from Yorkshire that local peasants had recommended it to General Lambton, saying, 'We like it very much. You have a great estate, General; we shall soon divide it amongst us.'

The Earl of Abingdon called the abolitionists 'our Robespierres', and, denouncing the 'new philosophy' of the French Revolution, argued that abolition 'is actually founded on those very principles. What does the abolition of the slave trade mean more or less in effect, than liberty and equality; and what more or less than the rights of man? and what is liberty and equality; and what the rights of man, but the foolish fundamental principles of this new philosophy?'[3]

Wilberforce was not as inclined to panic as many of his circle, believing that British society was too stable for imminent revolution – though he did fear that in the long term Britain would face catastrophic judgment from God for its complacent godlessness. What did alarm him was the prospect of war with France, which he was determined to vigorously oppose. The powers of Western Europe were willing to unite against revolutionary France, an unprecedented opportunity for Britain against its traditional enemy; some conservatives wanted an ideological war against revolution and Pitt was not prepared to let the

French control so much of the Belgian coastline, which was just across the North Sea from England. But to Wilberforce's mind, if the French were acting aggressively it was partly the first flush of revolutionary fervour and partly foreign provocation; leave them alone and they would calm down. The French rebels could hardly think it was in their interests to take on the whole of Europe in one go; nor was it in Britain's interests, or the interests of justice, to go to war unless attacked. He was sure that negotiations would prevent war, but not sure that Pitt was pursuing them with enough determination. 'War I consider at all times the greatest of human evils,' he told parliament when it opened in January, 'and never more pregnant with injury than at the present moment.' Hoping that the news would mollify the French, Wilberforce implored Pitt to announce that he (Pitt) had been secretly negotiating a decree with other European powers which stated that if France did 'not molest her neighbours, she should be suffered to settle her own internal government and constitution without interference'. But Pitt refused.

Another wedge between Wilberforce and the prime minister came in the shape of parliamentary reform. Both had been keen reformers until now, but amid such unrest and on the eve of war, Pitt rejected it as a recipe for 'anarchy and confusion'. Charles Grey, a young MP and a leading member of the 'Friends of the People', a pro-French revolution group, had been pushing for immediate reform in 1792, and in January 1793 Wilberforce's friend Wyvill offered his own reform bill. Wilberforce supported it as enthusiastically as ever, arguing that reform would defuse republicanism, which if suppressed now would only rise again more threateningly afterwards. The bill was soundly defeated.

The French government was no more peaceful than Pitt, seeing war as a defence against anti-revolutionary Europe, an opportunity to spread the revolution abroad and, above all, a way to unite France behind the new regime. When they executed Louis XVI on 21 January 1793, it was as much an act of foreign policy as it was domestic: 'Let us fling down to the kings the head of the King,' as Danton – a leading members of the assembly – said. Wilberforce still opposed war, and when it was debated in parliament he was on his feet ready to proclaim his reasons when he was passed a message from Pitt 'earnestly desiring me not to do so that day, assuring me that my speaking then might do irreparable mischief, and pledging himself that I should have another opportunity before war was declared.' He sat down, 'sadly distressed', and before he had another chance to speak, the French declared war on Britain. For the time being, Wilberforce thought it his duty to support the war.

'It will be a very short war,' Pitt assured people, 'and certainly ended in one or two campaigns.' And if that sounds rather like 'It will all be over by Christmas', the following twenty-two years bear up that impression. As with the revolution itself, it was Burke's pessimism that proved more foresighted: 'No, sir, it will be a long war, and a dangerous war, but it must be undertaken.'[4]

War did no favours for the struggling abolition campaign. In February 1793, Wilberforce tried to arrange what he thought should have been the formality of further discussions on how to implement the gradual abolition that they had agreed in principle, but MPs voted to postpone the debate until the following year. In the Lords, Abingdon raged against abolitionists as a fifth column of French revolutionaries, arguing that their petitions against the trade had been illegal, not being in defence of the petitioners' own rights. 'Humanity is a private feeling,' he said, 'not a public principle to act upon.' He informed the peers that the abolitionists looked forward to the day when 'all being equal, blacks and whites, French and English, wolves and lambs, shall all, merry companions every one, promiscuously pig together; engendering... a new species of man'. The Duke of Clarence agreed that they were all 'either fanatics or hypocrites', singling out Wilberforce by name, though when Grenville replied insisting that he was 'an ornament to human nature' the noble lord humbly apologized.[5]

Grenville and Pitt assured Wilberforce that the Lords would at least complete their inquiry the following year (1794) and that the bill could get moving again, but Wilberforce queried this. The Lords seemed to be making no progress at all in their perfunctory inquiry, and the deadline for the completion of gradual abolition was getting closer. New propaganda was coming from Jamaica all the time, and the public – whom the abolitionists needed to put pressure on parliament – were getting tired of the subject. Sarah's husband told Wilberforce:

'I do not imagine that we could meet with twenty persons in Hull at present who would sign a petition, that are not republicans.'⁶ The effects of the war on Pitt's liberalism were not all bad, and in an attempt to stop them joining the French against Britain, for the first time Pitt gave the vote to Irish Catholics.

Wilberforce had no intention of giving the campaign a rest, but he did have other plans too. These were early days in the globalization of Christianity, and Protestant mission was largely confined to German and Danish pietists in North America, Greenland, the Caribbean and India, and British missionaries who had been sent to North America by the SPG and evangelical groups. The charter of the East India Company was coming up for renewal in 1793, and this seemed like the perfect time to organize a Christian mission to India.

One rising star of the company was Charles Grant, 'the long-faced, blue-eyed Scotsman', an evangelical friend and soon-to-be tenant of Henry Thornton's; he suggested that Wilberforce persuade parliament to add some clauses into the company's charter requiring it to provide teachers and chaplains for its dominions and committing it to the 'religious improvement' of Indians. The company had been founded in the last years of Queen Elizabeth as a trading station in Bengal, armed for its own protection; but, after continual fighting with the French, it came to rule the region as an autocracy answerable directly to the British parliament. A desire on the part of the directors to spread the gospel could have a great impact.

In truth, the East India Company was appalled by the idea. The presence of missionaries and the disturbance of Indian religion threatened to disrupt a region that the colonists found quite volatile enough already. Wilberforce got the approval of the Archbishop of Canterbury for the scheme and Dundas promised to support it in the House of Commons. It caused little stir when he first introduced it there, and although Lord Carhampton said that he was clearly insane to want to Christianize the Hindu, the bill quietly passed through the early stages.

But by the third reading the alarmed directors of the East India Company had organized serious opposition to the bill. Wilberforce insisted that he did not mean to 'force our faith upon the natives of

India; but gravely, silently, and systematically to prepare the way for the gradual diffusion of religious truth'. If the British refused to do this, they might as well admit that their attachment to Christianity was not because they believed in its truth or even its benefits but merely because it was the national religion. But to his disgust he got no support from the bishops, and even Dundas, 'most false and double', agreed to drop the amendment. Wilberforce protested bitterly that 'our territories in Hindostan, twenty millions of people incorporated, are left in the undisturbed and peaceable possession, and committed to the providential protection of – Brama'.[7]

Wilberforce was devastated by this failure. Unlike the slave trade, the charter of the East India Company was not an issue he could bring before parliament whenever he wanted. How could a cause so unequivocally right, so obviously the work of God, have been allowed to collapse? He could only think that it was because he was unworthy to take up such a hallowed cause, and had felt too proud about it. The Lord had rejected him – 'Yet where can I go but to the blessed Jesus?'

He did not give up on the idea of mission. With India on the backburner for a while, he turned his attention to a mission field closer to home, the heathen in the Church of England. In Bath that August, he started writing a short book aimed at the upper and middle classes of Britain who were Christians, to his mind, in name only. He meant to analyze their religion, compare it to the religion of the Bible, and show how far short it fell. The writing was a greater struggle than he expected, however, and in the end it took four years to complete.

French politics continued to alarm the British parliament. After a purge by the artisan-class army, the convention introduced a new constitution, involving land redistribution, universal education, the annual re-voting of every law and an end to property qualifications in elections. The regime tried to replace Christianity with the cult of reason: Christian festivals became fruit and flower days, Notre Dame Cathedral became the Temple of Reason, and notices appeared in cemeteries saying 'Death is Extinction'. Facing food crisis, civil war and invasion, the convention decreed 'the Terror' – the execution of anyone hoarding grain. In a wave of bloody panic, 40,000 suspected traitors went to the guillotine, including the remainder of the royal family.

In San Domingo, the slave revolt had turned into a war in the north between the French authorities on the one hand and, on the other, slaves and French radicals resourcefully led by Toussaint L'Ouverture, a black coachman. The convention sent the commander Léger Felicité Sonthonax to contain the revolt, and to persuade the authorities to accept new French laws (such as equal rights for free blacks) and stop them declaring independence from France. He did well, but then British and Spanish ships arrived, seeing an opportunity to take the island from the divided French, and once again Britain claimed to offer freedom to all slaves who joined its forces. Sonthonax, who hated slavery anyway, decided that the only way to secure San Domingo for France was to declare all slaves on the island free, which he did single-handedly on 29 August 1793. The British invaded the following month, welcomed with open arms by many of the French, but they faced an army of freed slaves under Toussaint which they were shocked to find invincible.

And so it was that the French government was finally persuaded to accept that slavery sat uneasily with its manifesto of liberty, equality and fraternity, and it decreed the abolition of slavery throughout the empire on 4 February 1794. Clarkson was proved right: revolutionary France had beaten Britain to abolition after all. Thus the single most popular argument against British abolition, that France would take up the trade instead, was demolished – or so one might have thought. In fact anti-French feeling in the British ruling class, stoked by the war, by the increasing radicalness of the revolution and by the massacres, was so strong that to many the French abolition just reinforced the impression that abolishing slavery was a French idea, inseparable from ending the monarchy and washing the streets with aristocratic blood.

In the summer and autumn of 1793, Wilberforce collected evidence to be presented to the House of Lords' slave trade inquiry. Clarkson, increasingly frail mentally and physically, once again toured the country from September to February to find witnesses. The pair of them had something of a falling out – over Clarkson's request that Wilberforce help his brother, the governor of the Sierra Leone colony, achieve naval promotion. Wilberforce put his name forward to Lord Chatham, Pitt's brother and first lord of the admiralty, but Chatham declined.

Clarkson then wrote angrily to Wilberforce, complaining that he had not pressed Chatham hard enough. Wilberforce explained that he was constantly dealing with such requests; that he had recommended John Clarkson, but that it was against his principles to use his influence any more decisively than that, and that the fact that corruption was generally accepted did not make it right. Clarkson then retorted that he had expected more gratitude for all his work in their common cause. Wilberforce replied that this was the attitude he had come to expect from those who lost out as a result of his scruples: 'They always, like you, seem rather to approve of one's delicacy in general, but claim a dispensation from it in their own particular instance.'[8]

The Sierra Leone Company ended up sacking John Clarkson as governor, and replacing him with Zachary Macaulay. Clarkson, it seems, was rather critical of the Company; for example, over its insistence on taking a substantial land tax from settlers in partial return for its substantial outlay, after he had told them there would be none. Macaulay was far more 'one of us' for Wilberforce's circle, an 'austere and silent' 24-year-old Scottish evangelical. He had invincible powers of logic and an extraordinary capacity for reading, digesting and remembering state papers, becoming the human encylopedia of the abolition campaign. He was also Babington's brother-in-law and convert, and a useful addition to the abolitionist cause in that he had been a Jamaican plantation manager from the age of sixteen to twenty-three.

After the five-month journey that Clarkson had taken to get witnesses for the House of Lords inquiry, the Bishop of Rochester proposed restarting the inquiry in March, but the Lords refused and it remained on the shelf. Clarkson then had a nervous breakdown. Over seven years, he had travelled 35,000 miles, kept up correspondence with 400 people without a secretary, written a book a year, seen the people he had persuaded to testify persecuted and then come to him for redress, spent a considerable part of his wealth, and seemingly all for nothing. He left the abolition committee, which had now given up its rooms and from this point on only met twice a year. Wilberforce organized a pension fund for Clarkson, writing to his abolitionist friends for donations, and carried on without him.

While the Lords sat on the abolition bill, Wilberforce introduced a new bill in May 1794, to stop British traders supplying slaves to foreign powers in the meantime. As Pitt pointed out, war had naturally put a stop to this anyway, so all Wilberforce was asking the House to do was to forbid the future revival of a trade that they had already committed themselves to abolishing within a few years. Robert Peel, father of the future prime minister, opposed this restriction of the slave trade on the basis that 'emancipating those who are not sufficiently matured by civilisation to understand and feel the blessings of liberty, would be like putting a sword into the hands of a madman'.[9] Enough anti-abolitionists preferred Pitt's logic for the bill to be passed by the Commons, but the Lords were almost unanimously affronted by its interruption of their own urgent inquiry into the slave trade, and so put this bill on hold too. They revived their inquiry, interviewed a total of two witnesses, and then, having spent some part of just seven evenings in three years on it, abandoned it. The celebrated cartoonist Gillray published *Philanthropic Consolations, After the Loss of the Slave Bill*, picturing Wilberforce and the Bishop of Rochester carousing with half-naked black women.

Anxiety about the war with France, meanwhile, had brought to fruition a scheme that Pitt had long been working on in order to divide Fox's opposition. He persuaded the Duke of Portland, the nominal leader of that group, to join his cabinet with a mouthwatering selection of titles and appointments for his allies. Fewer than half of the opposition remained out in the cold with Fox.

The war with France expanded to take in British bases in Africa, the French navy bombarding slave-trading stations along the coast. The Sierra Leone colony was attacked in September 1794 and, after a ninety-minute bombardment, sailors burnt down their buildings, destroyed their crops and killed their animals. As well as rebuilding, Macaulay organized a militia in which, unusually to say the least, black officers commanded white troops.

John Newton

William Pitt

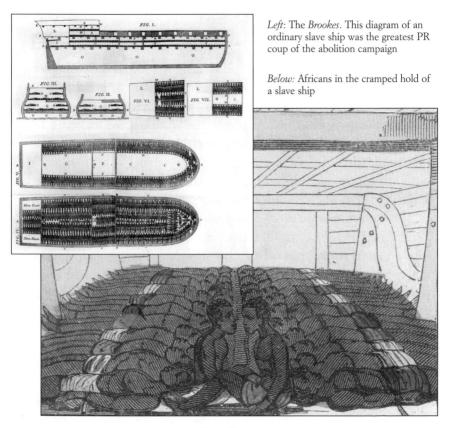

Left: The *Brookes*. This diagram of an ordinary slave ship was the greatest PR coup of the abolition campaign

Below: Africans in the cramped hold of a slave ship

The House of Commons. Pitt is speaking, and Wilberforce sits behind him, just in front of the pillar

This engraving by William Blake was produced to illustrate John Stedman's memoir of fighting against revolting slaves in Surinam (see page 145)

Josiah Wedgwood's design for the abolition campaign was the must-have fashion accessory of 1788, appearing on medallions, snuff boxes, brooches and cuff-links

12

In Opposition

Being in this dreadful captivity and horrible slavery, without any hope of deliverance, for about eight or nine months, beholding the most dreadful scenes of misery and cruelty, and seeing my miserable companions often cruelly lashed, and, as it were, cut to pieces, for the most trifling faults; this made me often tremble and weep, but I escaped better than many of them. For eating a piece of sugar-cane, some were cruelly lashed, or struck over the face, to knock their teeth out. Some of the stouter ones, I suppose, often reproved, and grown hardened and stupid with many cruel beatings and lashings, or perhaps faint and pressed with hunger and hard labour, were often committing trespasses of this kind, and when detected, they met with exemplary punishment. Some told me they had their teeth pulled out, to deter others, and to prevent them from eating any cane in future.
Ottobah Cugoano in Grenada, 1788[1]

If Wilberforce had felt that Pitt was too willing to go to war in February 1793, the two years of conflict since had hardly reassured him. For all Pitt's promises that the French rabble would quickly collapse before the shock and awe of the allied invasion, the French forces were now stronger than ever. Facing a coalition of fourteen kingdoms and smaller states (including Britain, Prussia, Austria, Spain, Portugal and the Dutch Republic), and civil war at home, only seemed to make the French revolutionaries more fervently determined to fight for their new freedoms.

Pitt had expected an even more decisive victory over the French than his celebrated father had achieved, but failed to grasp how profoundly the world had changed. Wilberforce, meanwhile, was more convinced than ever that if Pitt could persuade them that he did not want to interfere in their affairs then they too would mind their own business. Wilberforce said also that if Pitt was fighting for regime change in France, that very fighting was making a counter-revolution more and more unlikely as republicanism became synonymous with patriotism. If he did not end the war now, Wilberforce told friends, Pitt would find it ever more difficult to do so. Wilberforce even talked with Henry Bankes, a fellow independent MP and an old friend of both his and Pitt's from Goostree's, about helping to unseat Pitt if it became the only way to ensure peace.

So when Pitt began the new session of parliament on 30 December 1794, by scripting a depressingly gung-ho king's speech insisting that there could be no peace without counter-revolution in France, Wilberforce was forced to speak out. He had suspected it would come to this, and suffered a sleepless night before the opening of parliament, thinking not just of the pain of publicly deserting a friend but of the damage to his own reputation. His consolation was that 'perhaps my differing from Pitt, by lessening my popularity and showing me my comparative insignificance, may not be bad for me in spiritual things'.[2]

As parliament voted on a loyal address of thanks, he moved an amendment calling for peace, and criticizing the truculence of his honourable friend. He was supported by Bankes and his Yorkshire colleague Duncombe. As ever, Wilberforce lamented that it was 'a very incoherent speech… for want of preparation', but it delighted the opposition as much as it shocked and angered Pitt – 'You will soon see that you must join us altogether,' said Fox. Pitt's secretary at war rejected the call for what he called 'submission, humiliation, degradation before an inveterate and insolent enemy', while Pitt himself explained that in fighting French democracy and republicanism, the British were attacking 'new and monstrous systems of cruelty, anarchy and impiety'. The fact that war was not proving as easy as was first hoped was no reason to quit he said.

Wilberforce's laughable reputation in more conservative circles as an undercover revolutionary became all the more grotesque: 'Your friend Mr Wilberforce', Lady Spencer (wife of the lord privy seal) was warned, 'will be very happy any morning to hand your ladyship to the guillotine.' The king also publicly snubbed him. When the radical MP Charles Grey then brought a motion for peace negotiations in January,

Wilberforce supported it, though not without offering reflections on how much better his own proposals had been. His diary notes a party held for Pitt's political circle in February, adding, 'I not there.'[3]

Paradoxically, though, he enthusiastically backed Pitt's suspension of *habeas corpus* – the right of all subjects not to be imprisoned without trial – because of the war, as a result of which 2,000 people were now being held. He reasoned that as long as the country was at war, the government needed the strength to deal with any disorder and treachery.

While he was helping to get British workers chained indefinitely without conviction, he planned yet another new bill against the slave trade. The gradual abolition bill, which the Lords had now held up for almost three years, committed parliament – if it should be passed – to stop the trade by the end of the present year, so new legislation was needed to flesh out the details. As things stood, Wilberforce had little hope of getting the law passed in the Commons, let alone the Lords, but he was now thinking in terms of abolishing the slave trade by 1800 – Dundas's date. For that to happen, he would need to keep bringing the issue before parliament constantly, which in turn was the only way to keep it in the newspapers.

The new bill fell at the first hurdle, in February 1795. Wilberforce, asking permission to bring the motion, suggested that there was little need for protracted debate as their long inquiry had given them comprehensive information about the evils of the trade, and they had debated a remedy, deciding calmly and moderately on total abolition by 1 January 1795. For the many MPs who felt it dangerous to make such changes in times of war and revolution, he offered several thoughts: adding fresh slaves to the colonies only increased the danger of creating new slave wars like the one Britain had got embroiled in San Domingo; the naval protection of slavers was a drain on war resources; and such unstable times were not an occasion to make the people more disgusted with their governors by reneging on a firm commitment, or to provoke God by rehabilitating 'a system of greater cruelty and wickedness than ever insulted the forbearance of heaven'.[4]

A heated debate followed. Edward Hyde East complained that agreeing to gradual abolition had been a way of shutting Wilberforce up for five years, but he had betrayed that arrangement by bringing a new motion in every session since. The abolitionist Samuel Whitbread caused a scene by suggesting that if the Commons back-pedalled on abolition, they would be as 'lost to all sense of shame as the Lords appear to be'. Sir William Young, however, argued that if it would bring disrepute on the House to change its mind about gradual abolition, then Wilberforce should not be allowed to keep proposing the immediate abolition that parliament had firmly rejected. In the end, MPs voted to postpone all discussion of the issue to the next year. 'Shameful!' protested Wilberforce. Here we see the effect that his anti-war stance had on the flagging abolition campaign. The cartoonist Gillray depicted him clutching his peace motion as one of the pro-French opposition whom the warlike Pitt trampled with his horse. The plantation owner Stephen Fuller wrote home from London that abolition was defeated and they should hear no more of it.

In March, Wilberforce and Pitt met socially for the first time after eleven weeks of estrangement. They tried to be nice to each other, but it was embarrassing for both. Wilberforce was glad to see things thawing, and yet this did not stop him crossing Pitt again in April. The prime minister wanted parliament to vote for a vast increase in the allowance of the Prince of Wales, who was £600,000 in debt. Amid famine, the expense of war and the unpopularity of the monarchy, Wilberforce was by no means alone in opposing the grant – though his suggestion that it would benefit the nation spiritually if the aristocracy as a whole could live more simply was all his own. Pitt did not take this opposition personally though, and that summer found them both at Eliot's – who was now a neighbour of Thornton in Clapham, renting a house called Broomfield on his land – 'walking, foining, and laughing, and reading verses, as before'.

With Thornton, Eliot, Charles Grant and, for much of the year, Wilberforce living in Clapham, we have the genesis of what later became known as the Clapham Sect or 'the Saints'. It was never a formal organization, still less a sect, but it seems that Thornton deliberately created a community of evangelical activists on his splendid grounds at Battersea Rise. Charles Grant, the man behind Wilberforce's Indian mission, rented a second villa on the Thornton estate, like Eliot. Thornton also appointed the village rector, the like-minded John Venn, and another Clapham neighbour was William Smith who, though being a Unitarian and thus spiritually far removed from the evangelical enclave, was an abolitionist MP and had cross-examined witnesses alongside Wilberforce in the Commons inquiry of 1789–91. The observation of Logan Pearsall Smith, 'All reformers, however strict their social conscience, live in houses just as big as they can pay for,' sounds as if it could have been directed towards the Thornton estate of Battersea Rise.

The governor of the Sierra Leone colony, Zachary Macaulay, had to return to England because of health problems, and Wilberforce suggested that he make the most of it by coming home via the Caribbean. That way he could renew his acquaintance with the treatment of slaves there and bring back new evidence for his abolition campaign.

On 27 May 1795, Wilberforce brought before the House a bill for ending the war with France. He had shown it to Pitt beforehand, and found him very good-natured about it, though Pitt considered it misguided. He assured Wilberforce that France would be bankrupt so soon that he could almost calculate the day. Abbé De Lageard, the French émigré who had entertained them on their visit to Rheims, was sceptical: 'I should like to know who was Chancellor of the Exchequer to Attilla.' Presenting his motion, Wilberforce argued that a war, however it starts, is only just as long as it continues to be reasonable. The situation had changed in various ways since the start of this war – Prussia had quit the alliance, Spain and the Holy Roman Emperor were expected to follow; this, plus the end of the French civil war, had already released up to 3,000 French soldiers to fight the British. French morale was high and they were feeling the economic pressure less than the British, and a long war was more likely to encourage revolutionary ideas in Britain than to defeat them in France. Duncombe seconded the motion, answering those who objected that no peace with people as unstable as republicans could be lasting by asking when did we ever have lasting peace with France? In the last half-century, Britain and France had not seen seven consecutive years of peace. Pitt disagreed as good-naturedly in public as in private. He explained that continuing the war was for now the best prospect for a fair and honourable peace, and Wilberforce's bill was defeated by 201 votes to 86.

But that year, Prussia, Tuscany, Spain, Holland and Sweden all made peace with France. Holland actually joined forces with them, leaving Austria and two Italian states as Britain's only allies; and the French navy then seized Guadeloupe and St Lucia from Britain. A British fleet of 218 ships was sent to the Caribbean led by Thomas Maitland. San Domingo was proving to be Pitt's Vietnam, his forces unable to match Toussaint's ill-equipped army of former French slaves, dying in their tens of thousands by ambush and disease, by far the largest casualties of the war so far. In July 1795, tensions in Jamaica between the British and the free black Maroons broke out in fighting also. There were only 500 Maroon men, women and children, but it took 5,000 British soldiers and £500,000 in costs to subdue them. The British government promised to restore their traditional freedoms, but then deported them to Nova Scotia.

As Wilberforce warned, the anti-revolutionary war continued to encourage revolutionary politics in Britain. Bread prices had doubled since the start of the war and radical tracts streamed off the presses, arguing for democracy, republicanism and the redistribution of wealth. Posters appeared showing George III being guillotined. More than 100,000 people joined a demonstration in London against Pitt in October 1795; on another occasion rioters broke his windows at 10 Downing Street. Later that month the king's coach was mobbed, and he ran for his life – claiming he had been shot at – and was only saved by his life guards. Gillray the cartoonist published pictures of the outrage, with the mob led by Fox and friends, and Wilberforce helping to hold back the wheels of the coach.

The attack was the perfect excuse for Pitt to launch restrictions on political freedom. His seditious meetings and treasonable practices bills gave magistrates the power to disperse meetings of more than fifty people, break up small political clubs, and arrest those involved in either. They also imposed severe penalties for attacking the constitution. Just as he had confounded expectations by opposing Pitt over the war, Wilberforce now confused public opinion further by adamantly supporting this repressive legislation. By giving magistrates better powers to contain illicit political activity, he argued, they would actually defend legitimate debate and protest, and thus 'raise new bastions to defend the bulwarks of British liberty'.[5]

Wilberforce was as bitterly reviled in liberal circles for this as he had been in conservative circles for his one-man peace movement. His Yorkshire friends Duncombe and Wyvill opposed him, and Wyvill called a meeting of Yorkshire voters to protest the gagging bills: 'Come forth from your looms, ye honest and industrious clothiers... come forth in the spirit of your ancestors, and show you deserve to be free.' The declaration of a York county meeting would have a great impact on national opinion – a fact that Wilberforce had used to Pitt's advantage before – so Wyvill called it at only four days notice to stop Wilberforce interfering and trying to turn the meeting.

The news reached Wilberforce less than 48 hours before the meeting. It was a Sunday and he was on his way to church, and he took it seriously enough to turn home. Borrowing Pitt's carriage, as his own could not be got ready quickly enough, he set off at 2.30 p.m., and with the help of outriders to clear the road he achieved the amazing feat of covering the 160 miles to Doncaster by 9 p.m. on the Monday. He spent the rest of the evening and following morning surreptitiously rounding up supporters. When the meeting started, outside in the Castle Yard, Wyvill's opponents were surprised to find themselves in a large majority but worried about having no leader to take him on. In a great *coup de théâtre*, Wilberforce appeared from nowhere in the coach and four, and gave a thundering speech in defence of Pitt's security measures, reciting shocking passages from the radical tracts he had been reading on the journey, to huge applause and cheers and the air full of hats. 'You made my blood tingle with delight,' one voter, Colonel Cockle, told him.

Wilberforce had gone to Doncaster with only a small hope of winning round the antipathetic majority and believing that he was probably sacrificing his seat at the 1796 election due to his principles. Instead, because of Wilberforce's efforts, the county meeting voted decisively in favour of the bills, and he returned to London laden with petitions. The managers of the Yorkshire cloth industry became known as 'Billymen' for their conversion to his cause, and among

Wilberforce's supporters, the occasion was remembered as 'the glorious first of December'.

With this performance, Wilberforce transformed his standing in parliament, becoming for the moment a hero of the establishment. The announcement a week later that the government was seeking peace with France after the collapse of the alliance helped too – his own pressing for peace now seemed far-sighted rather than premature. And so when on 15 December 1795 he gave notice of a new abolition bill, he enjoyed more support from MPs than he had had for some years. Abolitionists thought that Wilberforce had finally saved the cause from the libel of revolutionary aims. On the other hand, the sugar market was recording record profits, so the resolve of colonists was as strong as ever.

The preliminary debate took place on 18 February 1796. Wilberforce began by assuring MPs that he would never get tired of banging the same old drum: 'This question differs fundamentally from all others, which have ever come under the cognisance of parliament,' because every failure and delay brought further disaster to African peoples. 'While the House sleeps, the mischiefs complained of are going on, and every year, nay every day, is adding to the guilt of this country, and to the calamities of that.' He pointed out that the situation was vitally different from what it had been last time they discussed it. Britain had lost several Caribbean colonies, precisely because of its slaves, whom the French had turned into rebel soldiers. The 150,000 Africans brought over in the four years since the gradual abolition bill was passed were an enormous liability. He also argued that those who equated abolition with French ideology were perversely making revolution seem more humane and honourable than British conservatism: 'Shall it be said that [the French] pour balm into the wounds of the Africans, whom we scourge and torment?'[6]

Tarleton commended Wilberforce on his eloquence (although his own estimation was: 'Opened the business coldly and indifferently'), but countered with another difference in the new situation – that the French attacks on the African coast had hit the profits of Liverpool, making abolition now particularly unfair. Sir William Young reported that the historian Bryan Edwards had researched the San Domingo uprising and found that it was directly caused by the abolition committee. Pitt replied that the problems of the Caribbean constituted an argument *for* abolition, slavery being the best breeding ground for dangerous principles. He pointed out the irony that in the years that the Commons had been committed to phasing out the trade, it had steadily increased.

To Wilberforce's surprise and joy, he won this first vote 93 to 67, and for the first time in almost four years he was allowed to draft the terms of a new abolition bill: it would make trafficking slaves illegal from 1 March 1797, punishable by transportation to Australia. That night he celebrated with Pitt. 'I staid too late, and my feelings too little of sacred joy and humble gratitude.'

On its second reading, the bill was ambushed by Young and Tarleton. When MPs expected a light evening's work in the House, they tended to turn up promptly to get on with it; when, as on this occasion, they expected to be pushing on into the morning they made sure of a hearty dinner first and drifted in later. Wilberforce was dining in Palace Yard when the news came to him that a skeleton House was about to throw the bill out. He rushed over in time to give a stirring speech warning the rump MPs that what they did in the name of the Commons must consider the dignity of both parliament and the good of mankind, and he kept speaking while the House gradually filled up, eventually carrying the vote 63 to 31.

When the bill was debated on the third reading, in March 1796, it faced an impassioned attack from Young: 'Every clause is replete with tyranny and oppression.' He protested that it was unfair on Caribbean planters, that all prosecutions would be heard in Middlesex, while the penalty was draconian: 'I beg the House to consider what must be the effect of such a sentence as that of fourteen years transportation to Botany Bay, to a gentleman of rank in society, of polished manners and of extensive connexions.' He decried the bill's ingratitude to 'the West Indian planters in the present war, who raised 3,000 blacks to act as pioneers and save the health of our army'.[7] The assumption that greater gratitude for that was due to planters than to the black pioneers themselves is an impressive example of the double standards of the slavery party.

John Dent protested that to allow only one year before abolition cut to the very root of the Magna Carta, the foundational charter of the British constitution. This provided a great source of entertainment for abolitionist speakers. The veteran MP Philip Francis then made his first contribution to the abolition debate with a personal testimony of how he had lost a major inheritance because he refused to oppose abolition; the moral he offered pro-slavery MPs howling about the injustice of abolition costing them money was: 'Do justice before you demand it.' Dundas told a different story, however, the moral of which was that Britain had £20 million at stake in the Caribbean colonies. This sentiment just about carried the day, and when Tarleton moved to defer their decision to the following session, he won by four votes.

Wilberforce felt sick with disappointment and resentment. 'Ten or twelve of those who had supported me were absent in the country, or on pleasure.' *The True Briton* reported 'a large and splendid audience' that night at the new comic opera *The Two Hunchbacks* by Portugallo; Wilberforce reckoned there were enough abolitionist MPs in the audience to have carried the bill. 'I am permanently hurt.' Burgh's conclusion was that Tarleton deserved mere contempt, and Young enough attention to forestall 'a shallow trick' like his ambush of the second reading; 'but against Dundas I recommend, and will cultivate in myself, direct hostilities'.[8] The following month, Francis closed his parliamentary career with his own bill for improving the conditions of slaves, presented with a very long speech, but even this failed.

The war was going badly enough for Pitt to make a serious attempt to discuss peace terms with the French, but it was also going badly enough for the French to accept nothing but complete capitulation. Negotiations quickly broke down, and Napoleon launched his devastating invasion of Italy.

Wilberforce's health went through a bad patch in April, and he was confined to his house, castigating himself for being 'secretly glad that I have a privilege to be idle. This is base!' He had little opportunity to canvas for the general election that summer, although he kept his seat anyway, and Pitt won by a landslide. Wilberforce's Yorkshire parliamentary partner Duncombe retired, replaced by Lascelles, a son of plantation-owning aristocracy.

Wilberforce spent the whole summer in Buxton taking the waters, and was pleased to receive many letters from constituents complaining that the war was now hurting their pockets and pressing for peace. In September he went to Holwood to discuss peace negotiations with Pitt. Along with others, including Eliot, in 1796 Wilberforce became a founder member of the Society for Bettering the Condition and Increasing the Comforts of the Poor, which as well as encouraging private charity in order to develop trust between rich and poor, subsidized shops and supported schools and friendly societies for saving.

Once again Wilberforce planned to harry MPs with his seventh slave trade bill in seven years. 'If the war continues I fear it will be in vain,' he told one correspondent. 'I have another idea about the slave trade, which I dare not here put down, not being sure of the safe arrival of my letter.' This idea was an international convention to end the traffic, and Pitt and Dundas were interested enough to sketch out plans, but it never got off the drawing board.

Wilberforce, however, had new hopes for Indian-based missions. The Scottish minister Robert Haldane approached him to get backing for an independent evangelistic expedition, and Dundas would have allowed it, if it had not subsequently turned out that Haldane and his friends were political radicals. Wilberforce argued, unsuccessfully, that Britain would be better off sending its democrats to Asia, and then set about trying to find more politically correct candidates.

With Napoleon clearly getting the better of Britain's last remaining ally, Austria, in Italy, the British began to expect a French invasion; an even greater threat since the naval power of Spain had now joined forces with the French. Pitt again tried to secure a peace, but during the negotiations the French launched a forty-three-ship armada to take Britain by the backdoor of Bantry Bay on the south coast of Ireland. Not one ship landed, however, thanks merely to the terrible December weather, but then a month later a massive Spanish fleet set sail to join the French in another attempt. This time British ships, under the command of Jervis and Nelson, intercepted the Spanish at

Cape St Vincent, and although outnumbered two to one, destroyed them. It seemed that for all France's irresistible dominance of the mainland, Britannia ruled enough waves to hold off invasion for the time being. In the Caribbean, British forces retook St Lucia from the French, 12,000 soldiers taking a year to defeat 2,000 freed slaves. They also went on to take Trinidad from the Spanish, and Demerara on the nearby South American mainland from the Dutch.

Wilberforce spent December 1796 working on the reform of hospitals, but then on new year's day he fell very ill. He thought he was revisiting 'the famous time' before his first slave trade motion; in fact, he thought his time was up, and though he faced death with equanimity, he was disappointed in himself for feeling 'no ardour or warmth' at the prospect. As it was, after an emergency visit to Bath, he recovered fully, and was back in action in good time to face a dangerous manoeuvre from the slavery party.

13

The Doldrums

The men-slaves were brought on deck for the first time since our sailing.
They seemed exceedingly dispirited, and drooped very much…

While the ship was on the coast they had made an unsuccessful attempt
to gain possession of her. After the insurrection had been quelled, the
captain, willing to show his valour, went among them with his drawn
sword. He gave one man a blow with it, which broke the sword in two.
He aimed a blow with his fist at the temple of another, with the intention
of knocking him down: but the man, turning his head suddenly, received
the blow on his teeth, which so disabled the captain's hand, that it is
doubtful whether he will ever recover the perfect use of it. The two
ringleaders are now chained to each other by the neck; besides having on
the same fetters which are worn by the others.
Zachary Macaulay's travel diary[1]

On 6 April 1797, the plantation owner Charles Rose Ellis brought
before the House of Commons a motion 'for the Amelioration of the
Condition of the Negroes in the West Indies'. He told MPs: 'I
reprobate the principle of the trade, and sincerely wish for its
complete termination.' The problem was that if it was outlawed as
suddenly as Wilberforce wanted, it would simply become, for want of
a better phrase, a black market. The solution, he argued, was for slaves
on the plantations to be kept alive for longer, through moral
instruction and better living conditions. But it was the colonial
governments' job, not parliament's, to make laws for the colonies, and
they were making excellent progress. So the one practical proposal of
the bill was for parliament to send a message to the planters telling
them to keep up the good work.[2]

It was an insidious piece of mischief. Not only, as Pitt objected, did it pretend to move towards abolition and improve slave conditions while making no real difference at all (offering a sugarplum to MPs' consciences) but – in theory at least – it set narrow limits on parliament's right to legislate about the slave trade. Still, compromise, as ever, appealed to MPs. Even Pitt had at first suggested to Wilberforce that they try to improve the bill by amendment rather than vote it out, but when Wilberforce insisted on opposing 'the abominable motion' head on, Pitt joined him. It was carried by 99 votes to 63. 'Ellis's motion till very late,' says the diary '– much hurt.'

There may possibly have been some tactical sense in Pitt's suggestion of limiting the damage of a motion that seemed likely to be passed whatever they did. But there seems to have been rather more a sense of fatigue. As eager and sincere as his opposition to the slave trade was, the abolition campaign had dragged on for ten years, swallowing up time and resources, and now divided parliament in the midst of a war that was gradually becoming a desperate struggle, all without any prospect of ever achieving anything. It is perhaps understandable that he should start to look for compromises.

The star on the colonists' side of the debate was the new MP Bryan Edwards. He had been a leading member of the Jamaican Assembly, and, after twice failing to win a seat in Westminster, was elected in 1796 to Grampound, a Cornish borough with about forty voters who were consequently able to charge as much as £300 per vote. His *An Historical Survey of St Domingo*, published in 1797, traced its slave revolution directly to abolition committee publications, which gave slaves ideas of equality and justice: 'In many of those writings, arguments are expressly adduced, in language which cannot be misunderstood, to urge the negroes to rise up and murder their masters without mercy.'[3] With Ellis's bill passed, Edwards in the House, and Edmund Burke dying, the prospects for abolition looked as bad as they ever had.

Wilberforce's own book, 'my manifesto' as he called it, four years in the writing, was published on 12 April 1797. It was called *A Practical View of the Prevailing Religious System of Professed Christians, in the Higher and Middle Classes in this Country, Contrasted with Real Christianity*, and it did what it said on the cover. Wilberforce had struggled to get it published, the wisdom of the industry being that there were no similar books being printed and therefore none wanted. His friends warned against it, and the printer, said Wilberforce, 'evidently regarded me as an amiable enthusiast', only risking 500 copies in the initial print run. The book was out of print in five days, however, and within six months it had sold 7,500 copies. It caused a sensation, being a condemnation of the religious status quo from a prominent member of the establishment, and offering a calm, compelling case for the evangelical faith popularly associated with firebrands and fanatics. The main thrust of the book was to show how much nominal Christians had underestimated the importance of Christianity, the value of religious fervour, their own spiritual corruption, the terms of acceptance by God, and the strictness of true Christian living. Newton called it 'the most valuable and important publication of the present age', and the Bishop of London prayed 'that it may have a powerful and extensive influence upon the hearts of men, and in the first place on my own'. Edmund Burke spent the last two days of his life reading it, before putting its contents to the ultimate test when he died on 9 July.

The war with France was reaching crisis point for Britain. Fear of invasion had been stoked by the pointless but alarming landing of 1,400 French bandits in Wales. A run on the Bank of England almost bankrupted the state, and Pitt only avoided economic collapse by creating paper money for the first time, a successful gamble that gave him, he later said, one of his three sleepless nights in government, another being his falling out with Wilberforce.

Then on Easter Sunday, 16 April 1797, the fleet at Spithead mutinied, demanding better pay, food and sick care. Pitt had little hesitation in agreeing – their last pay rise had been over 100 years ago – and for now the fleet put to sea again. But it was a frightening demonstration of the vulnerability of the British Isles. Pitt's position in parliament, however, had never been stronger. His incorporation of the Duke of Portland's party into his government had been so successful that Fox's opposition group was now less than half what it had been. Many of them, including Fox, no longer bothered turning up. After one debate, it was said that the united opposition left the House together in one cab.

It comes as something of a shock to read in Wilberforce's sons' record of his life – halfway through a paragraph about his travels that year – that Wilberforce married Barbara Ann Spooner on 30 May 1797 in Bath. Not only is it the first time that her name appears, but she offers the first ever evidence that, at the age of thirty-seven, Wilberforce was not, in the words of Shakespeare (the playwright whom Wilberforce adored just as much as he abhorred the theatre):

A man whose blood
Is very snow-broth; one who never feels
The wanton stings and motions of the sense,
But doth rebate and blunt his natural edge
With profits of the mind, study and fast.
Measure for Measure Act I, Scene 4

Whether this is simply because his sons had, predictably, no interest in documenting any attachments or flings before their mother, or because he had never been interested in romance before, we do not know. Wilberforce had made up his mind not to marry, given his fragile health and commitment to the abolition campaign, but the abolitionist James Stephen said that before his conversion he could pass as the lover of every woman with whom he talked. He certainly had many female friends and connections, from Hannah More to the 'beautiful and bewitching' Duchess of Gordon, who recruited for the Gordon Highlanders by offering the king's shilling between her lips. She was one of those he tended to steer clear of after his conversion, although she continued to invite him to her castle. Her cousin Lord Calthorpe wrote to Wilberforce from there: 'I feel how necessary your warnings against her fascinations were… She seems to be on the same kind of terms with religion as she is with her Duke, that is, on terms of great nominal familiarity without ever meeting each other.' It was her discovery of Windermere that persuaded Wilberforce to renounce his holiday home in Rayrigg because of the temptations of society.

As for Barbara Spooner, she was a beautiful, devout girl seventeen years younger than him, and it was a whirlwind romance. Babington introduced her to Wilberforce as a potential bride on 15 April, Easter

Saturday. On the Sunday, he confided to his journal: 'My heart has been tender, but I fear it has been too much animal *heat* and emotion.' They spent the week getting to know each other, and thoughts of her kept him awake every night. 'Captivated with Miss Spooner,' he wrote. 'My heart gone.' Seven days after meeting, he proposed and she accepted.

'She fell in love very suddenly,' according to Henry Thornton's daughter Marianne, 'being the only religious member of a worldly family, and she confided to Mr Wilberforce all her persecutions and difficulties. She was extremely handsome and in some ways very clever, but very deficient in common sense.' They spent many delicious hours in conversation over the next few days, 'one of Barbara's hands in mine; the other in her mother's'.[4]

It would have taken them nothing like five weeks to marry at this rate of courtship, but to Wilberforce's dismay – and the relief of his alarmed friends – Pitt called him back to Westminster. The Austrian forces were on their last legs, and Wilberforce was needed to help get a subsidy of £3.5 million passed in the House to keep Austria in the war. This was duly done, but to no avail – by the time the British representative had reached Austria, they had already made peace with France, ceding the Netherlands. The British lost their last ally and Napoleon took charge of the invasion forces. On 12 May 1797, further naval mutinies broke out on the Thames thanks to Pitt's delays in getting the pay rise he had promised through parliament. This time one of the disputes dragged on for eight weeks and ended in executions, by which time Pitt was talking seriously about resigning in favour of Henry Addington, the speaker in the House of Commons.

Wilberforce's forced cooling-off period in no way dampened his passion for Barbara, but it did allow him to reflect. Whipped on by 'the forces of affection or impulse of appetite', he felt that he had been too hasty, and should have given it more than a week before popping the question. He certainly did not regret his engagement, but did regret the way he had gone about it, believing he should not have let his head be overruled by, for example, his heart.

He took the opportunity while he was in town to make his seventh abolition motion, which he duly lost on 15 May 1797, saying 'I have been too long used to it to feel much disappointment.' Playing up to his role as a celebrity evangelical, he warned the House that the present disarray of the Caribbean colonies was divine vengeance for the slave trade. His more down-to-earth opponents warned MPs that the motion contravened Ellis's resolution. Young took a leaf out of Edwards's new book and denounced it as 'a bill for enacting a revolution in the West Indies' while Edwards himself suggested that if Wilberforce 'is desirous of exercising his humanity... he has nothing to do but walk the streets, and he will even meet a race of blacks as worthy of his benevolent attention as those of the West Indies, namely the chimney-sweepers'.[5] While being interminably harangued, Wilberforce caught up with some correspondence – possibly with Barbara, whom he sent a feverish stream of letters.

After a month's absence, Wilberforce was back in Bath on 29 May, and he and Barbara were married the following morning. 'In evening to Beacon Hill. My dearest B desired me to join in prayers with her. Retired to bed early.' Their honeymoon was a few days spent at Hannah More's house, and a week after the wedding Wilberforce was back to work in London, scolding himself for 'not having been duly diligent'.[6] The newly married couple settled in Broomfield, the house which they took over from Edward Eliot on Henry Thornton's Clapham estate.

Thomas Clarkson was now a married man as well, and had settled down in the Lake District, investing his abolitionist pension in farming and writing a three-volume *Portraiture of Quakerism*. He was a friend and neighbour of Wordsworth and Coleridge, and was evidently moving on from the collapse of the abolition movement to which he had given so much. He was not the only one. The abolition committee now met for the last time, and closed their books on the honourable failure of the campaign.

Wilberforce's book and marriage cheered him up personally after a dispiriting political season and an alarming military one. The former ended with two more failures. He managed to get a bill passed to allow Roman Catholics to serve in the militia, but it was thrown out by the lords and bishops, to his outrage. Then at the end of the parliamentary session, he stayed in London in the hope of getting a clause on abandoning the slave trade inserted into the latest treaty that

Pitt was desperately trying to agree with the French, but once again negotiations failed, this time because, at the last minute, the French government was overthrown by a pro-war coup. There was nothing for it but to dig in for a long war, and considering the economic devastation of the last five years something radical was needed to provide for it financially. So Pitt created income tax, which started at less than half of 1 per cent for the lower middle class, rising to 10 per cent for the richest, raising £5 million or so a year. (The war had increased the national debt by £120 million so far.)

As popular as radical politics had been at the start of the war with France, the defence of the sceptred isle 'against the envy of less happier lands' had quite smothered the movement. Coleridge reflected a common mood swing, having initially celebrated the French revolution by picturing himself joining the rampage for liberty:

Red from the tyrants wound I shook the lance,
And strode with joy the reeking plains of France;

[and now repenting:]

Forgive me, Freedom!...
... Forgive me that I cherished
One thought that blessed your cruel foes;

[and cheering on the home front:]

Stand forth! Be men! Repel an impious foe![7]

Fox's radicalism, however, though milder than some, never abated, and was increasingly out of step with the national mood. When he proposed a toast to 'Our sovereign's health: the majesty of the people,' Pitt discussed with Wilberforce the possibility of putting him in the Tower for treason, but was satisfied in the end with removing him from the Privy Council.

In September 1797, Edward Eliot died. He was not only a close mutual friend of Pitt and Wilberforce dating back to the earliest days,

Pitt's brother-in-law and a sometime host and neighbour of Wilberforce, but he was also a vital third strand holding their relationship together, and now that strand was broken. Equiano died around the same time and thus the abolition campaign lost another invaluable voice. How much would it take to persuade the happily married Wilberforce that there were now better things to be doing with his time?

In the spring of 1798, Irish rebels rose up against British rule. It had long been recognized that further Irish reform was necessary, not least because the Catholic majority, though they now had the vote, were not allowed to take public office, including seats in their own Dublin parliament. But Pitt had just blocked the latest reforms, so he now faced not just French forces ready to seize Ireland from the British, but Irish rebels ready to help them. Thanks to the British naval blockade, however, the French troops that managed to land were far too few and too late to swing the campaign. The uprising was brutally supressed and 30,000 Irish were killed, compared to 1,000 British troops. But the question of how to stablize Ireland had not been resolved.

Wilberforce's Proclamation Society was doing its bit to defend the bulwarks of British liberty by prosecuting booksellers dealing in material inciting readers to political radicalism and religious scepticism. Paine's writings were illegal on both counts, and the Society had the penniless London bookseller Thomas Williams prosecuted for trafficking in *The Age of Reason*. He was convicted, but a year later the prosecuting counsel, Thomas Erskine, met Williams, who was still free and awaiting sentence, and Erskine repented. The family of five lived in a 10-foot hovel 'emaciated with disease and sorrow', and William's main line of business was sewing up religious tracts. Without any talk of mitigating his sentence, Erskine said, Williams asked whether Erskine would burn the offending books for him if he could get them back. Erskine concluded that only destitution could have driven such a man to sell Paine's books, and he appealed to the Society for mercy, 'the grand characteristic of the Christian religion'. The characteristics of the Society's Christianity differed, however, and they refused Erskine's request. Williams was subsequently fined £1,000 and imprisoned until he could find the money.

A couple of events around this time suggest that Pitt's commitment to abolishing the slave trade was not as strong as it had been for the last ten years. First, the government issued an Order in Council giving slave traders permission to supply Spanish colonies. Wilberforce wrote Pitt a respectful note suggesting that the legislation had understandably slipped by him unnoticed and gently reminded the prime minister that the Commons had passed a bill abolishing the foreign slave trade, and Pitt duly rescinded the order.

Secondly, Pitt gave his support to a plan to prohibit the import of new slaves to cultivate the new British territories such as Trinidad, but which allowed their transfer from existing British plantations. The man who stood most ardently against this was James Stephen, a barrister who had returned to Britain in 1794 after a decade spent in the Caribbean. With a soap-operatic past, fathering an illegitimate child with his best friend's fiancée while himself engaged to the friend's sister, he was now an evangelical convert. 'Stephen is an improved and improving character,' said Wilberforce, 'one of those whom religion has transformed and in whom it has triumphed by conquering some natural infirmities.' He had been one of Wilberforce's information sources in the colonies throughout the abolition campaign, having turned against slavery as soon as he arrived in Barbados after attending a trial where two slaves were convicted of rape on trumped-up charges and burnt to death. He was an intense-looking man, with shadowy deep-set eyes under a vast forehead, and was a close friend of Zachary Macaulay. Stephen was as fiery and volatile as Macaulay was steely and placid ('I would rather be on friendly terms with a man who had strangled my infant son than support an admission guilty of slackness in suppressing the slave trade'[8]), and he lived for a time in the evangelical capital of Clapham.

Stephen persuaded Wilberforce that while the government's proposal to transfer slaves instead of buying new ones sounded like abolitionist principles in action, it would actually be the opposite in practice. The cultivation would require vast numbers of slaves; it was considerably more dangerous than ordinary sugar farming, so numbers would fall sharply; and this would allow the colonialists to tout it as a failure of abolitionist principles. Meanwhile, it would cause misery to slaves, and managers would simply replace the slaves they had transferred with fresh imports to the old colonies anyway, so the prohibition was meaningless. 'Lloyd's Coffee House is a roar of merriment, at the dextrous compromise,' he told Wilberforce.

Wilberforce said nothing in public, but privately appealed to Pitt to stop the proposals, which he did finally in April the following year. It was not enough for Stephen, however, who accused him of putting personal friendship with the prime minister and allegiance to his cabinet – 'those high priests of Moloch' – before duty: 'I clearly think you have been improperly silent... You are bound by the situation wherein you have placed yourself to cry out loud against it.'

Wilberforce warmly welcomed such criticism. 'Go on, my dear sir, and welcome. Believe me, I wish you not to abate anything of the force or frankness of your animadversions. I have not yet had the opportunity of deliberately and fully questioning myself on the charge you have brought, but I mean to enter into as impartial a self-examination as I am able on that head.' And Stephen was not the man to decline such an invitation. But Wilberforce confided in his diary, 'I trust that I have preserved the due medium: all think me wrong.'[9]

Wilberforce's abolition motions had become something of an annual rite, but not yet a hollow gesture. His eighth, on 3 April 1798, brought an impassioned speech from him. Once again he confronted MPs with reflections on the effects of the trade on West Africa: 'What greater reproach could attach to the British name, than... that our interference tends only to corrupt, darken and barbarise?' The trade constantly increased the danger of insurrection in the islands, he argued, while British slave ships captured by the French supplied them with 2,000 black soldiers a year: it furnished the enemy 'with the best instruments they could employ for the subjugation of our islands, and against whom we would have to wage unequal war in a climate which would continue to prove, as it had been, the grave of our brave countrymen'. And as for Ellis's resolutions, Wilberforce argued that since they were expressly intended as a step towards abolition, he was not infringing them, but simply fleshing them out.[10]

Wilberforce had considerable support in the House, but Edwards led a counter-attack, decrying his motion as adding to 'the torrent of revolutionary ideas that overwhelm half the earth'. Just as the French were raising the lowest of mankind to the level of the greatest, so Wilberforce wanted to turn slaves into masters. 'He tells the poor innocent negroes, that they are unjustly and inhumanly brought into their present condition, and of course they have nothing to do but to murder their masters, and plant the tree of liberty on their graves.' Edwards admitted the horrors of the slave trade, but insisted that Ellis's tactics would entirely eradicate it soon enough. Wilberforce's instant abolition proposals were 'downright insanity. For what else but insanity could think a race of ignorant savages fit for the complicated relations of civil society, without some sort of previous instruction?'[11]

George Canning, the rising star of Pitt's party, came out for abolition for the first time, but the abolitionist Windham defected out of anxiety about 'French ideas'. Henry Thornton replied to Edwards by reading a report from Sierra Leone. Edwards had argued that the trade rescued African captives from execution but Thornton demonstrated that captives were taken purely to supply the trade and were killed if unsold. Fox then responded to Edwards's protestations of hatred for the trade by concluding that the House was 'so lost to every sense of virtue, so lost to hypocrisy, that, notwithstanding we are so loud in sounding our detestation of the practice, we have not yet abandoned the course which we so unanimously condemn'.[12]

'Thought we had carried it,' said Wilberforce, but the vote slipped away, 87 to 83. He consoled himself by reflecting that the slavery party had entirely conceded on the issue of the evil of the trade and the need to end it, and were now forced to evade him by pretending to be subtler-than-usual abolitionists. 'On the whole we got ground,' he said. Thornton then brought before the House a less ambitious abolitionist bill to shut certain parts of the African coast to the slave trade, but Pitt put it off to the following year. 'Greatly provoked me,' said Wilberforce.

On 25 May 1798, Pitt brought the emergency bill to the Commons, to reduce the number of professions that were exempt from military service. In the absence of Fox, George Tierney led the opposition to it, which an exasperated Pitt attributed to 'a desire to obstruct the defence of the country'. Such language was clearly against parliamentary rules forbidding comments on the motives behind MPs' speeches, and Tierney appealed to the Speaker. Addington equivocated, and Pitt then repeated the charge. Tierney's response was to challenge the prime minister to a dual, and Pitt accepted.

Wilberforce was appalled. He vehemently opposed duelling on moral grounds; he feared for his friend's safety; his mind boggled at the cost of losing a prime minister in a pointless squabble during a war for national survival; and as if that was not enough, the dual took place on a Sunday – adding insult to God to any injury that the prime minister might suffer. About Pitt's safety, there was little cause for concern – as several people noted, with Tierney's corpulent bulk against the prime minister's own wiry frame, Pitt had good odds. As in most duels, no one was actually hurt, but Wilberforce still wanted to make his feelings known, and a man-to-man confrontation was not enough – Pitt had had quite enough of those already. So he brought a motion before parliament to outlaw duelling.

Wilberforce insisted, doubtless to himself as well as to others, that apart from a general reformation of manners, his only motivation was concern for Pitt's safety; but this is hard to accept. The duel was over and unlikely to be repeated, so any good that the bill could do for Pitt's physical well-being was hugely outweighed by the political damage of what was obviously a public censure in which Wilberforce was asking the whole of parliament to join. Pitt certainly shared this interpretation and was livid. Wilberforce may have subconsciously meant to punish Pitt, perhaps for shooting at the opposition on the sabbath or perhaps because he could not help feeling that Pitt was drifting away from what was left of the abolition movement. Pitt then told Wilberforce that he would resign if he even proposed the motion in the House. Wilberforce continued canvassing MPs, but he had almost no support, and so gave up.

Shortly after parliament finished for the summer, Wilberforce's mother died, and he returned to Hull for the funeral. Seeing her body lying in the bed where he was born gave him more food for self-critical reflection on sin, death and judgment than perhaps he needed, but he was back in Clapham just in time for the birth of his first son William.

Extraordinary news then arrived from Egypt. Napoleon had invaded, in order to hamper British Indian trade; but Nelson found the French fleet in Abu Qir Bay on the Nile Delta, and destroyed it. Napoleon abandoned his army and sailed home. Wilberforce was overjoyed about 'Nelson's glorious victory', telling his friend Baron Muncaster that it was 'the most signal victory with which a gracious Providence ever blessed our arms', and he was almost equally delighted that Nelson's official report likewise gave the credit to God.

In October 1798, British troops finally withdrew from San Domingo. The abolitionist prime minister, in pursuit of his belief that the war against the French was to be won in the Caribbean, had sent 40,000 soldiers to their deaths in just five years against slaves fighting for their freedom. He had also allowed slaves in the colonies to be used as soldiers, and there were now about 30,000 black regulars fighting for the British.

Over the winter, Wilberforce turned his attention back to the reformation of manners. He starting planning a new magazine, *The Christian Observer*, with Babington and Thornton and worked on a scheme to set up a Sunday school in every parish. In November he came to London to petition Dundas, successfully, on behalf of some Methodists in the Jersey home guard who were being banished from the island for refusing to drill on Sundays.

14

Quiet Time

I saw a black man suspended alive from a gallows by the ribs, between which was first made an incision, and then clinched an iron hook with a chain. In this manner he kept alive three days, hanging with his head and feet downwards, and catching with his tongue the drops of water (it being the rainy season) that were flowing down his bloated breast.
Captain John Stedman, 1798, *Narrative of Five Years Expedition Against the Revolted Negroes of Surinam* [1]

When parliament met in November 1798, Pitt had another momentous proposal to present to MPs. Having already been led by the war into the creation of paper money and income tax, he now wanted to establish the United Kingdom by merging Britain and Ireland, for the sake of security. Wilberforce was initially cool towards the idea, not least because it would bring vast numbers of Catholics into the kingdom and presumably necessitate giving all Catholics full political rights. He was gradually won round over the following months by the hope that it would broaden the political franchise in Ireland. If he had foreseen the impact that union would have on the abolition campaign, however, he might not have felt so ambivalent.

A couple of debates in this session show the less appealing side of Wilberforce's politics. Discussing the renewed suspension of *habeas corpus* (a 'seasonable sacrifice' of civil rights for the long term good, Wilberforce argued), he got into an argument with the opposition MP John Courtney. Courtney argued that the incarceration of 80 people without trial for the past two years in the Dickensian-sounding Coldbath Fields prison in Clerkenwell was a bleak indictment of the suspension, especially as he had investigated their conditions and found them to be miserable. Wilberforce, being interested in prison reform, was one of the magistrates of the prison, so Courtney took the opportunity to deplore the fact that 'the honourable gentleman, celebrated for his humanity' had never visited it, perhaps because he believed in subjecting prisoners 'to so much pain this world, that the less punishment may be inflicted on them in the next'. Wilberforce replied that he had indeed visited the prison, as had other magistrates who believed that conditions were fine. When Courtney insisted on raising the subject again the following week, complaining of the 'Christian rancour and religious facetiousness' of Wilberforce's previous speech, the attack on his faith stung as no other could, and Wilberforce crushed him with the observation that while 'a religious man may sometimes may be facetious… the irreligious do not of necessity escape being dull'.[2] He was deceived about Coldbath Fields, however, as was Courtney, because official inquiries eventually unearthed far greater abuse of prisoners than either had been led to suspect after their visits. And yet, whatever sympathy he may have felt for the victims of national security, Wilberforce continued to support imprisonment without trial both during and after the war.

The second debate centred around mill-builders who wanted their workers' trade union to be banned. Wilberforce's contribution was to suggest that parliament go further and outlaw trade unions in general, which were 'a general disease in our society', especially in wartime. The naval strikes had made MPs especially sensitive about being held to ransom, but they were less sensitive to the grinding poverty produced by a series of disastrous harvests on top of wartime inflation. And so parliament passed the Combination Act, giving local Justices of the Peace the right to send all union members to prison. Wilberforce gave a considerable amount of money away to people who were struggling and urged the government to do more for them, but he was not prepared to let them fight their own battles.

In between these two debates, Wilberforce brought his ninth bill for the abolition of the slave trade before the House on 25 February 1799. It was hardly a brash speech. Even the date for abolition so cautiously proposed by Dundas nine years ago was at hand, and Wilberforce said: 'I see less appearance of that event being brought about by the

House than at any time [since then].' Planters had had time to improve conditions and had failed, he said, proving that MPs had been duped by Ellis. The Jamaicans had reported to Westminster that they had passed some feeble resolutions, but insisted that they would continue to buy slaves until all the island was cultivated, which, Wilberforce calculated, was a matter of 2.68 million more acres, and would take 300 years and 2.8 million slaves.[3]

In reply, the anti-abolitionist MP Petrie recycled the story about slavery offering salvation from African barbarity, with an impressively perfect inversion of reality: 'The abolition would be the scourge of Africa; as a planter, I wish it to take place; but as a cosmopolite, I desire its continuance out of humanity to the inhabitants of the coast of Africa.'[4] Colonel Isaac Gascoyne, MP for Liverpool, conceded that the trade was 'unjust and inhuman', but then various other things were too, he said. Dundas made a more substantial defence. He argued that abolition would be a disaster without the consent of the colonists because they would just buy African slaves from foreign traders, and then how would parliament regulate the trade? The Jamaicans' resolutions were sound and substantial, he said, but their report showed increasing irritation at abolitionists' interference. Parliament should let them continue to make progress.

Now Canning came into his own as an abolitionist MP, with a long satirical speech, demolishing Dundas's defence as Fox once had. What had the Jamaicans actually done in their resolutions? Increased clergy wages, stopped the import of slaves older than twenty-five, but nothing else. Their report explained that these measures 'have been actuated by views of humanity only, and not by view to the termination of the slave trade' – an unnecessary clarification, jeered Canning, 'because they might have defied the ingenuity of man to discover what there was in them that could, by any possibility, tend to its termination.'[5] And yet Dundas had urged the House to accept this as unfeigned progress towards abolition – reinterpreting their explanation by ignoring the word 'not'. But despite Canning's intervention, the abolitionists lost once again, this time by 84 votes to 54.

More positively, two older abolitionist motions were revived: William Smith renewed Francis's slave-carrying bill, and Thornton resubmitted his own slave limitation bill. Pitt angered both of them and Wilberforce by casually postponing the latter after some baseless accusations without letting Wilberforce reply, but both bills were eventually passed by the Commons before being defeated in the Lords.

When the Lords read the slave-carrying bill, they insisted on hearing witnesses again, so James Stephen interviewed them for the abolitionists' side. One vital witness was Zachary Macaulay, back just in time from a Caribbean fact-finding excursion, with notes taken in Greek to avoid detection. All he wanted to do was to go to Somerset and marry Hannah More's pupil Selina Mills, but the Saints' three-line whip kept him in London. In the ensuing debate, the Duke of Clarence, in a surreal outburst, extravagantly praised Dolben's original Slave-Carrying Act ('Let foreign nations make no regulations for their own vessels... we, thank God, are actuated by other considerations than mere gain'), though he perversely attributed it, according to the report, to the pro-slavery Lord Liverpool. Because of this, he concluded, the new bill was redundant. The Earl of Westmoreland called the bill to improve shipboard conditions 'an organisation of bloodshed, and a bounty upon enormities'. Thurlow ridiculed the Sierra Leone Company and its plan to send 'missionaries to preach in a barn of Sierra Leone to a set of negroes, who do not understand a word of his language' – 'profane balderdash' was Wilberforce's summary. And yet for once, there was enough of a conscience among the Lords for the bill to have been passed – if the abolitionists had not mislaid 14 proxy votes. 'Never so disappointed and grieved by any defeat,' Wilberforce said.[6] Macaulay was then allowed to marry and moved to Clapham.

That summer Pitt spent £1.5 million of government funds buying the acquiesce of MPs in Dublin to the proposed union in which they would be absorbed into the Westminster parliament. The one great sticking point was the granting of fuller political rights to Catholics. For Pitt and some of the Irish MPs it was a sensible way of securing acceptance of the union, the peace of Ireland and the security of the United Kingdom; for many others, most ominously George III, it was both religiously and politically impossible. Pitt's risky answer was privately to assure those who thought like him that union would include emancipation, but to make no official mention of it.

The Saints founded the Church Missionary Society on 12 April 1799, in the hope of sending missionaries to India. As well as all the usual names, it involved Charles Simeon, a Cambridge member of the Clapham Sect particularly devoted to foreign mission. The Society initially only had the permission rather than the backing of the bishops who were cautious about disrupting the increasingly important Bengali colony, and it would be many years before they had any success in sowing, let alone reaping, the seed of the gospel in India.

In August 1799, Wilberforce celebrated his fortieth birthday in Broomfield. His marriage was very happy, though Barbara's letters reveal little more than a woman whose chief pleasures in life were piety and fretting. The couple now had a baby Barbara to go with their baby William. Wilberforce's reflections on reaching this great milestone, and the end of the century, are unrecorded, but were doubtless intense, unsatisfied and unforgiving. It was fourteen years since his evangelical conversion, and he had never been content with the changes he had seen in his life since.

And yet to outsiders he was one of the great saints or, depending on perspective, religious fanatics, of the age; a soul-winning philanthropist or bleeding-heart God-botherer, but a towering figure from either direction. Beyond his parliamentary campaigns he was famous throughout Britain for his evangelical bestseller, his frustrated plans for India, the Sierra Leone project, the Proclamation Society, the Poor Society, prison work and Hannah More's rural regeneration project. And yet the public didn't know the half of it. Not only did he have several new plans on the drawing board, but privately he was a major charity himself. The following year, Wilberforce would overspend his income by £3,000 having given more than that amount away, but rather than cut back his giving amid such need he considered giving up Broomfield. He regularly gave a quarter of his income away. Thornton was also known as a fount of charity, giving up to 85 per cent of his annual income away; but, as Macaulay noted, whereas the great banker carefully investigated his causes to make sure he put his money where it would be productively and worthily spent, Wilberforce happily gave to anyone who could convince him that he or she was not a complete crook. He gave to schools and missions, debtors and struggling farmers, supporting hospitals and dispensaries, all the more now he had children, and could imagine what it must be like not to be able to afford the medicine they needed. When practical, he gave anonymously, if necessary posting a large gift in separate amounts to avoid being noticed.

The generosity of his political influence is more ambiguous. He would eagerly support any measures he saw as providing more adequately for the common people materially or spiritually, and agitated for better poor relief; but he did so of course from a position of power, and sharing that power with the lower orders was another matter. He had always, unlike most MPs, wanted to broaden the franchise, but the political turmoil of the last decade and his increasing years now made him feel a little less certain. 'In the early part of my life,' he told the Commons during the Irish union debate, 'I zealously supported the cause of a reform in parliament, and particularly the plan of my right hon. friend [Pitt]. Much undoubtedly has passed in the course of sixteen years, to justify him for any change which may have taken place in his opinion on that head. An alteration, however, it seems must be made.'[7]

His contribution to Pitt's suppression of civil rights, on the other hand, had been unambiguously pernicious. He liked to see himself as the voice of reason between the hysterical reactionaries who saw revoluntionaries under every bed and the reckless radicals who wanted to put them there – not an entirely unreasonable assessment. But imprisonment without trial and the criminalization of campaigns for political reform and labour rights were themselves panicked overreactions, and Wilberforce was instrumental in them. His reasoning was that it made sense to sacrifice some of 'our liberties' for the sake of the war effort, instead of losing all liberty under a French conquest; but then it was not his own liberty that he was sacrificing. Moreover, the repression continued long after the war, creating violent conflict for the rights of ordinary British people.

And then there was the slave trade. It was ten years now since Wilberforce's first celebrated motion to abolish it. In that time he had presented nine more motions (one a year except during the parliamentary inquiry of 1790), spent thousands on the campaign, devoted countless hours to it through sickness and health and even missed church for it. And for what? In that time 400,000 slaves had been taken from Africa to feed the Caribbean plantations, an 80 per cent increase on the previous decade. The Americas as a whole had absorbed 10 times that number. For all Clarkson's and Wilberforce's insistence (in 1789) that it was a 'losing trade', profits had increased by 37 per cent per head since then. The single positive improvement directly achieved by this unparalleled endeavour was a reduction in shipboard overcrowding, passed before Wilberforce's first speech. (Indirectly, conditions in the colonies had improved a little; and attempts to increase slave importation had been held off for the time being.)

When Wilberforce made that great speech of 1789, he had behind him a huge popular movement, a brilliant campaign, and the greatest speakers of the age. Now, the abolition committee had folded. Clarkson was a Lakeland farmer and family man, Sharp was in his sixties, Newton in his seventies, and Ramsay and Equiano were dead. The abolition movement had long run out of steam, after years of failure and concerted opposition, and anxieties fuelled by revolutionary war. And of the big four in parliament, Burke was dead, Fox was in semi-retirement (though still showing up for slave trade debates), and Pitt was increasingly impatient with the whole thing. And yet Wilberforce continued year after year, bringing forward his bills, hatching his plans, gathering information and organizing inquiries. He did not stand completely alone, as he had the Saints with him: MPs Thornton and Smith, his old taskforce Babington and Gisborne, and the invaluable newcomers Stephen and Macaulay. But still he must have felt like a marathon runner pressing on as the others fell away – only with no known finishing line. Wilberforce may not have exhibited the drivenness of Clarkson, the PR acumen of the Quakers, the pioneering spirit of Sharp or the rage of Stephen, but he did have stamina.

A bout of illness took Wilberforce to Bath for four months that autumn. Returning to London for parliament in January 1800, he crossed swords with Pitt several times: the prime minister was not doing enough for the poor after yet another failed harvest; he planned a bill to limit the numbers and freedom of non-conformist preachers as a further homeland security measure, which Wilberforce eventually persuaded him not to pursue; and he turned down peace with France.

Napoleon had seized power in France, becoming first consul, and had offered to end the war with Britain; but in protest against the coup, and because Austria and Russia were now fighting with the British, Pitt superciliously rejected the offer – to Wilberforce's dismay – although Pitt eventually convinced him that the offer had been a con.

When it came to the slave business, Wilberforce had his own surprising peace proposal to weigh up. In February, Pitt received a proposal for stopping the trade from the unlikeliest of all sources – a group of leading Caribbean magnates, including Sir William Young. Rapidly increasing competition had brought sugar prices crashing down; in Hamburg, the main market for British sugar, eighty-three trading houses collapsed in just three months in 1799. Young hoped a five-year ban on new slaves would protect his market. Wilberforce held off presenting any other abolition motion while the two sides talked, but then at the end of the session the West Indian parliament threw out the proposal. It did such a good job of keeping Wilberforce quiet for a whole year that some have since seen it as a scam which he fell for. But the planters' problems with overproduction were quite real, much more so than the dangers of Wilberforce bringing yet another bill to be defeated. With the idea now raised, he tried to persuade Pitt and Dundas to suspend the trade themselves, but without success.

In 1800, James Stephen married Wilberforce's widowed sister, Sarah, and both families spent June boating on the Thames. Sarah fitted perfectly into the Clapham Sect environment. Stephen's grandson Leslie reports that she spent £10 a year on clothes and gave the rest of her income away to charity. Staying at Gisborne's in ever-declining tatters, she provoked him into tearing her dress in half, saying, 'Now, Mrs Stephen, you *must* buy a new dress.'[8] 'She calmly stitched it together,' says Leslie Stephen, 'and appeared in it next day.'[8] Wilberforce hinted to James about a new scheme: 'If you knew all I do, you would think you saw streaks of light indicating the opening day, and rewarding all our past sufferings.' He had contact with the writer Francis Hare Naylor, who after years living in Italy had forged personal connections with Napoleon himself. Confident that peace talks would come soon enough, Wilberforce wrote to Naylor asking him to present proposals for multilateral abolition to

Napoleon, to be worked into any treaty. 'Would I were the starling to hollow "Abolition" in the Grand Consul's ear,' said Wilberforce. 'Oh, that he might be sensible of the opportunity Providence puts into his hands; it would be worth almost the endurance of all that is past to effect such an object.'[9]

Barbara was seriously ill in the summer, and Wilberforce told Hannah More that he thought she might be dying, but a visit to Bognor seemed to revive her. In November 1800, he got into a rather ugly fight with Grey, Tierney and the opposition MP and playwright Richard Brinsley Sheridan, over a parliamentary motion on the high price of provisions which had more than tripled since the start of the war. And yet, dissatisfied by the government's moderate measures, he helped found the London Committee for Poor Relief.

The Act of Union being passed, the House of Commons in that session had expanded from 558 to 658 MPs with the Irish influx. It was now time to move on to Catholic emancipation, but the king stood resolutely against it and Pitt's cabinet was divided. Seeing no way to keep his word on the matter, Pitt resigned on 5 February 1801 and Addington became prime minister. Pitt left office personally £45,000 in debt and facing bankruptcy. He refused a gift of £30,000 from the king, but accepted a loan of £11,700 from 14 friends including Wilberforce, which to no one's surprise was never repaid. Wilberforce was impressed that Pitt had stepped aside so 'magnanimously and patriotically'. It was widely reported that Addington would end the war and give Wilberforce, who liked the pious minister very much, an office in his cabinet. 'I was for a little intoxicated,' confessed Wilberforce, 'and had risings of ambition.' His long commitment to peace appealed to Addington, but his determination to use any position of power to attack the slave trade did not, and so he continued as one of what he called the 'independent characters'.

Negotiations began with Napoleon at Amiens immediately. As all the slave powers were involved, Wilberforce had great hopes for his 'grand abolition plan', incorporating into the treaty multilateral abolition of the slave trade. He was hopeful enough to go for a second year without bringing before parliament a new abolition bill, to calm the waters. After parliament had approved of the preliminary agreements in Amiens, Wilberforce wrote a long letter to Addington laying out his proposals and entreating him to try them. He pointed out that the credit for abolition would then go to him: 'It is not... without emotion that I relinquish the idea of being myself the active and chief agent in terminating the greatest of all evils.'[10] But it was credit that Addington could do without, and he refused. Wilberforce warned Addington that he would console himself by bombarding the Commons with all kinds of anti-slavery bills.

In 1802, the Religious Tract Society received an appeal for Bibles from a Methodist minister who complained about the scarcity of them in Wales. The society approached Charles Grant, who arranged an audience with Wilberforce, and they put to him the idea of a new society being set up to print free Bibles for the poor throughout the UK and the wider world. Wilberforce told them to organize a survey, identifying areas of Bible shortage. They felt frustrated by his discretion, but the British and Foreign Bible Society was eventually established two years later, with Sharp as chair and most of the Clapham Sect on board. Within twenty years it had distributed over 4 million Bibles and New Testaments, in 140 languages, fifty-five of which had never before had Christian scriptures.

The Clapham Sect launched *The Christian Observer* in 1802, a monthly magazine edited by Josiah Pratt, following the trail blazed by *The Gentlemen's Magazine*. Like the *Magazine*, it offered articles, reviews, parliamentary reports and international news. The differences were its evangelical spin, abolitionist propaganda, rather duller style ('It is heavy,' Wilberforce conceded), and far cheaper cover price. Wilberforce then helped found the Society for Suppression of Vice to take over the work of the Proclamation Society for no clear reason, prosecuting the pedlars of obscene, blasphemous or 'democratic' books. He supported Robert Peel's Factory Act, which vastly improved working and living conditions, but only for Poor Law apprentices, which he thought was a pity.

Wilberforce planned a new abolition bill for early February, but despite his threat to Addington, for a third time he let the session pass without one. The reason this time was that Canning was planning a motion to outlaw the introduction of slave plantations to the newly acquired island of Trinidad, and as such a vast increase in the number of slaves was at stake Wilberforce decided that the most constructive thing he could do would be to let Canning have the stage to himself, and then bring forwards his abolition bill soon after.

In the meantime, the Treaty of Amiens was concluded on 25 March 1802 and a decade of war was at an end. The Wilberforces were at Gisborne's when the news came through, and let off fireworks. The British gave up a number of their Caribbean gains, but kept Trinidad. As for San Domingo, which after a two-year civil war was united under the draconian regime of Toussaint, which was only marginally better than slavery, Napoleon reasserted French claims to the island. Addington, seeing a peaceful 'black empire' as a greater threat to British interests than the French expansion, gave his full approval to the recapturing of the slaves, and Napoleon prepared an army of 35,000. In May, before landing, Napoleon declared that slavery was officially reinstated on the island.

Canning finally brought his motion before the House on 27 May 1802, arguing that the cultivation of Trinidad, by bringing vast numbers of new slaves into the Caribbean, would place British territory under huge danger of uprisings. Without the slave trade, Trinidad could become a new thing in the Caribbean, 'a bloodless, guiltless colony'. At the very least, Canning argued that no cultivation should be allowed until parliament had consented. Addington replied that no new proposal was needed, because the wonderfully fertile island was still being surveyed and he expected there to be a parliamentary debate on the matter next year. Wilberforce responded bitterly that no good could come from Addington's expectations judging by his past record, and the matter was left up in the air.

It was dispiriting enough to stop Wilberforce bothering with an abolition bill at this late stage of the parliamentary session. He did, however, contribute to an attempt to outlaw bull-baiting. Dismayed that the bill's sponsor seemed to have no interest in animal welfare and only saw it as a social problem, he spoke passionately in defence of the bulls. It was a rousing performance, despite the fact that he had lost his notes, but the bill was still defeated. In the general election that summer he was re-elected without opposition, and his second son, his biographer Robert, was born.

Stephen published *The Crisis of the Sugar Colonies*, making the familiar case that the slave trade was a liability to colonial security, but doing so with the relentless logic and expertise of a major maritime lawyer. Moreover he made no mention of the evils of the trade, appealing 'not to the conscience of a British statesman, but to his prudence alone'.[11] Stephen published it anonymously to dissociate it from the abolition campaign, and it made quite an impact.

Early in 1803, the vast French reconquest force started assembling off San Domingo. 'We are lost,' said Toussaint. 'All France is come to St Domingue.' Wilberforce was dumbfounded to hear that Napoleon was hiring British ships to transport men and arms. It offended against a sense of patriotism, compassion towards the islanders and the honour of British agreements with Toussaint. He protested, but could get no one – from Addington to Fox – as worked up about it as he was, except for Stephen who was angry that Wilberforce was not doing enough about it. Toussaint resorted to a scorched-earth guerilla war in order to make French victory as costly as possible.

Wilberforce was about to bring his tenth abolition bill before the House in February 1803 when he went down with flu. Before he had recovered, the king announced that Napoleon was once again preparing an invasion force and the country should get ready to defend itself. New sea forts were to be built, old ones strengthened, volunteer regiments organized and trained. And so for the fourth year in a row Wilberforce could not present a slave trade bill. 'My poor slaves!' he cried; it would be 'improper to bring forward my intended motion... when the whole attention of government is called to the state of the country'.[12] Proper or not, it would be quickly and overwhelmingly defeated, while making a dire impression on all those Irish MPs who were new to the debate and needed to be carefully cultivated.

In May, Addington's government declared war on France, once again opposed by Wilberforce before a hostile House. By the start of 1804, Napoleon had 2,000 ships and 100,000 soldiers ready on the coast; but British defences were in good shape, one in five men was mobilized and the navy was strong enough for Admiral St

Vincent to proclaim, 'I do not say the French can't come, I only say they can't come by sea.'

At the same time, some major plantation owners started talking again about temporarily suspending the slave trade. Wilberforce heard that the next conference of planters in London was expected to agree unanimously to this. He believed that Addington would bring the proposal before parliament, and encouraged him 'to make himself the head of a suspending party for five years'. He expected him to recommend it as an antidote to 'the wild enthusiasts who are for total Abolition'; he expected others, assuming the proposal succeeded, to contrast Addington's successful practicality with his own ineffectual idealism; and of course for most people 'it might perhaps... not be very pleasant to have the chief object and endeavour of their whole public life taken out of their hands'.[13] But Wilberforce insisted that none of this mattered in the least, if someone could just stop British sailors taking men, women and children from Africa to the brutal degradation of the plantations. But again Wilberforce had put too much faith in a prime minister to whom the brutality was of no consequence, and he refused to have anything to do with it. On 17 May the plantation owners' conference again rejected a suspension of the trade, for fear that it would never be restarted.

It looked as if Wilberforce had let a fifth parliamentary session pass without bringing forwards an abolition motion. But the day after the conference, Pitt returned to office as prime minister, after a combined attack from him and Fox had forced Addington to resign, and two weeks later, on 30 May 1804, Wilberforce finally presented his tenth bill.

There were so many new MPs since Wilberforce had last addressed the subject five years before that he felt it was worth going back over the well-worn arguments and counter-arguments: the conditions in the colonies and in the Middle Passage and the problem of foreign slave traders. He returned to his opponents' claim that colonists just needed more time to improve conditions and wind down the trade, arguing that they had been given it, and yet had only grown more addicted. It was folly to be pouring capital into such vulnerable islands given the prospects for renewed war, and to be adding 30,000 unbroken captives each year given the danger of slave risings. He ended with a direct appeal to the Irish, calling them 'a brave, a generous, a benevolent people'.

Tarleton replied that the slave trade was just one of those evils humans were obliged to endure – in which, thanks to Pitt's fiscal policy he could now compare it to income tax as well as war. John Fuller argued that, like Indians, if Africans were capable of civilization they would have resisted British dominion better. Wilberforce was then outraged by a 40-second 'speechling' from Addington, in which he dismissed instant total abolition as impracticable, mendaciously passing over Wilberforce's offer of suspension. William Smith offered a caustic assault on the arguments and motives of the slavery party, Fox was as robust as ever, and the cause had a new convert in John Foster Barham, a Caribbean magnate who believed that the collapse of sugar prices made abolition practicable for the first time.

The result of the vote astonished both sides: every one of the Irish MPs present supported Wilberforce and the first reading was carried by 124 votes to 49. Wilberforce was immediately deluged with congratulations. 'On all sides, and in all directions, letters are lying around me unanswered, and many of them unread.' He told the eighty-year-old Newton: 'I fear the House of Lords! But it seems as if he, who has the hearts of all men in his power, was beginning to look with pity on the sufferings of those poor oppressed fellow-creatures whose cause I assert.'[14]

He knew that it was not time to celebrate yet though. All was nearly lost when the Irish MPs decided to go home for the summer, but he persuaded them to stay a week. In the second reading and subsequent committee stage, anti-abolitionists did everything they could to slow the bill fatally, but on 27 June it was finally passed by the Commons by 69 votes to 33. Wilberforce and Pitt then took it to the House of Lords, where it passed its first reading the following day.

On the way, however, Pitt broke the news to Wilberforce that the cabinet had decided to abandon the bill. The Lords would never pass it without letting the slavery lobby give evidence, and it was hopeless trying to squeeze that into the butt end of the session. The upper chamber duly laid aside the bill on its second reading – though not before another anti-abolitionist, the Earl of Mulgrave, voiced his increasingly mixed feelings on the subject, conceding that abolition might have some advantages after all. 'It quite lowers my spirits to see all my hopes for this year blasted,' confessed Wilberforce, 'yet I can't help myself.'

The abolition bill was expected to sail through the Commons again in 1805, and then make it through the Lords also, because of the large Commons majority. Wilberforce as usual was more wary: 'We know not what may happen in the interval.'[15] But with the prospects for abolition now looking realistic for the first time in a decade, Granville Sharp, now sixty-nine years old, along with the Quakers, revived the abolition committee after its long hiatus.

After the disappearance of his bill, Wilberforce moved immediately on to the question of opening up new land, on islands such as Trinidad and Demerara, to British slavery, an issue which the government had still not resolved, and which was now claiming 1,000 new slaves every month. He pressed Pitt on the matter, who said he would organize a royal proclamation to stop it and insisted that it should not therefore be brought before the Commons. Wilberforce was in two minds, but discussing it with the Clapham circle, decided that he could achieve nothing in parliament with Pitt's opposition, and so left it up to him.

At the start of 1805 Wilberforce was still imploring Pitt to move on the issue, but slaves were a lower than ever priority for the prime minister. He had returned to office in a weak position: he had lost support on one side through his political lynching of Addington, and on the other side Grenville had joined Fox because he had not done it sooner. The king was less help to him as his sanity was becoming more and more patchy. Moreover, Pitt was increasingly hampered by a chronic stomach ulcer, and the threat of invasion by the French hung as ever over the British coast. He had to start winning back the House, and an issue as divisive as the slave trade was not going to do it. In fact he even pushed Wilberforce to postpone his abolition motion. Wilberforce, of course, refused outright to 'make that holy cause subservient to the interest of a party'.

So in February 1805, Wilberforce presented his eleventh abolition bill. The first reading was unopposed, and on Thursday 28 February he had a quick dinner before the second reading, expecting a short evening with a comfortable majority. Instead of his usual speech he said he had nothing to add to last year's.

It was overconfidence. The slavery party had subtly gathered up a good attendance from supporters and had had persuasive words with fence-sitters, tactics that Wilberforce had not imagined would be necessary on his side, and they took the floor in force. Charles Brooke reported that the French slave trade was resurgent, so that abolition would merely hand British commerce over to the enemy. Young gave a long speech detailing the horrors of the San Domingo revolt, barbarity in Africa, and the financial losses that could be expected from abolition.

Belatedly, Wilberforce returned with the rallying cry that had been missing at the start:

> The opportunity now offered may never return, and if the present moment be neglected, events may occur which render the whole of the West India islands one general scene of devastation and horror. The storm is fast gathering; every instant it becomes blacker and blacker. Even now I know not whether it be too late to avert the impending evil, but of this I am quite sure – that we have no time to lose.[16]

For the first time Pitt declined to help him out. Gascoyne proposed putting off the question till next session, and won the vote by 77 to 70. 'Sad work!' Wilberforce wrote in his diary that night. 'Though I thought we might be hard run from the face of the House, I could not expect the defeat, and all expressed astonishment.' He slept little that night or the next. Lying awake, 'the poor blacks rushed into my mind, and the guilt of our wicked land', and when he slept it was to visit 'scenes of depredation and cruelty on the injured shores of Africa'. He told Muncaster: 'I have had a damp struck into my heart.'[17]

When he had picked himself up from his devastating defeat, Wilberforce returned to the issue of taking slaves to Trinidad and Demerara – 'an affair, probably of no less than 12 or 15,000 human beings annually, and of suffering so much capital to be invested in a foreign settlement which we must relinquish at peace.' He moved on from entreaty to threat, telling the ailing Pitt that he had waited long enough and was going to take it to parliament with or without his support. Pitt came back to him two days later saying that the cabinet had unanimously agreed to stop the traffic to Demerara and neighbouring Surinam by an Order in Council, and Wilberforce was to help with the decree.

A scandal then broke in April 1805, when it emerged that Dundas, now Viscount Melville and first lord of the admiralty, had allowed subordinates to embezzle naval funds. To Pitt he was a close friend and ally, and vital to the war effort, but to Wilberforce he was a sinner. Samuel Whitbread brought before the House a motion of censure against Dundas and the subsequent debate was so close that Wilberforce's denunciation swung the vote against him. Friends ushered Pitt out of the chamber in tears, and Dundas was replaced by Charles Middleton.

The delays over the Order in Council dragged on until Wilberforce saw the final version on 11 May 1805. He was dismayed to find it riddled with loopholes, and implored Pitt not to publish it after all, until it had been revised. After two weeks – in which time he helped to defeat Fox's bill to grant political rights to Catholics – Wilberforce submitted the revised text. In June, he was complaining, however, as 'Pitt has not yet settled it – too bad… I write and call again and again.'

After six years, the Church Missionary Society sent a missionary to India for the first time. There were already a few unauthorized British missionaries there, including the Baptist cobbler William Carey, who had translated the New Testament into Bengali. The Society's contribution was to get Henry Martyn appointed as chaplain to the East India Company. Coming, as you would guess, from a somewhat different class to Carey, Martyn was a Cambridge philologist and a protégé of Simeon's. More impressed by Carey's efforts than by his grammar, Martyn joined in the translation work, and produced a New Testament in Urdu.

On 13 September 1805, the Order in Council against the cultivation of Demerara was finally issued, not by Pitt, but by his anti-abolitionist secretary for war, Lord Castlereagh. In the same month, news reached England that the combined fleet of thirty-three French and Spanish ships had been seen off Cadiz. Nelson took a fleet of twenty-seven ships, and in the Battle of Trafalgar on 21 October destroyed the enemy, who lost all but eleven ships. The British lost none, although Nelson was killed. Wilberforce, reading the report, was 'so overcome that I could not go on reading for tears'. Any prospect of that long-promised invasion was finally destroyed, and British rule of the waves was complete.

Celebrations were dampened by news of the Battle of Austerlitz. Pitt had spent over a year negotiating a new alliance with, amongst others, Austria, Russia and Prussia, in order to attack France, and finally it was agreed, though without Prussia as yet. Then on new year's day 1806, an official report arrived in London that Napoleon had demolished the combined Russian and Prussian army on 2 December, as decisively as he had lost at sea. France now ruled Europe. 'Apparently we shall be in the most imminent danger,' reported Wilberforce.

Pitt was in Bath when the dispatch came, and this time the healing waters failed to help. Returning home he reportedly saw a map of Europe laid out and said, 'Roll up that map, it will not be needed again these next ten years.' Wilberforce called his haggard, thin, frail appearance 'the Austerlitz look'. Then, on 23 January 1806, Wilberforce heard from the Bishop of Lincoln that Pitt had died at half past four that morning. 'Pitt killed by the enemy as much as Nelson,' concluded Wilberforce. Others said the Melville affair had as much to do with it.

Pitt died £40,000 in debt. It was proposed that the state pay his creditors, which Wilberforce vehemently opposed, fearing that a precedent might be set for wild-living ministers. He tried to raise the money privately from among Pitt's friends, but managed only a quarter of it. At Pitt's state funeral, Wilberforce was a pallbearer, and cried throughout the service. He told Muncaster: 'I own I have a thousand times (aye, times without number) wished and hoped that a quiet interval would be afforded him, perhaps in the evening of life, in which he and I might confer freely on the most important of all subjects. But the scene is closed – forever.'[18]

15

Abolition

The place allotted to sick negroes is under the half deck, where they lie on the bare planks. By these means, those who are emaciated, frequently have their skin, and even their flesh, entirely subbed off, by the motion of the ship, from the prominent parts of the shoulders, elbows, and hips, so as to render the bones of these parts quite bare... The utmost skill of the surgeon is here ineffectual.

Alexander Falconbridge, a slave ship surgeon, 1788[1]

For all Pitt's services to the campaign, and for all Wilberforce's love and devotion to him, his death was, to put it brutally, the best thing that could have happened to the abolition campaign. Too politically weak to support divisive motions and too physically weak to attend to secondary issues, his administration had become an obstacle, which Wilberforce's deference magnified.

His successor was Lord Grenville, who along with Pitt had first put the idea of abolition to Wilberforce and constantly championed it in the House of Lords. Fox became foreign secretary and leader of the House for a third time, although the previous periods had amounted to less than a year in total. The chancellor of the exchequer, Lord Henry Petty, was another ardent abolitionist. Where abolition had been a personal ambition for Pitt, it was now a political priority. Abolitionists could hope for a decisive majority in a full House of Commons, thanks to the Irish influx; West Indian opposition was becoming less intransigent; the abolition committee was resurrected and now met frequently at Wilberforce's; and even in the Lords the balance was more promising.

Still, the opinion of Fox and Petty was that 'we might certainly carry our question in House of Commons, but should certainly lose it in the

House of Lords'. And with Addington, now Viscount Sidmouth, as lord privy seal, the cabinet was still not united against the trade. Grenville's tactic was to go for the less controversial abolition of the foreign slave trade first, reinforcing and extending the Order in Council which would at least test the water for total abolition.

This bill was debated throughout April 1806 in the House of Commons, without arousing widespread interest. An MP called Rose prophesied that if it were passed 'the manufacturers of Manchester, Stockport, and Paisley, would be going about naked and starving'. Peel warned that abolishing the sale of slaves to foreign powers would 'bring all human misery into focus, and that that focus shall be Great Britain! If we are to philosophise, let us do so while our looms are full.' And yet William Young was heartily in favour, claiming that most plantation owners saw the bill as deliverance after the collapse of sugar prices. It was passed by 35 votes to 13 on 1 May. In the Lords, there was a proposed amendment to add the words 'until 1 July 1807' to the date of the ban, but it was a token gesture, and the bill had enough support for Grenville to toughen up its wording. 'I saw our strength,' he told Wilberforce – and the reinforced bill became law. It was the first legislation against the slave trade to get through parliament since Pitt drove Dolben's bill through, eighteen years previously.

Wilberforce found himself in a paradoxical position. There was little love or understanding between him and Fox: politically, socially and religiously they were aliens, and tended to suspect the worst of each other. Meanwhile, Grenville had throughout most of Pitt's life been just a friend of a friend to Wilberforce, who had never much liked him and after his conversion thought less of him still. So their joint administration was hardly one to appeal to Wilberforce. It was Pitt that he had admired as a man and as a politician, and not least as an abolitionist; and yet Pitt's twenty years in office had achieved almost nothing in the way of abolition, while Fox and Grenville had swept away the foreign slave trade in their first few months, and looked to total abolition with increasing confidence.

Wilberforce wanted to move on to it immediately, but Grenville sensibly enough insisted on waiting until the next session, for fear that haste would cause the bill to be defeated in the Lords. Instead, Fox proposed that parliament agree a statement of intent before the end of the session, condemning the slave trade as 'contrary to the principles of justice, humanity and sound policy' and agreeing to abolition in principle. It was not a manoeuvre to bring out the big guns of the anti-abolitionists, but was another weapon to use against them in the new year. The resolution was carried overwhelmingly: by 114 votes to 15 in the Commons; and by 41 votes to 30 in the Lords. Wilberforce added a second resolution, that the king be asked to negotiate multilateral abolition with other slave powers, and this was also passed without opposition.

Stephen suggested to Wilberforce one last piece of business for this session to stop the panic buying of slaves. He warned that traders facing imminent abolition would send every ship they could get hold of to Africa in a last minute rush, so Wilberforce and Fox hurried a law through parliament that forbade any ships being brought into the trade for the first time. During the same session, Wilberforce also sat on a committee for five weeks discussing the woollen trade, and successfully opposed a tax on unwrought iron, on behalf of his constituents. It seemed to Wilberforce that there was room finally for optimism. 'If it please God to spare the health of Fox...,' he told Stephen, 'I hope we shall next year see the termination of our labours.' On 27 June, William Smith announced in tears that Fox had dropsy. 'Poor fellow,' was Wilberforce's reaction, 'how melancholy is his case! He has not one religious friend.'[2]

In August, Wilberforce retreated to 'the snug and retired harbour of Lyme, for the purpose of careening [turning a ship on its side] and refitting'. He also wrote a book there, *A Letter on the Abolition of the Slave Trade* – a title that shows how it rather ran away with him in the writing. For what he hoped might be one last time, he laid out the evidence and arguments for abolition comprehensively and compellingly – the vast unjustifiable injustice and political pointlessness of it.

Fox then 'followed his great rival', as Wilberforce put it, dying on 13 September 1806. He found a salutary moral in the thought that Fox had finally got a secure grip on the power he had pursued all his life, only for God to say to him, 'Thou fool, this night thy soul shall be required of thee.' He added, 'I am verging towards the close of the piece.'

An unexpected general election took Wilberforce to Yorkshire in October, and it looked for a while as if he would have to defend his seat against an opponent for the first time in twenty years, until his rival realized he would be throwing away £50,000 on a hopeless contest. Where their petitions had put enormous but ultimately fruitless pressure on parliament in 1789, the political nation now made abolition a major issue in the election, with tremendous effect. 'Newspapers teemed with abuse of this trade,' complained Gascoyne. Seats changed hands over it, even in Liverpool, further strengthening the cause in the Commons.

On 1 November 1806, Napoleon unveiled a new strategy, the Continental System. Thanks to its seas and navy, Britain had proved the one indomitable nation of Europe, and, without fielding its own troops, repeatedly funded anti-French forces on the continent. Now all nations under French influence were forbidden to trade with Britain, starving British resistance and stopping it from throwing its money around.

During the recess, Grenville had two new proposals for the abolition. One was to wear the slave trade down with punitive taxation rather than immediately abolish it. Wilberforce, however, was appalled. This would gradually diminish what he believed they could kill with one blow, and in the process legitimize it. Grenville was not convinced by Wilberforce's arguments, but deferred to him anyway – Wilberforce was to have nothing officially to do with the bill, but everyone recognized it as ultimately his. Grenville's other idea was to take the bill to the Lords first, at the start of the parliamentary session, and only after that to the Commons. This would give much less opportunity for aristocratic anti-abolitionists to drag out the business beyond the end of the session, and if time became tight the bill could be debated in the Commons concurrently.

So Grenville brought the bill for abolishing the slave trade to the Lords on 2 January 1807, and Wilberforce watched from the public gallery. Thanks to the evolving membership of that House, there were a significant number of new voices against the trade since the Lords had rejected Smith's slave-carrying bill in 1799. The first reading was unopposed, but then delaying tactics held off the second reading for a month. Both sides drummed up all the support they could manage, and yet Grenville told Wilberforce they had less than a third of the House on their side. At the second reading on 4 February, anti-abolitionists brought in witnesses for the British and Caribbean merchants, to testify about the amount of capital they stood to lose. Grenville objected that, after twenty years of discussion, they knew everything they needed to know about the slave trade. 'Their lordships were not now to determine, if a few more or a few less ships were devoted to this commerce, but to wipe away the disgrace of this country.' And of course Britain had capital employed in the slave trade, he said; if it did not they would not need to abolish it. His objection sustained, the crucial debate began.

Both sides made their familiar cases at length. Wilberforce called Grenville's long speech 'one of the most statesmanlike I ever heard'. Westmoreland decried Wilberforce's campaign as religious and political fanaticism: if the bill was passed 'no property could be reckoned safe... and the very freehold estates of the landholders might be sacrificed to field-preaching and popular declamation'. Admiral St Vincent insisted that 'the West India islands form a paradise itself to the negroes, in comparison with their native country', blaming Grenville's abolitionist folly on a witch doctor's spell. But the new Duke of Gloucester, the nephew and son-in-law of the king, broke ranks with the royal family, declaring, 'My Lords, I cannot find language sufficiently strong to express my abhorrence and detestation of this abominable traffic in human blood.'[3] As the night wore on, such sentiments were clearly in the majority. The House divided at five o'clock in the morning, and – including proxies – the bill passed by 100 votes to 36.

The committee of peers decided the precise terms. The slave trade would become illegal from 1 May 1809, in ten weeks' time, although ships that had already set off by then would be allowed until the end of the year to finish their business. Westmoreland made one last protest at the final reading on 10 February, saying that as the bill's preamble declared the slave trade to be contrary to 'justice and humanity', it logically follows that all slaves taken by this means must be freed. Grenville replied that he was glad to see that that was the only argument left against abolition, but he rejected it nevertheless. Abolition was about justice for Africa, 'but in giving liberty to the slaves of the islands, we should do the greatest injustice to them in giving them that which they would not know how to use'. Whether this stunningly limited appreciation for the dignity and faculties of slaves genuinely reflects the limits of Grenville's abolitionist goals or was mere pragmatism, it reassured his peers, and this time just one other person voted with Westmoreland against the bill.

Congratulations poured in for Wilberforce – 'as if all done' he said. 'Yet I cannot be sure.' Grenville was again not confident of a majority in the Commons, even though they knew that a number of colonial magnates were with them. 'Our opponents are making their utmost exertions,' Wilberforce reported to Muncaster, 'and by what I hear are proceeding with considerable art and plausibility.'[4]

The day the bill was passed by the Lords, it was brought before the Commons on behalf of the government by Charles Grey, now briefly known as Viscount Howick (soon to become Earl Grey of tea fame). The debate started with an embarrassing maiden speech from George Hibbert, who said that the bill risked being carried on the strength of Wilberforce's elevated reputation – 'but if he would descend and fight this battle upon the level plain of fact, and experience, he should feel it his duty to assume the courage to meet him'.

Gascoyne complained that 'the church, the theatre, the press, had laboured to create a prejudice against the slave trade.' But no one was going to try to throw out a bill which had won such a majority in the Lords without a proper hearing, so the debate over the second reading was fixed for 23 February. The abolition committee compiled lists of the probable voting intentions of each MP. 'A terrific list of doubtfuls,' said Wilberforce, 'yet I think we shall carry it.'

The morning of the great debate, 23 February 1807, Wilberforce spent with Grey. Despite nineteen prominent years in parliament, he was very nervous about making the most momentous speech of his career so far before a packed House. It was by all accounts a clunky performance, though Wilberforce was pleased with the case he made. He dealt mainly with the commercial benefits of abolition as his opponents had entirely given up trying to justify the slave trade on moral grounds; and he noted that slave populations were growing naturally everywhere except the Caribbean, because the endless supply there made plantation managers reckless. Nevertheless he did allow himself a flourish of indignation against those who complained about the preamble to the bill, whose condemnation of the trade on grounds of 'justice and humanity' would, they warned, incite slaves to rebellion. The fact of the injustice and inhumanity of a slave's treatment is written on every slave's heart by God, Grey said: 'If he cannot see it upon the wounds inflicted on the back of his fellow sufferer, if he cannot hear it in the cries of his fellow slave, are we supposed to believe he will read it in the preamble of the bill?' Finally, he looked forward to the abolition of slavery itself more hopefully than Grenville: 'I trust that by this measure slavery will gradually wear out without the immediate intervention of any positive law.'[5]

It seemed that everyone in the House wanted to contribute to the great occasion, six or eight MPs standing up ready to speak whenever one finished. A few remaining pro-slavery voices got a word in. Gascoyne conceded that freedom was better than slavery, all other things being equal, but the British ought to consider their own interests before others'. Addington, whom Wilberforce even now saw as an over-moderate friend to the cause rather than an inveterate enemy, once more appealed for gradual abolition, by which of course he meant gradual non-abolition.

But it was a last stand, and their callous murderous cause was finally lost in an abolitionist stampede. It was not so much a debate as a celebration – of the triumph of abolition and of the work of Wilberforce. One speaker after another, MPs old and new, paid tribute to 'that exalted and benevolent individual', to 'his indefatigable zeal, and his impressive eloquence', to the hero 'whose name will descend to the latest posterity, with never-fading honour'. Wilberforce himself made a short speech, refusing to blame Caribbean managers who were made cruel by their upbringing, circumstances and power, but only those who had the knowledge and opportunity to abolish such cruelty in parliament, and yet obstructed abolition.

The most memorable tribute to Wilberforce came from the solicitor general, Sir Samuel Romilly, who, adding one last peak of eloquence to the nineteen-year campaign in parliament, compared Wilberforce to Napoleon.

When I look to the man at the head of the French monarchy, surrounded as he is with all the pomp and power, and all the pride of victory, distributing kingdoms to his family, and principalities to his followers, seeming, when he sat upon his throne, to have reached the summit of human ambition, and the pinnacle of earthly happiness, and when I follow that man into his closet or to his bed, and consider the pangs with which his solitude must be tortured, and his repose banished, by the recollections of the blood he has spilt, and the oppressions he has committed; and when I compare with these pangs of remorse, the feelings which must accompany my honourable friend from this House to his home, after the vote of this night shall have confirmed the object of his humane and unceasing labours; when he shall retire into the bosom of his happy and delighted family, when he shall lay himself down on his bed, reflecting on the innumerable voices that will be raised in every quarter of the world to bless him; how much more pure and perfect felicity must he enjoy in the consciousness of having preserved so many millions of his fellow creatures, than the man with whom I have compared him, on the throne to which he has waded through slaughter and oppression.[6]

It was all far, far too much for a man of Wilberforce's sensibilities, who since the age of thirty had been opposed in parliament as a misguided do-gooder and derided as a treacherous fanatic – not least because Romilly had so perfectly described Wilberforce's own feelings a couple of weeks before, after the bill's success in the Lords. As MPs rose to their feet, applauding and filling the chamber with their cheers – a display unprecedented in living memory – he sat there in a daze, tears streaming down his cheeks. When Dr Hey asked him afterwards if it was true that the Commons had given him three cheers, Wilberforce could not, or would not, say. 'I was insensible to all that was passing around me.'

The vote was carried by 283 votes to 16. Afterwards, Wilberforce went back to Palace Yard with Thornton, Sharp, Macaulay, Grant, Smith and others, and we can imagine the atmosphere in which they saw the new day dawn. The bill had two more formal stages to go through in the Commons, but after such a triumph they would surely be formalities. The twenty-year struggle for Wilberforce had been shorter for some of them, but in the case of Sharp lasted almost forty years. It had consumed a fortune in time and money; it had, in some cases, threatened health, welfare, and reputation; it had taken eleven bills from Wilberforce plus more from the others; and it was finished.

'Well, Henry,' grinned Wilberforce to Thornton as they sat down, 'what shall we abolish next?'

16

'What Shall We Abolish Next?'

We will be slaves no more,
Since Christ has set us free,
Nailed our tyrants to the cross,
And bought our liberty.
Slave hymn[1]

The cup was so close to Wilberforce's lip that there was only time for one last slip. The *Edinburgh Review* celebrated 'the greatest battle ever fought by human beings' and British schoolchildren enjoyed a week's holiday. The United States abolished the slave trade in March with effect from 1 January 1808; but again compromise with the southern states allowed them to sell any slaves seized in transit, rather diminishing its force. The committee stage of the British abolition bill was set for 6 March 1807. Grenville suggested two amendments to the bill: it had decreed no specific punishments for those convicted of slave-trading, but considering the invincible support for abolition, they could afford to stipulate fines (£100 for each slave being carried) and the confiscation of ships. Conversely, why not sugar the pill by removing the phrase about 'justice and humanity', which made no practical difference but had proved a stumbling block during the debate. Wilberforce was happy with both, and the committee passed the amended bill without a division.

Meanwhile, Grenville and Grey (who was now Earl Grey) pressed on with another measure of justice closer to home – political emancipation for Catholics. Wilberforce vehemently opposed this, as did many politicians, including George III. The king grudgingly agreed to a bill opening lower-ranking military commissions to Catholics, but Grenville extended it to include all ranks. The king forced the government to withdraw the bill, but Grenville wanted to make a public statement of commitment to the cause to mollify Catholics. The king replied on 17 March that he would dismiss the government unless they promised never to raise the issue again, a promise which would probably have been unconstitutional and certainly impossible. Grenville's government was effectively finished, and he would be replaced within days. Would anti-abolitionists have enough influence in the new cabinet to trip the bill up even now? Wilberforce was certainly worried by the possibility of watching the bill die at the finishing post.

The following day the abolition bill had its last reading in the Commons, and Wilberforce took the opportunity to join the discussion about where this left them with regard to the abolition of slavery itself:

> If that measure [the present bill] is to be shortly carried into execution, I shall think that my labour for these nineteen years past has been amply rewarded: but still, I must confess, that I shall have another object after that in view, and that I look forward to a still more happy change in the state of the negroes of the West Indian islands.[2]

While the prime minister-in-waiting, Spencer Perceval – to Wilberforce's great approval, an evangelical, abolitionist Pittite – negotiated a new cabinet, Grenville drove the bill through the concluding debate in the Lords, obtained its royal assent as law, and resigned the same day – 25 March 1807. Perceval's ministry was the first in almost a century in which the majority called themselves 'Tories', in antagonism to Grey's Whigs.

Within weeks of the outlawing of the slave trade, Wilberforce nearly lost his seat in parliament, as Perceval, struggling to establish a government, called a general election in order to boost his ranks. This time two of the great aristocratic families of Yorkshire stood against him: Henry Lascelles, son of the Barbados tycoon the Earl of Harewood, and Lord Milton, son of Viscount Fitzwilliam. Wilberforce had the reputation, but they had the money, and the professional political machinery. He had no taste for such a contest, but then not standing would suggest a low view of the saleability of his constituents' principles and smack of gutlessness. Counties having two seats, voters had two votes; and Lascelles and Milton being political enemies, Wilberforce could expect the votes of his own supporters plus the second votes of the others.* Until, that is, it turned out that some of Wilberforce's supporters had been cooperating with Lascelles's men (he might be a slave-driver but at least he was not a Whig). Milton decided that they had made a secret pact to exchange second votes to defeat him, and his supporters withdrew their second votes from Wilberforce. They printed fliers denouncing Wilberforce as a hypocritical double-dealer, and published poems in which he told the West Indian 'friend of plunder', 'If you but tickle pious Billy/He in turn will tickle you.' Their 'bruisers' disrupted Wilberforce's speeches and intimidated his supporters. The *York Herald* reported: 'Nothing since the days of the revolution has ever presented to the world such a scene as this great county for fifteen days and nights. Repose and rest have been unknown to it, except it was seen in a messenger asleep upon his post-horse.' In the end it was a close-run contest. Wilberforce won and Milton beat Lascelles by 0.5 per cent of the votes to win the other seat. Wilberforce told Hannah More that he had been defrauded of two-thirds of his votes. He also spent two-thirds less than the others, and was able to return half of his donations.

After a short parliamentary session, Wilberforce joined his family in Brighton, where he spent five or six hours a day finally answering his letters. Newton, aged eighty-two, said that he himself was 'packed, sealed, and waiting for the post',³ and died in December 1807. In his epitaph he described his pre-conversion self as 'once an infidel and libertine, servant of the slaves in Africa'. Despite his services to his protégé's cause, it is not clear whether he ever entirely understood what the fuss was all about. Clarkson was now writing his personal account of the history of the abolition movement which would so outrage Wilberforce's sons, and published it the following year.

* This was nicely illustrated in their campaign songs: Milton's was 'Milton and Wilberforce Forever', Lascelles's was 'Lascelles and Wilberforce Forever', Wilberforce's was just 'Wilberforce Forever'.

After Napoleon annexed half of Prussia to France, the Danish expected a French invasion. The prospect of Napoleon gaining their fleet alarmed the British, who took the precaution of attacking Denmark, a neutral power, in September 1807. The Danish army being busy at the Prussian border, the British bombarded Copenhagen until General Peymann surrendered the 60 ships. A third of the city was destroyed and 2,000 people were killed. At first Wilberforce was appalled. 'They must think us the most unjust and cruel of bullying despots.' But then, after talking with Perceval, he decided that, however horrible, it was a necessary and just act of self-defence; and by March he was telling parliament that the 'ministers had conscientiously and ably discharged their duty towards the country'. Either way, he helped raise funds for the Copenhagen poor.

Slave-trading in the British Empire became illegal on 1 January 1808, and on the same day Sierra Leone became a crown colony, under the direct rule of the British government. The question of Catholic emancipation, which had unseated both Pitt and Grenville, had not gone away, and the Whig opposition continued to agitate for it. For men such as Grenville and Grey it was unjust and absurd that Irish constituents could only vote for representatives of a minority religion. Absurdity and injustice were a greater issue for some than others: many Irish MPs were reluctant to compete for their seats with Catholics; many English MPs were reluctant to tamper with the constitution that had put them in power; and the English in general had a residual fear and loathing of Catholicism. It was seen as the inspiration behind Bloody Mary's bonfires, James II's bid for absolute power and repeated Jacobite risings – and more basically as the religion of incomprehensible, barbaric, bloody-minded foreigners. As with most issues, Wilberforce took an independent view. He distrusted the motives of the opposition, without sharing the self-interest of the conservatives. He did, however, share their phobia of Catholicism, magnified by evangelical fervour. For him, taking Christ seriously meant taking popish distortions of Christ seriously, and he was genuinely concerned that giving Catholics better representation would encourage their dangerous error, while converting them to true Christianity would cut out the parliamentary middleman, not to mention saving their souls and transforming their 'degenerate' society. They needed charity and evangelism, not politics.

The issue heated up in May 1808, firstly over proposals to increase the subsidy to Maynooth College in Country Kildare. Maynooth trained Catholic clergy, as Oxford and Cambridge trained Anglican clergy, and Wilberforce was shocked at the idea of a grant for the propagation of papistry. 'No man is a greater enemy to persecution,' he insisted, like genial persecutors before and since, 'or a greater friend to toleration, than I am.' He argued that no other country in the world would subsidize a college that teaches non-established religion, skating over the fact that Britain, having incorporated a Catholic majority in Ireland, would have to fund their colleges unless it planned to systematically extirpate their faith. Smith spoke against him, while Barham retorted: 'Of the religion of the honourable gentleman I have at times been inclined to think well, but if bigotry and Protestantism have so much blinded him that he cannot see that the Catholics worship the same God with himself, his is not a religion in which I would either wish to live, or be content to die.'[4]

The debate seems to have made Wilberforce think further, and he came to believe in Catholic emancipation after all – not because they deserved it, apparently, but because Irish Protestant MPs were already defending their interests so effectively that one might as well give them Catholic MPs and remove their supposed grievance.

And yet when Grey and friends presented a raft of Irish petitions for Catholic emancipation on 25 May, Wilberforce vehemently opposed them. After presenting himself as a 'prodigious friend to the education of the Catholics', he received a long diatribe against his hypocrisy from George Ponsonby, MP for Wicklow. Wilberforce urged the House to put off all discussion till next year, arguing that no reform would be completed in the present session, so debate would only raise false hopes and encourage Catholic uprisings; even if passed it would provoke them to make more and more outrageous demands for freedom, he said. It was all too much for those who had helped get his slave trade bill passed only to see him transform into a second William Young when they tried to extend freedom to Catholics: 'Good God!' cried Whitbread. 'How often has this senseless answer been given in this House upon other occasions, and how often have we heard in discussions upon the abolition of that detestable traffic, the slave trade… you will kindle a rage in the breast of the negroes…; for the negroes will be content with nothing short of total emancipation.' Wilberforce accused the Whigs of caring for nothing but bolstering their own ranks with grateful Catholic MPs – a misjudgment entirely typical of his attitude to politicians more liberal than himself. 'The very men who were allowed to be perfectly consistent in their support of him in the abolition of the slave trade,' protested Whitbread, 'and allowed to have genuine feelings of humanity towards the African negroes as their fellow creatures, if they presume to express a fellow feeling for their fellow creatures in Ireland, are now to be charged by him with agitating a dangerous question upon party spirit.' MPs cried 'Hear! hear!'[5]

It was 'a very long and most unpleasant debate', recorded Wilberforce. 'I was extremely abused.' And in an oracle worthy of Young, he said: 'Alas, they are driving the Catholics to rebellion. How mad to be thus stimulating them, by telling them they are slaved and oppressed!'[6]

What would make a man who had just become immortal in the history of social justice use the moral authority he had gained by it in parliament to assail against the rights of another abused group? The answer is, of course, religion – his and theirs. While Africans were selected for slavery purely by the accidents of place and vulnerability, Catholics were disadvantaged, as Wilberforce saw it, by superstitious beliefs that they could and should abandon. Meanwhile his own commitment to 'true Christianity' gave him, he believed, an urgent moral imperative to oppose and hinder false Christianity – an imperative shared by all of his evangelical friends. To his mind, politicians who declined to give truth greater rights than falsehood could not really believe the truth, and were Christians in name only. It was the same powerful conscience that had driven him to assault the slave trade for twenty years which now made him so uncomfortable about Catholic rights, and which overcame any sense of gratitude to the abolitionists on the other side of the House, telling him that it was wrong for public policy to bow to personal obligations.

And yet his more humane compulsions were every bit as strong and as real as the more reactionary ones. In the midst of all this, he cautiously supported Whitbread's unpopular Poor Laws bill which proposed two years' free education for all children; he enthusiastically supported reductions in the death penalty; he backed a hefty grant to Edward Jenner for developing the smallpox vaccination; and he even defended a sugar distillation bill because it offered financial relief to his enemies – the struggling plantation owners.

When Portugal refused to join Napoleon's trade boycott of Britain, the French invaded, taking Lisbon on 1 December 1807. Napoleon took the opportunity of deposing the Spanish king on the way through, and replaced him with his own brother, proving himself 'absolutely intoxicated by his prosperity' in Wilberforce's judgment. However, he saw the hand of God in 'the destruction of Spanish political despotism', hoping that it would also be the end of Spain's 'popish bondage and darkness'. Napoleon provoked a vast patriotic uprising in Spain, followed by a brutal war. British forces, led by the Duke of Wellington, joined the Portuguese and Spanish in August 1808, while the Wilberforces holidayed in Eastbourne, eagerly following their victories: 'the glorious achievements of our brave soldiery… *vainqueur des vainqueurs du monde.*'

In the winter of 1808–89 the Wilberforces gave up Broomfield and Palace Yard and moved to Kensington Gore, a house on the present site of the Royal Albert Hall, in three acres of beautiful garden, with mulberry bushes and walnut trees – one of which the children called their father's office because of the amount of time he spent reading under it. Wilberforce decided he could do without the extravagance of two houses, and being one mile from Hyde Park Corner this just about felt like countryside while being only two miles from Westminster. He would save money (to give away) and see more of his growing family.

He and Barbara now had six children, their full complement, and William, the eldest, was eleven. It was a happy family and – extremely busy as he was – it was important to Wilberforce, and enjoyable, to spend time with them, walking in the garden, reading, playing cricket, marbles and blind man's buff. He had always liked children – he wrote from Berne in 1785 to Muncaster with a message for his son Gamel that 'if he will meet me at Spa, I will turn him into a pancake as often as he will'. In their first summer in Kensington, William put his father out of action for a week with a cricketing injury.

Sunday was their family day, providing Wilberforce with another justification for his strict sabbatarianism. The day started with family prayers, which included the servants, followed by church, and an afternoon spent in the garden before a relaxed dinner. 'Never was religion seen in a more engaging form than in his Sunday intercourse with them,' enthused Robert. 'A festival air of holy and rational happiness dwelt continually around him'; and yet, he remembered, their father was 'always on his guard against forcing their religious feelings'.[7] Marianne Thornton left a less reverent memoir of their family hymn-singing, describing mama as 'dreadfully out of tune' and papa making 'dreadful faces', 'waving his arms about, and occasionally pulling the leaves off the geraniums, and smelling them, singing out louder and louder in a tone of hilarity'.[8] He was, as we would expect, not one to spoil his children; but it made him miserable to punish them, and he made a point of rewarding their moral victories as well as penalizing their failures.

Cost-cutting as he was, Wilberforce was still able to buy the cottage next door, which he called 'the Nuisance'. 'Mr So-and-so is not at home' was, of course, a genteel fiction for unwanted visitors among Wilberforce's class, but it roused his scruples. How could he expect servants to lie for his benefit and then not lie for their own? And yet he was perpetually besieged by an army of callers: friends, would-be friends, constituents, lobbyists, financial suppliants and MPs. 'You can little conceive how difficult it often is for me to force my way out of my own house.' He took on more work than most MPs and believed in replying to all letters – the comment above is from an eleven-page reply to a man who complained about him missing an appointment – and yet just imagine the volume of fan mail and political protests someone like him would have received. He was also constitutionally incompetent at turning anyone away. Hence the Nuisance. He could get work done and see his family, while honestly not being at home.

Perceval continually consulted Wilberforce as Pitt had done, and they discussed strategies for further hampering the slave trade.

Wilberforce tested his influence over the prime minister by persuading him to move the opening of the 1809 parliament from a Monday to a Tuesday in order to stop MPs having to travel on a Sunday.

The major business of the parliamentary session was one which Wilberforce found profoundly distasteful, but nevertheless took a leading role in. The Duke of York, the king's son and commander-in-chief of the army whose reforms helped pave the way for Wellington's success in Portugal, had been having an affair – something no less common among nineteenth-century royalty than twentieth-century film stars, but less widely publicized. When he and his mistress Mrs Clarke fell out, he cancelled her allowance and she published his letters, and the grand old duke was publicly accused of allowing her to arrange military promotions in return for bribes. It became the most popular scandal of the age, and when Mrs Clarke was called before a Commons inquiry, Wilberforce had the proceedings moved from the public view to a committee, fearing that 'the people may be inflamed to madness'. Mrs Clarke made no secret of her guilt, but tried to implicate the duke as far as possible. Wilberforce pressed that the motion against the duke should acquit him of knowing about Mrs Clarke's crimes, but not of suspecting them, and that he should therefore be relieved of his military command. The motion was roundly defeated, but Wilberforce was confident that parliament would remove the duke if he did not resign, which he did. 'The king and all of them [are] extremely angry at me,' reported Wilberforce. 'Yet what could I do as an honest man, short of what I have done?'[9]

Thornton's answer to Wilberforce's question 'What shall we abolish next?' had been a po-faced, 'The lottery, I think.' Wilberforce shared his condemnation of raising state funds through the abuse of the false hopes of the neediest people in society. In 1809 he passionately supported Whitbread's attempt to abolish it, calling it 'the most forcible appeal I have ever heard made in this House', but the bill was soundly defeated. He also supported a mild reform bill to ban the sale of parliamentary seats, warning both those who opposed it and those who supported it immoderately that they were inciting more radical reform than he thought wise. After his fortieth birthday, he spent a wonderfully quiet summer in a parsonage in the Buckinghamshire village of Newport Pagnell, reading *Arabian Nights* to his children and walking as a fan in the footsteps of William Cowper.

He gave more examples of his independent and idiosyncratic spirit in the 1810 parliamentary session. He once again drew a cutting rejoinder from Ponsonby about his blinding self-righteousness when he disparaged the opposition's motives for not joining a committee to investigate a radical MP's misdemeanours; he also crossed Perceval by supporting an inquiry into the government's conduct of the mismanaged military expedition against the French to the River Scheldt. He supported another inquiry into abuse in the navy, and warmly backed the solicitor-general's bill to remove the death penalty for the more trivial of the 220 offences that it currently punished (more than any other regime in history). He supported another mild reform bill, justifying himself to a concerned constituent as 'one of the most moderate of all reformers', who loved and admired the present constitution, and believed that 'the danger of going too far was far greater than that of not going far enough'.

17

Bramber and Bengal

They then came to us in the reeds, and the very first salute I had from them was a violent blow on the back part of the head with the fore part of a gun, and at the same time a grasp round the neck. I then had a rope put about my neck, as had all the women in the thicket with me, and was immediately led to my father, who was likewise pinioned and haltered for leading. In this condition we were all led to the camp. The women and myself, being pretty submissive, had tolerable treatment from the enemy, while my father was closely interrogated respecting his money which they knew he must have. But as he gave them no account of it, he was instantly cut and pounded on his body with great inhumanity, that he might be induced by the torture he suffered to make the discovery. All this availed not in the least to make him give up his money, but he despised all the tortures which they inflicted, until the continued exercise and increase of torment, obliged him to sink and expire. He thus died without informing his enemies where his money lay. I saw him while he was thus tortured to death. The shocking scene is to this day fresh in my mind, and I have often been overcome while thinking on it...

Prince Boteer, afterwards called Venture Smith, describes his capture by African traders in Guinea[1]

In these early years after the passing of the Slave Trade Act, the abolitionists started to learn the truth of their opponents' warning, that outlawing the trade was not the same as abolishing it. Some British traders carried on supplying slaves despite the law – in 1810 a ship was found in the Thames with 660 padlocks, 93 handcuffs, 197 shackles, 13 cwt of chain and 'one box of religious implements'.[2] The new Whig MP Henry Brougham then obtained a resolution from parliament to investigate violations of the Act. The French, Spanish and Portuguese showed no interest in following the UK, the United States and Denmark in abolishing the slave trade, and their commerce thrived – as indeed did that of the United States. One happy prospect was that, having been deprived of their own slave supply, British colonists threw their formidable weight behind any attempts to stop the foreign trade.

When the Act was passed, the abolition committee was replaced with the African Institution, a glittering organization combining the members of the old committee with more or less the entire Clapham Sect, plus Perceval, Grey, Grenville and the Duke of Gloucester. It aimed to replace the slave trade with other African commerce, making reparations to Africa, replenishing the loss to British merchants, and making abolition irreversible. This goal was seriously hampered, however, by the continuance of the slave trade, so they directed their efforts at enforcing abolition itself. The Institution worked for new laws and promoted abolitionist negotiations with other countries. Wilberforce himself wrote to President Thomas Jefferson suggesting a treaty whereby each nation could arrest the other's slave traders.

It was not enough for James Stephen, now an MP himself, who again complained bitterly about Wilberforce's recalcitrance:

> If you, who must be the public leader, are to be only a battering ram to be pushed forward instead of a fore-horse in the team to pull as well as guide the rest, the cause is lost, the abolition is undone. It will sink under the weight of your daily epistles... Millions will sigh in hopeless wretchedness, that Wilberforce's correspondents may not think him uncivil or unkind.[3]

Approving of his frankness, Wilberforce helped to achieve a treaty with Portugal, although it proved meaningless. He had an unlikely friend in the Venezuelan revolutionary General Miranda, who got the trade abolished there, and Chile and Buenos Aires soon followed. In May 1811, Brougham got slave-trading upgraded to a felony punishable by fourteen years' transportation to Australia. This proved such an effective deterrent that the first prosecution was brought thirty-three years later, by Stephen's son George, who praised it as 'the second great measure of the cause'. Wilberforce persuaded the first lord of the admiralty to send ships to sweep the coast of Africa for traffickers; he supported Barham's proposals for introducing paid labour to the Caribbean islands and he continued in fruitless dialogue with Portugal. Sweden, meanwhile, abolished its smaller slave trade.

By 1811 the 73-year-old blind, mad king was ill enough for the Prince of Wales to gain the regency he had been seeking for a quarter of a century – although he was ill enough himself for some to suggest that his father ought to be the regent's regent. Napoleon's Continental System was seriously hurting Britain and prices soared, while exporting industries collapsed. The economic crisis of Pitt's days was back, and with it the inevitable unrest. In November 1811, Nottingham weavers smashed up the mass-production looms that were putting them out of work, under the leadership of Ned Ludd, who may or may not have existed, and Luddism proved infectious. Lord Byron used his maiden speech in the Lords to support it, but of course Wilberforce and the establishment in general denounced them unequivocally, and industrial sabotage was made yet another capital offence. Troops were mobilized against them including, at one point, 15,000 in Yorkshire alone – as many as Wellington took to Portugal in 1808. Activists for universal suffrage followed abolitionist strategy, sending parliament hundreds of petitions, while Wilberforce helped found the Association for the Relief of the Manufacturing and Labouring Poor.

Brougham's felony law left one gaping loophole – the supply of slaves from Africa to Jamaica might have dried up, but it was very easy to buy them from Cuba, where the supply was limitless. Stephen came up with a scheme to stop this, however. In 1812 he composed an Order in Council for the prime minister requiring all the slaves on Trinidad to be registered in order to make the abolition watertight. St Lucia and Mauritius voluntarily followed suit, and Wilberforce planned a bill imposing registration on all the colonies. The government, however, was uneasy about interfering with colonial independence, and Perceval persuaded him to postpone it for a year. Then on 11 May, John Bellingham, a ruined trader who had been falsely imprisoned for debt in Russia and failed to get compensation from the government, walked into the lobby of the House of Commons with a pistol and shot Perceval through the heart. He was the only British prime minister ever to have been assassinated. His widow led her children in prayers for the forgiveness of Bellingham, to Wilberforce's great admiration – 'Oh wonderful powers of Christianity.'

By the summer of 1812, Wellington had secured Portugal from the French, and led his soldiers – or 'the scum of the earth' as he called them – into Spain. For the first time the British were making gains against Napoleon on land. Napoleon's actions against Spain are generally seen as his first fatal mistake of the war, and now news was coming of a second. Russia had had enough of the Continental System and reopened trade with Britain; the Tsar was also challenging French power in central Europe, and so Napoleon marched on Russia.

As if to keep the navy occupied during Napoleon's absence, the British got into a 'perfectly horrible' war, in Wilberforce's words, with the United States. Perceval had, on the inspiration of Stephen, ruled that any neutral ship trading with Britain's enemies without British permission could be seized. This made European commerce impossible for the United States, whose government was also looking for a pretext for taking Florida and Canada from Spain and Britain respectively. Typically, Wilberforce had predicted and opposed the war, 'between two nations, who are children of the same family, brothers in the same inheritance of human liberty'.

At home, industrial unrest spread, and a panicked parliamentary committee reported that all working class protest was part of a huge revolutionary conspiracy. Its evidence was that, apart from the violent demonstrations – which were inexcusable – the demonstrations were peaceful – which could only mean they were organized.

Perceval was succeeded as prime minister by Lord Liverpool, with Castlereagh as foreign secretary and Sidmouth (Addington) as home secretary. All had been notable anti-abolitionists in the past, but things had changed now: abolition was a *fait accompli*, and if the British economy was to be deprived of slave trade revenue, then Lord Liverpool wanted to persuade countries such as France and Spain to give up their own share, just as much as abolitionists. The government had less interest in enforcing abolition on British territory, however – Liverpool refused to support Wilberforce's slave registry bill, and Stephen threatened to quit parliament in disgust.

Wilberforce was also, more calmly, thinking of quitting parliament. He was fifty-three, and feeling his age. On top of all his familiar frailties, he found his memory increasingly unreliable, and his voice was not the great instrument it had once been. The blunt Stephen pointed out 'symptoms of deterioration in your bodily appearance, as if you were getting old faster than I could wish. Your spirits, too, I have thought not uniformly so high and so long on the wing as they used to be.'[4] The crucial consideration for Wilberforce was spending more time with his family, to give more of himself to their raising and training and to themselves: 'They claim a father's heart, eye, and voice, and friendly intercourse.' He canvassed his friends and Grant and Thornton urged him to stay but Babington urged him to go. Stephen pressed for the compromise that he eventually plumped for – leaving Yorkshire and taking a less demanding seat – and Barbara's cousin Lord Calthorpe offered him the pretty little Sussex village of Bramber. When the general election was announced for October 1812, he had cold feet for a moment, knowing that whatever his moral authority in the Commons, he would never again have the power of representing 20,000 Yorkshiremen. 'I feel somewhat like an old retired hunter, who grazing in a park, and hearing the cry of the hounds pricks up his ears and can scarce keep quiet or refrain from breaking out to join them.' More bleakly he reminded himself in his diary: 'It is not annihilation.'[5]

Which was more than could be said for Napoleon's invasion force in Russia. The Russians' willingness simply to withdraw ever further, scorching the earth as they went, meant that – having taken the empty shell of Moscow in September – Napoleon's army had nothing to do but return home, starving, frozen and harried by ambushes. He had led 600,000 men into Russia and brought home 50,000. The invincible emperor, defeated by his own megalomania and the weather, took his place in European mythology.

The question of Catholic emancipation came before parliament in 1813, again unsuccessfully, but this time Wilberforce spoke in favour, although not as a way to effectively empower Catholicism but instead the reverse. The Saints were dismayed and angry, but he was ready for them. When he visited the More sisters, as soon as Patty launched into a basting, he scolded her: 'How shocking it is that you who know so much of the misery which Popery has brought on Ireland, should advocate a system which perpetuates its galling yoke.' His argument is unconvincing enough, however, to suggest that maybe it was the justice of emancipation which really moved him, and that this convoluted logic appeased his Protestant conscience.

The East India Company's charter came up for renewal in 1813, and this time Wilberforce was determined to get mission to the Indians included in it. The loss of Perceval was a blow, and when the charter debate opened on 22 March Wilberforce saw the 'dreadful truth... that the opinions of nine-tenths, or at least of a vast majority of the House of Commons would be against any motion which the friends of religion might make'. But he was not put off. If he had swung MPs round on the issue of the slave trade, the same techniques and same vigour could do so again. It was, after all, 'the greatest object which men ever pursued'.

Wilberforce encouraged the Saints to mobilize their potential supporters, writing letters and pamphlets, organizing meetings and drawing up petitions on the same scale as for abolition, eventually delivering 500,000 names on 837 petitions. 'And can you venture thus', Wilberforce hectored one correspondent who declined to take part, 'to add your sanction to the opinion... that our East India empire is safer under the protection of Brahma with all his obscenities and blood, than under that of God Almighty?'[6] His speeches drew influential admirers to high-powered meetings of the Church Missionary Society. *The Christian Observer* then launched a sister paper, *The Missionary Register*. Wilberforce personally buttonholed cabinet members, and finally persuaded Castlereagh to propose the change to the charter, allowing missionaries into British India.

Castlereagh brought the proposals before the Commons on 22 June 1813, and Wilberforce gave MPs one of the most celebrated and powerful speeches of his life. For three hours, he condemned Hinduism in an explosion of righteous indignation, as not just undoing the immortal souls of the Indians under British rule, but utterly depraving their society and ruining their lives. The 'cruel shackles of caste' were worse than slavery; the unnatural evils of infanticide and euthanasia were prevalent, as was the more natural sin of polygamy; 10,000 widows a year were killed in the 'horrible exhibitions' of suttee; 100,000 people a year were sacrificed to the god Juggernaut; their idolatrous ceremonies were 'obscene and bloody'; 'their divinities are absolute monsters of lust, injustice, wickedness and cruelty', a 'rabble' of 33 million. It would be 'almost morally impossible' for India not to be vastly improved by willing conversion to Christianity, he said. 'Our religion is sublime, pure beneficent. Theirs is mean, licentious, and cruel.' He closed with a tribute to the work of William Carey, the 'consecrated cobbler' in Sydney Smith's words, who had now translated the New Testament into Sanskrit and Marathi, and the whole Bible into Bengali.[7] In reply, MPs with Indian interests defended Hindu society and warned that attacks on the religion would provoke Indians to disorder; but the campaign had done its work, and the proposals were carried by 89 votes to 36. The bill created a bishopric of Calcutta, and though the Saints were disappointed the post did not go to an evangelical but instead to Thomas Fanshawe Middleton, the bishop ordained their society's missionaries. It also granted funds for the education of Indians.

With this crowning triumph for the Clapham Sect, the circle started to break up. John Venn, the rector of Clapham and chaplain to the Saints, died in 1813. Granville Sharp, the father of abolition, died the same year, aged seventy-eight. Two years later Henry Thornton died of tuberculosis.

It was the end of an era, not just for Clapham, but for Britain and for Europe. Broken by the Russian retreat, Napoleon still managed to defeat a new alliance of Prussia and Russia, but Castlereagh persuaded them to form a coalition with Britain and Austria in return for a financial grant. Others joined them, and Napoleon was defeated at Leipzig in October 1813, in the largest battle ever seen in Europe before the First World War. In 1814, Wellington invaded France from Spain, while Prussia and Russia entered from Germany, and Napoleon abdicated and retired to Elba. Two decades of war were over, and most of France's conquests were returned. The war with the United States continued, however, with British forces entering Washington in August 1814, burning the capital and, after eating the President's dinner, the White House. The fall of Napoleon had removed the reason for the war though, and it was over by Christmas, the treaty of Ghent being signed on 24 December.

When the powers met to negotiate peace and remake Europe for the next 100 years, the abolitionists realized that this was the greatest opportunity history would ever offer for an international convention against the slave trade – three or four potentates, as Thornton put it, seeming to hold the earth in their hands. Wilberforce, however, was annoyed that they had not seen it coming and had tracts translated into all the relevant languages; he made up for lost time by writing to the Tsar, the King of Prussia and the French leaders. Clarkson presented the Tsar with a copy of the 1791 abridged evidence which he said, sailing for France, 'made me more sick than the sea'.[8] The Saints sent Macaulay to the peace talks in Paris to supply Castlereagh with information and put pressure on him. He failed, as the treaty obliged the French to give up the slave trade, but not for five years, after they had fully restocked their colonies. Castlereagh's treaty was loudly acclaimed in parliament, but Wilberforce said, 'I behold in his hand the death-warrant of a multitude of innocent victims, men, women and children, whom I had fondly indulged the hope of having myself rescued from destruction.'[9]

Nevertheless, the Paris talks were followed by the Vienna Congress. Once again the abolitionist network got busy, and the Commons received 806 petitions in one month, containing one million signatures, one for every ten British adults. Castlereagh conceded, 'The whole nation is bent upon the subject,' and he and Wellington had no choice but to press the matter at the Congress. Russia, Prussia and Austria, having no slave trade, were happy to outlaw it. The government of Louis XVIII in France was violently against it as abolition not only smacked of the revolution but of bowing to English imperialism. Spain and Portugal also had too much to lose to agree to it. The compromise of the Congress was to condemn the slave trade without requiring anyone to stop it.

Then to the abolitionists' aid came Napoleon himself. Escaping from Elba, he seized power again in France, and, in a bid for British acquiescence, the man who had single-handedly restored slavery to the French colonies abolished the slave trade. Wilberforce felt distinctly cool about the allied attack, but was delighted when Napoleon was quickly beaten – especially when the restored Louis

XVIII was so dependent on allied forces that he had to maintain Napoleon's edict. 'I have the gratification of acquainting you,' wrote Castlereagh, 'that the long desired object is accomplished, and that the present messenger carries to Lord Liverpool the unqualified and total abolition of the slave trade throughout the dominions of France.'[10]

18

The Enemy Within

Being afterwards brought upon deck, he (Mr Arnold) was ordered to examine his wounds; he found his skull fractured in consequence of the blow he had received; his body was wounded also in many places by the cutlasses of the seamen, who had followed him into the hold, and pricked him as opportunity offered, while he was skulking among the casks; a great part of his skin was additionally peeled off by the scalding fat and water mentioned before to have been thrown upon him; the blood was dropping from his wounds, so that on the whole he was one of the most miserable objects he ever saw in his life, and he has seen many during the late war.

... [captain] ordered the mate to put an iron collar around his neck, and to chain him to the foremast, ordering him (Mr Arnold) at the same time to give him no medical assistance, and forbidding all who heard him at their peril to give him any sustenance whatever.

A rebel slave, defeated after an eight-hour siege in the hold of the *Little Pearl*. Testimony of James Arnold, surgeon, to the Privy Council, 1789[1]

The end of the war brought food flowing back into Britain from the continent, which should have been great news after two lean decades of war. However, the rural landowners who dominated parliament could only see the disaster of plummeting prices. So Liverpool's government introduced the controversial Corn Laws to keep prices up and imports out. In Wilberforce's eyes, this self-inflicted Continental System was a grim necessity to vote for quietly and with a heavy heart; but he held such sway over swayable MPs that the government pressed him to speak for it, offering to support his bill for the registration of Caribbean slaves in return. (Wilberforce had been meaning to bring the registry bill since the death of Perceval had scuppered the Order in Council, but the possibility of an international convention had taken priority.) Uniquely in his parliamentary career, Wilberforce cut a deal and gave his voice to the bill, which became law. The next morning, in Covent Garden Market, his former servant was told, 'Your old master has spoken for the corn bill, but his house shall pay for it.' The family was advised to evacuate, but instead Wilberforce hired five soldiers to guard them. Wilberforce brought the registry bill to the Commons on 5 July 1815, but there was considerable opposition, it was late in the session, and Castlereagh persuaded him to leave it till the following year while he collected evidence of illegal trafficking. It was one too many deflections for Stephen, however, who resigned his seat in protest.

Wilberforce sent an ambassador to Rome armed with abolitionist tracts to try to get papal pressure put on Spain and Portugal. He was pleased with the response, although it took twenty-four years to get an official condemnation of the slave trade from Rome. In 1815, the Portuguese government agreed to a major restriction of the slave trade – it would take slaves only for its own Brazilian plantations, and only from sub-equatorial Africa, protecting the lands vacated by the British and French. This concession was bought by the British government for £750,000.

News of the continued abolition campaign reached the slaves in a garbled state. 'Mr Wilberforce has sent out to have us all freed,' said one report on Barbados. The slaves there decided to seize what was coming to them, and on Easter Sunday 1816 they set fire to the fields across the island. Fifty slaves died in the ensuing fighting and 200 were executed. A quarter of the sugar crop was destroyed. In Jamaica, slaves were punished for singing:

Oh, me good friend, Mr Wilberforce, make we free!
God Almighty thank ye! God Almighty thank ye!
God Almighty, make we free!
Buckra [white man] in this country no make we free:
What negro for to do? What negro for to do?
Take by force! Take by force![2]

Bryan Edwards's predictions seemed to be coming true – though Wilberforce blamed them for putting the idea of revolt into slaves' minds.

The slavery party had been campaigning hard against the registry proposals, and the uprising gave them the perfect weapon to destroy it. At the same time, the Spanish government was considering an abolition deal offered by Castlereagh, backed by abolitionist tracts and letters. Wilberforce decided that a parliamentary debate on the registry would give the slavery party a platform to accuse them of fomenting insurrection, and scare off the Spanish, so he postponed the bill again – consoling himself with the thought that Moses was eighty before he led the Israelites out of slavery, so it was never too late.

He became a friend and supporter of the King of Haiti (San Domingo as was), Henri Christophe. While guarding the island from French reconquest, Christophe established a successful school system, and abolitionists were excited 'to see a set of human beings emerging from slavery, and making most rapid strides towards the perfection of civilisation.'[3] Wilberforce sent him books and ploughs. 'Oh how I wish I was not too old and you not too busy to go,' said Wilberforce to Macaulay, but he rounded up some teachers for the schools. However, Christophe was overthrown in 1820, and his school system abolished.

Wilberforce's sister, Sarah Stephen, died in 1816. 'How affecting it is,' he reflected, 'to leave the person… on whom we should have been afraid to let the wind blow too roughly, to leave her in the cold ground alone!'

As ever in these hungry years, Wilberforce gave sacrificially and worked hard to raise poor relief, but his traditional combination of patriarchal charity and support for repressive legislation was more and more questioned. William Cobbett's radical journal the *Political Register* attacked him as the embodiment of everything that was worst about Britain – piety and sentimentality as masks for oppression. He wanted to 'render the whole nation effeminate… in complete subjection to your will', Cobbett said. 'You do the labourers of England… all the harm in your power… [and] describe their situation as desirable, by putting it in contrast with that of the blacks.'[4] In July

1816, a grand public meeting which he arranged in support of urban workers who were being starved by the Corn Laws, boasting such glitterati as the Duke of York and the Archbishop of Canterbury, was broken up by hecklers. A terrible harvest in 1817 then provoked radical political meetings and rioting. Radical papers such as the *Leeds Mercury* sprang up denouncing the Corn Laws and the corrupt, corpulent establishment. The MP Francis Burdett, backed by 700 petitions, proposed a committee to look into parliamentary reform and was defeated by an unusually decisive count of 106 votes to zero. Angry workers' marches and meetings were broken up by the militia. The prince regent's carriage window was smashed on the way to parliament. Nottinghamshire workers marched on London, but were intercepted, and had been – the *Leeds Mercury* discovered – incited by an agent of Lord Sidmouth to give the government an excuse to suspend *habeas corpus* and execute revolutionary leaders. It did both, and put restrictions on meetings severe enough to close societies for philosophy, literature and even mineralogy. And once again, fearing a civil war more bitter and cruel than Cromwell's, Wilberforce supported the repression with a passion, protecting British freedoms from the British rather than the French this time. Burdett asked, 'How happened it that the honourable and religious member was not shocked at Englishmen being taken up under this act and treated like African slaves?'[5] Wilberforce replied that Burdett was opposing the government in a deliberate scheme to destroy the liberty and happiness of the people. When the opposition called for an inquiry into the use of *agents provocateurs*, he insisted on Sidmouth's trustworthiness with a naivety that gives blind faith a bad name; and with the kind of moral convolution that repeatedly maddened both sides of the House, he gave a blistering indictment of the use of spies, while opposing the inquiry.

Not wishing to add insult to his injury of urban workers and traders, Wilberforce postponed the registry bill once again. 'It would betray an ignorance of all tact', he told Macaulay, 'to talk to them in such circumstances of the sufferings of the slaves in the West Indies. We should specially guard against appearing to live in a world of our own, and to have little sympathy with the sufferings of our own countrymen.'[6] The previous year's postponement had paid off, however, as the Spanish agreed to the same restrictions on the slave trade as the Portuguese, for a consideration of £400,000. 'We cannot afford unnecessary expenditure,' protested one MP, 'and I am averse to granting 400 pence to any potentate in Europe.'[7]

Where fear of revolution did not divert him, Wilberforce worked for social justice as heartily as ever. Between 1817 and 1819, he presented a Quaker petition against the bloodthirsty penal laws, twice supported bills to improve the atrocious treatment of chimney sweeps, twice attacked the insane game laws which punished all sale of game birds with seven years' transportation, and twice backed Sir Robert Peel's factory reforms which aimed to bring the working day down to 10 1/2 hours, but had to make do with 13 1/2. He talked to Elizabeth Fry, the Quaker, about prison reform, but felt too old to take on the demands of such a campaign himself.

Just when the abolitionists seemed to have given up on the registry scheme, it finally came to fruition. In 1818, both houses of parliament asked the prince regent for new measures against the illicit slave trade, and in the following year a naval squadron was sent permanently to West Africa. To protect themselves from more direct interference, most of the twenty British colonies started registers for themselves. They assumed that in their own hands this would be a hollow gesture, but the following year the British secretary for the colonies announced that duplicate copies would be kept in England, and with that, twelve years after abolition, an official annual register of all slaves in the British colonies at last became a reality.

On 16 August 1819, eight days before Wilberforce's sixtieth birthday, 60,000 working men, women and children met peacefully and quietly in Manchester to hear the radical reformer Henry Hunt speak. The local magistrates sent amateur guards to arrest Hunt, and their horses trampled a girl to death in the process. The crowd stampeded, so 600 regular cavalry were sent in, killing 11 and injuring 421, 162 with sabre wounds. Sidmouth congratulated the soldiers for acting 'with the greatest spirit and temper', hoping that the massacre would 'prove a salutary lesson to modern reformers'. Less celebratory, the *Manchester Observer* was inspired to name it the

'Peterloo Massacre'. Burdett called it 'a reign of terror and of blood', for which he was sent to prison for two months. Grey and Tierney proposed parliamentary inquiries, which Wilberforce opposed. He had no thoughts to share on whether the magistrates were right or wrong, but urged that an inquiry would discourage the forces of law and order and encourage 'those bad men who wished to produce anarchy and confusion', ultimately causing 'discord and bloodshed' itself. 'Was anybody punished for killing and wounding them?' demanded Cobbett. No? 'Well, then, this was all right, was it?... [Then] pray tell us, Wilberforce, why a person should suffer any fine for accidentally killing, for punishing unto death a runaway negro.'[8] Wilberforce, however, heartily supported the government's Six Acts which banned the public from attending meetings outside their own parish, as well as giving magistrates greater search powers and raising tax on newspapers.

The unrest was brought to a head by the unlikeliest of insurgents, the queen. George III died in January 1820, and his son finally became George IV. He had been estranged from his wife since the moment he met her, thanks to what Wilberforce bemoaned as the unnatural and unchristian traditions of royal marriage, and both had led busy emotional lives with others. Almost the first thing George IV did as king was to ask the government for a divorce. They proposed a secret committee to, in effect, try Queen Caroline for adultery, but Wilberforce persuaded them to wait and see whether the couple could not come to a private agreement first. The king wanted her to lose her title and her place in prayers for the royal family and never to re-enter the country, in return for a continued paper marriage and allowance.

Any victim of king and cabinet was a hero of the reform movement, and the queen returned to London to public adulation and lived with the radical leader Alderman Wood. Wilberforce tried to negotiate a compromise between her and George but failed, so the government prepared a divorce bill, involving a House of Lords inquiry in August – 'long, painful and disgusting' as Wilberforce described it. While an overcrowded and overheated Lords heard endless details about the queen's affairs, thousands surrounded parliament and rallies met throughout the country. 'If the soldiers should take up her cause,' worried Wilberforce, 'who knows what may happen – and is it very improbable?'[9] Brougham not only demolished the government's evidence against the queen but threatened to impeach the king. The divorce bill was finally dropped, and Caroline accepted a settlement of £50,000 a year plus a house, which rather demolished her credibility as a figurehead of radical reform.

19

The Last Crusade

Considering... that Auguste, slave of Jean Louis Diott, has had seven of his teeth torn out by pincers or broken in his head...;

Considering that it is proved that the said Auguste has had his flesh torn from the shoulders to the breech...

We request that the civil commissary of the district may carry a particular watchfulness on the conduct of the said Diott towards his slaves in general; and that, as to Auguste in particular, he be required to sell him within a fortnight.

Sentence of Mr Justice Christie, on J. L. Diott, for disproportionate punishment of a slave who took too long to fetch water, in River Rempart, Mauritius, 22 May 1817[1]

The Spanish completely outlawed the slave trade in 1820, leaving Portugal as the last major power with a legal slave trade. But 'legal' is the important word here, as without such powerful abolition movements as Britain's behind them, the French, Spanish and Portuguese governments were a lot less rigourous in the hard task of making sure their colonies were not buying slaves and their ships were not carrying them. As one British historian of slavery put it: 'It soon appeared that prohibition and authorization as understood by the Spaniards and the French were pretty much the same thing.'[2] In the coming decade the number of slaves arriving in Brazil doubled while the number entering the French Caribbean tripled. Hundreds of slaves landed in Cuba every week. Macaulay reported a French company fitting out twenty-four ships to take up any supply abandoned by the Spanish and Portuguese. And the argument that abolition would force managers on British plantations to treat slaves better, however logical, was simply not coming true. Reports from the British colonies showed that nothing had changed – the overwork and underfeeding, the savage punishments for black listlessness and the fines for white murder, all continued as ever. 'The habit of daily cruelty is more incurable than any other,'[3] explained James Stephen's son George. He had been a teenage secretary for the Clapham abolitionists, and now at twenty-four he was becoming one of their legal advisers. Later, at the age of sixty, he was to write the best of the abolitionist memoirs in the form of letters to Harriet Beecher Stowe, the author of *Uncle Tom's Cabin*.

And so the abolitionists decided the time had come to move on to the abolition of slavery itself. It was not only right in itself, but the only way to improve plantation life and ensure a complete end to international trafficking. In his sixties now and with his strength declining, there was no way Wilberforce could lead the parliamentary campaign himself; so, with the help of his usual counsellors, he looked around for someone to pass the mantle on to. His choice was Thomas Fowell Buxton.

Buxton was, not surprisingly, an evangelical Christian, although his wife and mother were Quakers, the former being Elizabeth Fry's sister. He was a solemn young backbench MP, a foot taller than Wilberforce, and a partner in Fuller's Brewery. He was already a campaigner, like Fry, for reform of prisons and penal law and for better poor relief. He came to a meeting of the African Institution in January 1821, and criticized members for failing to get anything done. With anyone else, Buxton might have blown his chances, but the outburst had the opposite effect on Wilberforce. Buxton was astonished to hear himself commended by him a few days later for his 'boldness and openness'. On 23 May, Wilberforce heard him speak magnificently against the death penalty in parliament, and the following day asked him to lead the emancipation campaign. Buxton said he would think about it, which took him eighteen months. In the meantime, Macaulay and Stephen – both of whom had gravitated to Kensington, the new Clapham – set about collecting evidence once again.

By now the Wilberforce children were aged between thirteen and twenty-two, and William married the daughter of the secretary of the British and Foreign Bible Society in 1820. He caused his father more trouble than the rest of the family combined, and Wilberforce had to remove him from Cambridge after a year of expensively riotous student life, but trusted that he was now settling down to legal studies. The family's entourage of servants grew ever greater, not out of a love of grandness, but because Wilberforce could never bring himself to dismiss anyone for mere incompetence. His secretary James Burningham had almost lost his eyesight, but remained in Wilberforce's service for years, playing the organ at prayers. Marianne Thornton described the house as 'thronged with servants who are all lame or impotent or blind, or kept from charity'; one would 'despair of getting one's place changed at dinner and hear a chorus of bells all day which nobody answers'.[4] 'Provided the servants have faith,' concluded the poet Southey after seeing them in inaction, 'good works are not to be expected of them.' Their daughter Barbara died in 1821, aged twenty-two, but William and Barbara were consoled by the conviction that she was 'prepared for the great change'.

In the 1822 session Wilberforce protested about the use of slaves in South Africa, and persuaded the Commons to request royal action against illegal trafficking by the French and the Spanish. The Whig abolitionist Stephen Lushington failed to get a slave trade consolidation bill passed, to iron out inconsistencies between existing laws.

In August 1822, Castlereagh shot himself. Wilberforce was devastated: 'Alas! Alas! poor fellow! I did not think I should feel for him so very deeply.' If only he had observed the Sabbath, Wilberforce lamented to Stephen, he would not have cracked under the pressure. One man who did not mourn his death was George Canning, who had once tried to do the job himself (they duelled in 1809), and refused to join Perceval's government because he hated Castlereagh too much to share a cabinet with him. He now took over the vacated posts of foreign secretary and leader of the Commons. Castlereagh had been the man to negotiate international agreements after the British abolition, but only in Canning did the abolitionists have an insider in Lord Liverpool's government. Another piece seemed to be in place for the abolition of slavery.

Buxton finally agreed to take on the 'holy enterprise', and in January 1823 he met with Wilberforce and Macaulay at Kensington Gore for a 'secret cabinet council'. The strategy they came up with was in many ways very familiar: they would publish tracts, form committees and stir up the nation, and on the strength of that support bring a bill before parliament. They decided to ditch the African Institution: its heavyweight aristocratic and episcopal membership had been ideal for getting existing legislation enforced, but as most of them gravely disapproved of rousing the common people, they would not be much use in helping to abolish slavery. As George Stephen said, 'When agitation became the order of the day, it was a necessary consequence that the African Institution and all its aristocracy should be thrown overboard.'[5] In its place, Macaulay set up in London the Society for the Mitigation and Gradual Abolition of Slavery throughout the British Dominions, commonly known as the Anti-Slavery Society. This mild-sounding organization included the surviving members of the abolition committee, as well as all the familiar Clapham circle names, with two for one in the shape of Thomas Babington Macaulay, Zachary Macaulay's 22-year-old son.

The name of the society highlights the most important and controversial decision of the secret cabinet: they were painfully aware that while their slave trade campaign had struggled for twenty years against the mighty wrath of the colonies before getting anywhere, only now for the first time were they directly attacking colonial rights to property and self-government. So, taking a leaf out of Dundas's book, they decided not to press for immediate abolition and release, but instead to work slowly but explicitly towards emancipation by improving slaves' legal rights. As well as the political reasons for gradual abolition, they genuinely felt that people who had lived their lives without formal education or religious teaching, or any kind of self-sufficiency, but only the brutalizing effects of violence and degradation, needed to be introduced gradually to normal freedoms if they were to cope.

On the same day as their secret cabinet council, Wilberforce started writing an anti-slavery manifesto, *Appeal to the Reason, Justice, and Humanity of the Inhabitants of the British Empire in Behalf of the Negro Slaves in the West Indies*. Though he complained 'I am become heavy and lumbering', it must have tripped off the quill rather more easily than his religious manifesto twenty-six years previously, because it was in print by March. To no one's surprise, but to Cobbett's disgust ('... this canting and rubbishy pamphlet...'), it was another bestseller. Macaulay, who had long been the managing director of the Sierra Leone project and sunk his personal wealth into it, now gave up that day job to devote himself to abolition, leaving the business in the hands of his partner Tom Babington, the elder Babington son. ('Day job' is perhaps inaccurate – he had given it from the hours of four to nine each morning to leave the rest of the day free for slave business.)

On 13 March, Wilberforce presented the first petition, from the Quakers, for the abolition of slavery, but being tired and muddled he forgot several important points and before he knew where he was Canning had moved on to other business. It seemed that the success of the campaign could not rest on the eloquence of Wilberforce or the collaboration of Lord Liverpool's leader of the Commons.

On 26 March, a victim of the Society for Suppression of Vice petitioned parliament. Mary Ann Carlile was a bookseller, taking over from her brother and sister-in-law who were in prison for selling politically incorrect material. The society in turn prosecuted her for selling Tom Paine's sceptical theology; she was fined £500 and imprisoned until she paid it, in other words, for life. Her petition was presented by the reformer Joseph Hume, who condemned the grossly disproportionate sentence and challenged the suppressors of vice 'to turn to the New Testament and show me one passage in which they were warranted in prosecuting men for the expression of opinions concerning religion'.[6] Ignoring the main drift of Hume's criticisms, Wilberforce replied that his organization did a vital job by prosecuting crimes against society, which otherwise would be overlooked because no individual was hurt. As for 'the unhappy woman', Wilberforce hoped she would receive mercy in heaven from the God she had so offended, but she could not be shown mercy in Britain without encouraging other blasphemers. As Robin Furneaux says, this was the logic of the Inquisition; one likes to think Wilberforce was feeling tired and muddled that day too.

More anti-slavery petitions came before parliament, and Quakers started the first local anti-slavery society. With the campaign starting to warm up, Thomas Clarkson, now sixty-three, published a booklet called *Thoughts on the Necessity for improving the Condition of the Slaves in the British Colonies, with a View to their Ultimate Emancipation*, and set off on another nationwide tour. For thirteen months, he toured cities and villages preaching the release of the captives and establishing more than 200 local abolition societies. He covered 10,000 miles; and the only problem he faced in mobilizing supporters was their over-enthusiasm. 'Everywhere people are asking me about *immediate* abolition, and whether it would not be the best.'[7] Macaulay published *Negro Slavery* in May, a sketch of the realities of slave life drawn from the colonial documents that he had such encyclopedic mastery of.

On 15 May 1823, backed by 777 petitions, Buxton brought his first anti-slavery motion before the House, condemning slavery as 'repugnant to the principles of the British constitution and of the Christian religion'. Buxton laid his cards on the table: his society's aim was 'nothing less than the extinction of slavery – in nothing less than the whole of the British dominions: – not, however, the rapid termination of that state – not the sudden emancipation of the negro – but such preparatory steps, such measures of precaution, as, by slow degrees, and in a course of years, first fitting and qualifying the slaves for the enjoyment of freedom, shall gently conduct us to the annihilation of slavery.'[8]

The first steps he proposed were to free all infant slaves born after a certain date, so that slavery would quite literally die out, and in the meantime to allow them new rights – to have Sunday rest and religious education, to buy their freedom at the market rate, to give evidence in court, to marry and to own property inviolably.

Before Wilberforce could second the motion, Canning bowled him another spinner. He lauded their aims, but offered an alternative programme of reforms – very similar and again explicitly aimed ultimately at emancipation, but excluding the immediate release of the young, a measure he called inefficient and hazardous. The advantage of his proposals was that the government would introduce them immediately in the crown colonies – which included Demerara, Trinidad, Mauritius and St Lucia and contained a small minority of British slaves – and press for them on the self-governing colonies too.

Wilberforce decided to accept. The only alternative was losing the vote, and Canning was certainly offering concrete improvements – though little could be expected outside the crown colonies. More important, in Wilberforce's eyes, was the matter of principle that Canning had officially conceded: 'We now stand in a perfectly new situation,' Wilberforce declared. 'We have now an acknowledgment on the part of government that the grievances of which we complain do exist, and that a remedy ought to be applied.'[9]

A broadside of protests returned from the colonies. The Jamaican Assembly complained that they were 'to be offered [as] a propitiatory sacrifice at the altar of fanaticism', and of course they predicted slave revolts. And this time Wilberforce agreed: when he heard that Baron Bathurst, Lord Liverpool's colonial secretary, had started his reform programme by telling Demerara to ban the cart whip he was dismayed. 'Why, it is positive madness!' Removing this essential emblem of slavery was not preparing slaves for freedom, he said, it was telling them slavery was already finished. Bathurst followed it up with instructions for the full reform programme.

Some Demerara managers withdrew the whip while others sent slave drivers out with two whips. On the night of 18 August 1823, 1,300 slaves in Demerara revolted, putting plantation managers in prison, but refusing to kill anyone or to burn crops or buildings. 'It is contrary to the religion we profess' explained one Christian slave afterwards. 'We cannot give life and therefore we will not take it.'[10] The colonists, whose Christianity had a somewhat different timbre, quickly regained control and executed fifty slaves, sentencing others to 1,000 lashes. They arrested a British Independent missionary and former biscuit baker called John Smith for conspiracy. He had repeatedly been in trouble for teaching and preaching to slaves, and in November was court martialled and sentenced to death for his alleged part in the campaign. A military chaplain by the name of Austin suggested to the management that not only was there no evidence for conspiracy, but it was Smith who had saved their lives by preaching pacifism to the slaves. Austin 'is sunk beyond redemption,' replied the *Guiana Chronicle*. The case was referred to Westminster, but before parliament could investigate, Smith died in prison and the governor of the colony barred his wife from the burial service.

Further slave plots, largely fictional, were uncovered in Jamaica, St Lucia and Trinidad, darkening the prospects for abolition. Wilberforce was seriously ill and out of action for two months when the government reported on Caribbean reform in March 1824. Demerara had done little, Bathurst said; he had only expected slow progress, and following this unrest it would be a lot harder. Canning promised to press for immediate reform in Trinidad. Buxton protested that Canning's policy for the twenty slave colonies was 'frittered down to a single island', but despite 600 petitions, being amid slave revolts the abolitionists were in no position to demand a vote.

Then the London Missionary Society reported Smith's story. The death of a consumptive Briton in unjust captivity roused an outrage that the execution and torture of scores of Africans in unjust captivity could not hope to match. 'The day of reckoning will come,' brooded Wilberforce, who was well again in time for the Commons debate about Smith on June 11. Brougham, in a ferocious speech, pulled the legal justification for the trial and sentence apart limb from limb, and Wilberforce supported him. 'I quite forgot my topics,' he lamented again; but he made the impressive point that parliament had instructed Demeraran colonists to prepare the slaves for freedom through religious education and their response had been to kill a man because he was a missionary. But Canning once again had to balance justice with politics, and managed to defeat the motion.

Bathurst tried to enforce his reforms on the crown colonies through Orders in Council, and pressed them on the self-governing colonies; but even the crown colonies furiously resisted, so there was little hope for the others. Jamaica rejected virtually all the reforms, Barbados absolutely all. Two out of thirteen eventually allowed marriage; two abandoned the whip; none ever guaranteed slaves the right to buy their freedom.

Wilberforce was debilitated by pneumonia that summer, this time recovering just in time for the public meeting of the Anti-Slavery Society to discuss the Smith affair, chaired by the Duke of Gloucester on 25 July. The star of the show proved to be Thomas Babington Macaulay. The excuse the colonists had given for the court martial, he reminded listeners, was that Smith would not get a fair trial in a civilian court.

Sir, I have always lived under the protection of the British laws, and therefore I am unable to imagine what could be worse [than the court martial]; but… since the colonists maintain that a jury composed of their own body not only possibly might, but necessarily must, have acted with more iniquity than this court martial, I certainly shall not dispute the assertion, though I am utterly unable to conceive the mode.[11]

'Capital!', 'Wonderful', exclaimed Wilberforce throughout. Marianne Thornton describes him and Stephen forgetting the decorum of the platform and the royal presence in their excitement, 'catching hold of him as he was going back to his place, and keeping him there, each shaking a hand, while the very walls seemed to be coming down with the thunders of applause'. Macaulay senior sat 'with his eyes fixed on a piece of paper' throughout, and his only comment afterwards was to tell his son off for folding his arms before royalty.

Clarkson's local societies held less high-powered meetings throughout the country – taking advantage of a more relaxed attitude from the government towards seditious assemblies in these years of economic recovery. The Smith scandal brought them increasingly powerful support, most dramatically from Dissenting churches, and it is hard to see what the colonists could have done to injure their cause more. This time, however, the Church of England was less help. Porteus was dead, and the bishops could not see abolition in such stark terms now that it involved the sacred rights of property – including their own.

The most outspoken campaigner was the Leicester Quaker Elizabeth Heyrick. In 1824 she published the magnificent *Immediate, not Gradual Emancipation*, criticizing the Anti-Slavery Society's gradualism. Calling it 'the very masterpiece of satanic policy' – which she meant quite literally – she demanded to know whether 'emancipation… out of the jaws of a shark or a tiger, must be gradual'. She renewed the sugar boycott, on precisely the grounds that some abolitionists had disliked it: 'Why petition parliament at all, to do that for us, which… we can do more speedily and more effectually for ourselves?' She even offered support to the slave rebels of Demerara:

'Was it not the cause of self-defence from the most degrading, intolerable oppression?'[12]

In March 1824, Canning got slave-trading reclassified as piracy, which raised the deterrent from transportation to execution. Stephen published the first volume of *Slavery Delineated*, a text book for abolitionists, examining slave law and demonstrating that it was not just the abuses of Caribbean drivers but the institution itself that was essentially unjust. Wilberforce joined the MP Richard Martin and others in founding the Society for the Prevention of Cruelty to Animals (SPCA). It was not a cause that particularly exercised the public, but it had always mattered to Wilberforce. A story was told of him berating a cabbie for abusing his horse, which got him a mouthful back, until the moment the cabbie's friend whispered in his ear, 'That's Wilberforce.' The SPCA was the first animal welfare society in the world, and its initial aim was to enforce Martin's pioneering 1822 law to protect farm animals. It then gained its initial R from Queen Victoria in 1840.

After his first illness of 1824, Wilberforce's family had pressed him to retire from parliament. After the second, there was no escape. He decided that whatever loss he might be to parliament could be made up by writing, and he ought to spend more time with his family. Turning down a peerage from Canning, Wilberforce resigned his seat in February 1825 at the age of sixty-six, after forty-five years as an MP. Buxton replied to the news by quoting to him from the tomb of Hannibal: 'We vehemently desired him in the day of battle.' Canning's intervention seemed to have taken the campaign down a dead-end street and many abolitionists saw Wilberforce's withdrawal as 'ominous of its abandonment as a hopeless struggle', in George Stephen's words.

The Wilberforces sold Kensington Gore and moved to Mill Hill in Middlesex, it being at that point 'beyond the dirt of the metropolis', though they had to spend most of the year in a cottage waiting for the builders to finish, with the servants staying in the nearest inn. 'Here I am,' he told Marianne Thornton, 'a wreck left over for the next tide'; but her impression was that for all the thin, frail exhaustion of his body he was more keenly alive than ever: 'Really he is almost a proof already of the immortality of the soul.'[13]

On 8 April, 1825, Elizabeth Heyrick and others formed the Birmingham Ladies Society for the Relief of Negro Slaves. They promoted the sugar boycott, targeting shops as well as shoppers, visiting thousands of homes and distributing pamphlets, calling meetings and drawing petitions. They encouraged other women's societies across the country, and within six years there were seventy-three. Wilberforce was rather nonplussed, telling Macaulay that political activism was 'unsuited to the female character as delineated in Scripture', but Macaulay was not prepared to bow to his exegesis on this one.

Lushington's consolidation bill was finally passed in 1825, and he won compensation for two free black Jamaicans deported as aliens but there was no progress on abolition while Bathurst waited to see the success of his reforms, although petitions kept the subject more or less alive. In June, Zachary Macaulay launched the *Anti-Slavery Monthly Reporter*, a magazine which he largely wrote himself, constantly updating faithful readers on the evasions of the colonies and interpreting their prevarication – 'the sound of reform without a particle of its substance'.[14] Stephen wrote letters to the newspapers, getting friends to copy them out to vary the handwriting. Wilberforce was enjoying country life with his family, catching up on reading, visiting the poor, entertaining friends and bemoaning his idleness. He toyed with an invitation to tour Scotland, but decided he could not justify the waste of time. The Anti-Slavery Society arranged a public meeting for 21 December 1825, and pressed Wilberforce to chair it. He refused, feeling that it was an honour he no longer had the gifts to justify – 'I am a bee which has lost its sting' – but was eventually persuaded. The meeting declared that Bathurst's non-existent reforms proved that there was no hope of even improving slavery without direct intervention.

Wilberforce's youngest son Henry was now starting university; after William's disgrace at Cambridge, the other three all got firsts from Oxford and went into the church. William went into the dairy. His father was persuaded that he was too ill to become a lawyer and set him up as a dairy farmer instead, having to mortgage land in Yorkshire to do so.

Zachary Macaulay was proving to be the real manager of the emancipation campaign. He absorbed the entire documentary output of parliament as ever, providing intelligence for Stephen's writings and Clarkson's agitation, and for his own magazine. He helped co-ordinate the parliamentary campaigns of Brougham, Buxton and Lushington, and injected some placid optimism into it all. 'It was Macaulay that kept a steady look out from the mast-head,' says George Stephen, 'and shouted "Land!" buried as it was in mist and storm and darkness.'[15]

In 1826 650 petitions were brought before parliament, and on the back of the largest ever petition submitted, signed by 72,000 Londoners, Buxton demanded that, as Canning's approach had delivered nothing, the House either withdraw its pledge to dismantle slavery or take direct action immediately. Canning compromised by getting Bathurst's reforms passed unanimously by the Lords, making them yet harder for the colonies to ignore, and drawing up a reform bill, forcing each island to accept or reject it outright. The MP Thomas Denman protested about the execution of twenty-four Jamaican slaves in connection with a conspiracy fabricated by a butcher's boy. Buxton caused a scandal by accusing Sir Robert Farquhar, who had been not only the governor of Mauritius but also vice-president of the African Institution, of allowing a vast illegal slave trade in Mauritius. The Commons created a committee to consider the question, which got nowhere, so Buxton organized a private inquiry.

With parliament about to break for an election, Brougham told MPs that he would force the issue of Canning's 1823 pledge when they next met, and Stephen published *England Enslaved by her own Slave Colonies*, rousing voters to demand action. Macaulay prepared 'a pithy address' along similar lines, which appeared in every British newspaper on the day the election was announced. Heyrick pressed voters only to support immediate abolitionists.

Abolitionists then gained a valuable ally in the shape of the East India Company, who wanted to expand their own sugar production but faced what they saw as unfair taxation to protect the West Indians. So they added their voice to the anti-slavery campaign in order to hamper their Caribbean competition, while Macaulay's *Reporter* argued for a reduction in the tariff on slavery-free sugar. Giving up his Sierra Leone work for the campaign had meant many economies for Macaulay, including leaving Kensington, but he little guessed the full extent of his sacrifice. His wealth was still tied up in it, and in November it emerged that over three years the company had lost hundreds of thousands of pounds. Quite how was unclear – Tom Babington shut himself in his bedroom and refused to talk about it. Wilberforce lent Macaulay £10,000, but he had lost his fortune.

In February 1827, Liverpool suffered a stroke and Canning became prime minister, replacing extreme reactionaries like Wellington (who had quit) with Whigs like Tierney, on the condition that they made no attempts at electoral reform. Canning brought a moderation of the Corn Laws through the Commons, but it failed in the Lords. In August, Canning suddenly died, and was replaced, eventually, by Wellington in January 1828. This turmoil wrote off the 1827 session for the abolitionists, especially as no information had yet come through about the Caribbean reforms demanded the previous year.

Wilberforce took a tour of Yorkshire in the summer of 1827, and found it a dispiriting experience. He met a shopkeeper who had shared his roast ox in 1780, but whenever he asked after an old friend he was told, 'He died years ago.' He wrote to Hannah More, saying that: 'My friends are daily dropping around me.'[16] Thankfully one of his oldest friends, Thomas Gisborne, was still going strong, and he enjoyed a visit to Yoxall Lodge.

Wilberforce had largely faded from the abolitionist scene, but his life was not entirely without drama. In 1827 he started building a chapel – he had bought the new house on the understanding that one was about to be built, the parish church being three miles away – but no progress had been made. Apparently, the vicar Theodore Williams gave Wilberforce's project his blessing, but then had it stopped, and started denouncing him from the pulpit and in print as a hypocritical profiteer. Wilberforce exchanged letters with him, but could not get to the bottom of it, except by assuming that he was mad. He published their correspondence and appealed to the Church Commissioners, but the process dragged on for years.

The new prime minister Wellington was the kind of militant Anglican that the older generation of Clapham Saints so approved of, so it was a mark of the weakness of his government that its first major act was to repeal the Test and Corporation Acts, extending full political rights to Dissenters. The Whig Lord Russell brought it through, with such support both inside and outside parliament that Wellington was powerless. One of its effects would be to create more abolitionist MPs in the next election. The religious capitulation continued the following year with the Catholic Emancipation Act, forced by widespread violence in Ireland.

Finally, the response to Bathurst's reform bills for the Caribbean assemblies came back to his successor as colonial secretary, William Huskisson. When Brougham asked for his report in March 1828, Huskisson put an impressive degree of spin on it, but the fact was that not one of the twenty British islands had passed the bill, offering in its place their own flimsy scarecrow reforms. 'The progress of the colonies', Brougham replied, 'is so slow as to be imperceptible to all human eyes but their own.'

With the cause seemingly at a standstill in parliament thanks to colonial obfuscation and governmental patience, attendance at meetings dropped. George Stephen had to drag friends along to the Society's annual meeting 'to secure at least an apology for an audience'[17]. And yet the government's approach to Caribbean reform had obviously failed, and the great debates of Dissenting and Catholic emancipation were both resolved – in favour of freedom – so now would seem to be the moment to mobilize the nation and force the question. But instead the platform merely called for more petitions once again. Possibly it was because Buxton was patiently and quietly constructing something of a superweapon.

In December, William Wilberforce the younger approached his father for money, not for the first time. He was now in serious trouble, and the immediate problem was that a loan of £6,000 that he needed to pay off earlier debts had fallen through. Wilberforce, for once, could not afford it. He was spending a lot of money on the chapel, he was still supporting all his children, he was paying off the mortgage for William's dairy, and as ever he kept up colossally demanding commitments to charity. Even to deal with this immediate debt, Wilberforce saw no alternative but to sell the house in Hull where he was born, a painful parting at this stage of his life. And that was nothing to what he faced when the full scale of William's debts emerged.

20

The Chimes of Freedom

Well friends, I hope the time will soon come when we shall have privilege, and we shall drink our wine in free. I hope we shall soon have Little Breeches [their manager] under our feet... I hear him say, the king going to give us black people free; but he hope that all his friends will be of his mind, and spill our blood first. But I'll be first to do his business, though I am his slave. I'll give him a pill, as I follow him.
The slave George Guthrie on the eve of the Jamaican revolt[1]

Buxton's private inquiry into the Mauritius slave trade had amassed a vast body of explosive evidence from 200 witnesses, and though Farquhar himself was now dead, Buxton had managed to get at least a token parliamentary inquiry. The inquiry was unsympathetic, refusing to look at his evidence, but even so the information they uncovered themselves was horrifying and confirmed his allegations.

And so, four years after his original accusations in parliament, Buxton was ready to go public, his story incontrovertible. In the eighteen years that slave-trading had been a felony, more than 60,000 slaves had been imported to Mauritius from Madagascar and the Seychelles, representing a turnover of the entire slave population. How could so many replacements have been needed? George Stephen summarizes the stories Macaulay published in the *Reporter* from Buxton's inquiry: 'Slaves were murdered piecemeal, roasted alive in ovens; flogged, starved, dismembered, tortured, and slaughtered. Suicide and infanticide were the daily recourse of parents; mothers killed their children from humanity, and killed themselves from despair.'[2]

And yet when Wilberforce attended the sixth annual meeting of the Anti-Slavery Society in March 1829, it was just to see more motions passed and a disappointing audience encouraged to send more petitions. Something else was needed, and so to get their revelations and arguments beyond the faithful Buxton organized a team of speakers, briefed them – especially about the Mauritius story – and sent them out to the local abolition societies in the south-east to inform and 'inflame'.

It worked. When the Anti-Slavery Society met on 15 May 1830, the 2,000-seater Freemasons Hall in Holborn 'was crammed to suffocation,' George Stephen said; 'thousands were turned away'. Speakers failed to make the stage. Clarkson moved that 'my old beloved friend and fellow-labourer, Mr Wilberforce' take the chair. Now seventy years old, he did, with a few affectionate words for Clarkson, 'looking back to the days of our early labours... In that work, my friend preceded me.'[3]

Buxton tabled a motion 'to leave no proper and practicable means unattempted for effecting, at the earliest period, its entire abolition'. Thomas Babington Macaulay and others followed with more of the same, each passed unanimously. There was no more talk of 'gradual', but it still seemed pretty feeble to some. 'Admirably worded,' said George Stephen, 'admirably indignant, but – admirably prudent.' One of the committee in the side gallery, Mr Pownall, lost his patience, and, over Wilberforce's calls to order, shouted out an amendment, that 'after the 1st of January 1830, every child born within the king's dominions shall be free'. 'The shouts,' remembered Stephen, 'the tumult of applause... cheers innumerable thundered... hats and handkerchiefs were waved.' Wilberforce, Buxton and Brougham appealed for peace, but Stephen and friends ('the fuglemen of the mighty host') kept the disturbance going until Wilberforce officially proposed the amendment, which was carried with 'a burst of exulting triumph that would have made the Falls of Niagara inaudible at an equal distance'.[4]

Things were moving. George IV died in June 1830, which meant that his devoutly pro-slavery brother, the Duke of Clarence, became William IV, but it also meant a general election and a chance to boost the number of abolitionist MPs. Thomas Babington Macaulay gained a seat, and Brougham won Wilberforce's old seat for Yorkshire, telling him, 'The election turned very much on slavery; your name was in every mouth, and your health the most enthusiastically received.' Wilberforce's memories came flooding back: 'Ah! I hear that shout again! Hear! Hear! What a life it was!'[5] The tone of the election and the session was set by the July revolution in France, which provided exactly what many British had hoped for from the 1789 revolution, a transition from absolute to constitutional monarchy, and no more. Constitutional reform was the major issue of the election, newspapers freely agitated for change, and the new parliament was full of reformers. By the end of the year, Wellington was replaced by Earl Grey and the Whigs, the party of reform, were back in power for the first time since Grenville's abortive premiership, although without a workable majority, and Brougham became lord chancellor. Huskisson, the former colonial secretary, was then run over by Stephenson's Rocket, the first ever railway casualty.

In November 1830 Wilberforce's son William fled the country to escape debtors' prison, and Wilberforce called in Barbara's brother to investigate what the damage was and what could be done. The answer was a lot and not much respectively. William had accumulated £50,000 of debt – ten times the prime minister's annual salary – and it would cost most of what Wilberforce had. Six different people offered to pay off the whole amount, including Viscount Fitzwilliam whom Wilberforce had clashed with so unhappily in the 1807 election, but Wilberforce insisted that it was his responsibility and no one else should be put out of pocket by it. The only answer was to sell the house and let all his faithful, decrepit staff go, save a servant each for him and Barbara, and a reader. He had enough investments left to provide some income for the family, and the couple were to spend the rest of their lives travelling between Samuel, Robert and charitable friends.

'He is behaving beautifully on it they all say,' reported Marianne Thornton, 'as I might be certain he would. He comes to us with his train next week.' 'What I shall miss most,' he said 'will be my books and my garden, though I own I do feel a little the not being able to ask my friends to take dinner or a bed with me, under my own roof.'[6]

The new parliament received 2,600 petitions against slavery, twenty-six times the unprecedented number in the 1788 campaign. An estimated 2,200 were from Dissenters, thanks to John Smith's martyrdom. Buxton called for a debate on complete abolition, with a powerful speech on slave mortality figures, demonstrating that in the last ten years, after imports, exports and manumissions had been taken into account, the slave population of the fourteen sugar colonies had fallen by 45,800 – 14 per cent. The supply had finished, and yet the bestial planters were killing their slaves as recklessly as ever. 'If there were no other prospect of the extinction of slavery, it would be found in the rapid extinction of the negro race.'[7]

The chancellor, Lord Althorp, was sympathetic but, hampered by the realities of government, all he could offer was that Bathurst's reforms would finally be enforced on the colonies, whom he would pay to implement them. And yet once again, not one island took the bribe. The attitude of the colonies to the emancipation campaign has often been described as suicidal, and there is no better word. If they had only played ball they could surely have prolonged this gradualist campaign interminably – their delaying tactics had dragged out the campaign for the immediate abolition of the slave trade for nineteen years. And yet it was the colonists themselves who brought the emancipation campaign to a head, budging 'not by a hair's breadth'. Why? For one thing, protracting the earlier campaign had never involved the least compromise, so there was nothing new in their intransigence. They ferociously resented any attempt to interfere with their independence. Minority rule of their islands seems to have made the whites instinctively defensive, and the ever-growing alliance that they faced between abolitionists, the government, the East India Company, the British public and the slaves themselves seems to have created a siege mentality. Their obduracy made British demands more insistent, which only made them more obdurate. And to be blunt, one should not overestimate the average intelligence of the kind of men who became plantation managers.

Grey called an election for a reforming parliament in 1831, and abolition was high on the agenda. Every second MP, George Stephen said, claimed to have freed slaves, or addressed an abolition society, or had dinner with Wilberforce. Grey won a large majority, but the abolitionist majority was still not definite, and amid debate on constitutional reform the Society agonized over when to strike. George

Stephen and a couple of Quakers formed a more radical breakaway group, the Agency Committee, which paid six agitators, including Pownall, to stir up the local societies for immediate abolition and encourage new ones, to engage the kind of people who were soon to gain the vote, canvas door-to-door, and to heckle pro-slavery speakers. They annoyed Zachary Macaulay by meeting in the same building as his Society, but Wilberforce 'heartily acknowledged their value' and immediately gave twenty guineas. When the Agency attacked Macaulay and Buxton for apathy, Wilberforce was, in his words, 'more indignant than I can well express', but overall the two groups worked extraordinarily well together.

'I am but poorly,' Wilberforce told Samuel in October 1831. Suffering delirious seizures, he took the Bath waters, which once again restored him. 'I cannot understand why my life is spared so long.' One thing in his new wandering life remained unchanged since the heady days of forty years ago: 'I am bothered (a vulgar phrase, but having been used in the House of Lords I may condescend to adopt it) with incessant visitors.'[8] The reform bill brought out Wilberforce's conservative anxieties – 'I almost tremble for the consequences,' he told Samuel. 'I find myself now at seventy-one-and-a-half far more timid and indisposed to great changes.'[9] The bill was thrown out by the Lords in October 1831, and the rioting that had continued throughout the year culminated in Bristol, close enough to Blaise Castle, where Wilberforce was staying, allowing him to see the 'the horizon reddened with the lurid glare of these devastating fires'.[10] Barbara suggested that Samuel bury the family deeds and silverware in the garden against the threat of revolution, but order was soon restored.

In Jamaica, the slaves likewise moved for immediate emancipation. The black Baptist preacher Samuel Sharpe called a strike on the grounds that their release had been decreed in Westminster and denied at home. Managers, who more than ever saw slave Christianity as the root of their resistance, stoked it into revolt; 50,000 slaves broke free and burnt 160 properties. Ten white people were killed, two deliberately. In retribution, colonists executed 100 slaves and destroyed nineteen Baptist and Methodist chapels. In the wake of this political kamikaze attack, British missionaries returned home, giving loud and passionate new leadership to the abolitionists, and parliament heard how George Greathead Taylor was flogged to death by his master for refusing to stop preaching, saying 'I can't give over serving my God.'[11]

After a concerted attempt by Tory and plantation-owning MPs to bring down the government, the reform bill finally became law in June 1832, and the UK electorate increased by 45 per cent. In the face of incipient democracy, Wilberforce took comfort from the thought that 'the change will be for the benefit, and greatly so, of our poor West India clients'.[12] The first reformed election was in January 1832, and in a brilliant campaign, Stephen's Agency Committee and the Jamaican missionaries made abolition the predominant issue.

While negotiations rumbled on in Westminster, Wilberforce felt the conquest of personal decay. He was constantly drowsy and his memory was patchy. 'I feel myself becoming more and more stupid and inefficient,' he told Samuel.[13] To the end of his life though, he insisted that his homelessness was no trial: 'It has only increased my happiness, for I have in consequence been spending the winter with my son – the grateful witness of his gospel labours.' In 1832, Wilberforce's second daughter Lizzy died, and he was buckled with grief. James Stephen followed soon after. 'I have often heard that sailors on a voyage will drink "friends astern" till they are halfway over,' said Wilberforce, 'then "friends ahead". With me it has been "friends ahead" this long time.'[14]

Staying with Robert in April 1833, he was taken to Maidstone to propose one last abolition petition. The government finally brought the bill before the House in July, after constant pressure from Buxton, and yet it was – considering the hole the planters had dug themselves into – disgracefully generous to them. It abolished slavery and yet, thanks to the fear that free people would refuse to grow sugar, all slaves over the age of five became 'apprentices' for the next twelve years, working 71/2 hours a day unpaid, and 21/2 paid. Slave owners were granted a £20 million loan, about half the value of their half-freed slaves. Buxton got the apprenticeship term halved, but the lords and bishops added permission for the term to be extended for seven years for 'wilful absence'.

Still, thanks to the combined forces of the abolition campaign, the

UK public, the slaves, and their pig-headed owners, an end was in sight. It is the conundrum and irony of Wilberforce's story that this gradual abolition was achieved in half the time of his immediate abolition, which he fought so hard to save from the disingenuous lure of gradualism. Was Dundas right after all? Actually, neither Dundas nor the Anti-Slavery Society were right. They both saw gradual abolition working through colonial reform, but it was the colonists' absolute refusal to accept any sort of reform that finally forced the government to abolish slavery itself. It was, in other words, the failure of the gradual abolition campaign that was its success. Many since have expressed outrage that it was the owners and not the slaves who were compensated. Wilberforce was more realistic: 'Thank God, that I should have lived to witness a day in which England is willing to give 20 millions sterling for the abolition of slavery.' The Commons victory that made abolition certain took place on Friday 26 July 1833. Wilberforce died two days later, in the early hours of Monday. His last words were to his son Henry:

'I am in a very distressed state.'

'Yes, but you have your feet on the Rock.'

'I do not venture to speak so positively; but I hope I have.'[15]

21

The Long Run

My master then said, he would not be worse than his promise; and, taking the money, told me to go to the Secretary at the Register Office, and get my manumission drawn up. These words of my master were like a voice from Heaven to me; in an instant all my trepidation was turned into unutterable bliss; and I most reverently bowed myself with gratitude, unable to express my feelings, but by the overflowing of my eyes…

Heavens! who could do justice to my feelings at this moment? Not conquering heroes themselves, in the midst of a triumph – Not the tender mother who has just regained her long-lost infant, and presses it to the heart – Not the weary hungry mariner, at the sight of the desired friendly port – Not the lover, when he once more embraces his beloved mistress, after she had been ravished from his arms! – all within my breast was tumult, wildness, and delirium! My feet scarcely touched the ground, for they were winged with joy, and, like Elijah, as he rose to Heaven, they 'were with lightning sped as I went on'. Every one I met I told of my happiness, and blazed about the virtue of my amiable master and captain.

Olaudah Equiano, 1789[1]

'He is altogether a *double-entendre*,'[2] said the essayist William Hazlitt in 1825. Probably the accusation most often levelled at Wilberforce, both then and now, is inconsistency: defending the oppressed abroad and the oppressors at home; compassion for slaves, repression for workers. Eric Williams, the scholar and prime minister of Trinidad and Tobago, said in 1944: 'Wilberforce was familiar with all that went on in the hold of a slave ship but ignored what went on at the bottom of a mineshaft.'[3] Or as Cobbett – who was at least as inconsistent in the opposite way – put it:

You seem to have a great affection for the fat and lazy and laughing and singing and dancing negroes… I feel for the careworn, the ragged, the hard-pinched, the ill-treated, and beaten and trampled upon labouring classes of England, Scotland, and Ireland, to whom… you do all the mischief that it is in your power to do.[4]

Some have solved the contradiction by concluding that Wilberforce had no real compassion at all. To Cobbett his 'canting trash' about poor slaves was an opiate cynically prescribed to keep starved workers quieter. Coleridge believed it was sheer religious duty – he did not 'care a farthing for the slaves' if only '*his soul were saved*'.[5] Fox (who should have known better, but the misunderstanding was mutual) thought he cared more about keeping in with Pitt than the slaves themselves.

They were all wrong. Whatever the limitations of the records his sons have left us, his private journal and personal giving reveal a man whose compassion for both the slaves and the British poor was unquestionably real, heartfelt and costly. It was also practical, attempting reform of factories, penal law, chimney sweeping, poor relief, schools, and so on, and consistently opposing war. We should not forget that he was also a constitutional reformer for twenty years of his career.

This conversely tempts some to let the abolition, charity and reform eclipse Wilberforce's darker side, as it were. But he did real damage with the part he played in outlawing unions, introducing imprisonment without trial, reducing freedom of speech and assembly, and the individual prosecutions carried out by the Society for Suppression of Vice; the fact that he used his moral capital as the hero of abolition to do so makes it all the more bitter. To be sure, the scale of such injury is dwarfed by his achievement in stopping 40,000 Africans a year being made slaves of the British, but it does not diminish his achievements to ask how the same man could be responsible for both.

One suggestion might be that charity is more pleasurable and less expensive than giving away power. An uncharitable suggestion itself perhaps; but it is true that English radicals threatened Wilberforce's way of life in a way that slave revolts in the Caribbean did not. And yet his charity was not recreational, but made a significant dent in his standard of living, just as the slave business made costly demands on his time and wealth throughout most of his adult life. We should also bear in mind that Wilberforce's generation faced the plausible threat of revolution, civil war and invasion. Under those conditions it is perhaps not incomprehensible that a well-intentioned patriarch should do all in his power to improve the condition of the poor, while fearing their attempts to take that power to themselves.

But the real key to understanding the complexity of Wilberforce is his overriding sense of duty to God. It drove him to extraordinary lengths to defend the slaves and help the poor; it drove his efforts for mission in India and at home; but it also drove his assaults on British radicalism – which, being often coupled with attacks on traditional Christianity, made many religious people of Wilberforce's class feel like it was an assault on Christian values and society, as the French revolution had been. In fact, Wilberforce's problem was not so much inconsistency as being too consistent to this one principle of religious duty, as he understood it. When this sense of duty overrode his human sympathy, as with blasphemous booksellers, it could make him implacably tyrannous – especially when it persuaded him to support pious villains like Sidmouth. When sympathy overrode duty, as with his support for Catholic emancipation, he was more genuinely inconsistent, but also more human.

But when his sympathy and duty, his divinity and humanity, were working together, there was, in Macaulay's words, 'a splendour about Wilberforce'.[6] Sacred compulsion joined with a visceral revulsion against injustice to give him not just passion but unshakeable commitment. It is unfair to many people that his name is uniquely attached to the campaign to abolish the slave trade. He was not its prime mover or, in the earlier years, its driving force. He was not its martyr or its genius. But he kept it alive long after it was generally given up for dead, and brought it to completion. It took the greater part of his life.

Perhaps if it had not been for Wilberforce someone would have succeeded in getting the law changed sooner or later anyway. But not necessarily. And as the historian G. M. Trevelyan argues, later may not have been soon enough:

> If slavery and the slave trade had continued through the nineteenth century, armed with the new weapons of the industrial revolution and of modern science, the tropics would have become a vast slave farm for white exploitation, and the European races in their own homes would have been degraded by the diseases of slave-civilisation of which the old Roman Empire had died.[7]

As it was, the Atlantic slave trade – though illegal by the time Wilberforce died, in all participating countries, both buyers and sellers – continued for decades. Its suppression become central to British foreign policy – not least in order to open Africa up to commerce. Once again, the warnings of anti-abolitionists were proved right, as the illegal trade proved far worse than the legal. Abolition cut the price of slaves in West Africa and raised it in the Americas, making the traffic irresistible and intense. French ships were equipped with platforms three feet deep under which slaves were 'crowded together in one mass of living corruption'.[8] Cuba was importing 20,000 a year, Brazil twice that.

But by 1839, Britain had treaties with France and Spain allowing its navy to seize slave ships, and unilaterally extended that right to Portuguese ships also. Its West Africa Squadron started raiding African trading stations. In 1848, the French released its slaves. The British navy ended the Brazilian slave trade with a raid in 1850. After the United States freed its four million slaves in 1863, the United States and Britain united to crush the last remaining Atlantic slave trade, to Cuba. In fifty years, the British had spent £40 million seizing 1,600 ships in order to liberate 150,000 slaves, and the Atlantic slave trade was finished. Wilberforce would have been delighted with the way his baton was taken and run with.

The Clapham Sect cast a long shadow. The Church Missionary Society continues today, supporting 900 missionaries in twenty-six countries. The British and Foreign Bible Society gave away 180 million Bibles in the nineteenth century, and is today part of an international network distributing scripture in 2,300 languages. The RSPCA rescues 14,000 animals a year. The Society for Suppression of Vice is no more, but continued throughout the Victorian period, and in around 1870 it destroyed 140,213 obscene pictures, 21,772 books, and five tons of letterpress in the space of three years.

Thomas Babington Macaulay became the greatest Victorian historian, pioneering the 'Whig view' of history as a march of progress towards the 1832 British constitution. G.M. Trevelyan was his great-nephew. Charles Grant's sons were President of the Board of Trade and Governor of Bombay respectively. The Stephen family contributed to the government of Britain and Australia and to English literature, most notably giving the world Virginia Woolf, née Stephen. The Thorntons gave us Woolf's fellow Bloomsbury novelist E. M. Forster. Newton and Cowper's hymns are still sung today, as Newton's doubtless will be when every other word of the Saints is forgotten.

As for the Wilberforces, all four sons became high Anglicans, three of them ending up Catholic, and Henry being a confidant of John Henry Newman – which seems to say something about their evangelical upbringing, although it is not entirely clear what. (Clapham's second generation remained immune to evangelicalism, while the religion was taking the country.) The remaining Wilberforce Anglican, Samuel, became Bishop of Oxford and was best known for his spirited attack on Darwinism, which Darwin (himself the grandson of Josiah Wedgwood) saluted as 'uncommonly clever'.

Wilberforce himself was buried in Westminster Abbey, soon to be commerated with a rather alarming statue, and both houses of parliament were closed for the funeral. 'As I came down the Strand,' said one friend, 'every third person I met going about their business was in mourning.'[9] Slaves on the islands joined in.

Robert then set about his biography, drafting in Samuel when it got too much. Robert persuaded Clarkson to lend him all the correspondence between the pair of them, took the information that he wanted and then, it seems, destroyed the lot. Marianne had similar ambitions for the whole book: 'I wish you and I were rich enough to buy up his father's life and burn it, out of love for the great old man';

letting 'dull Robert' take custody of his memory, 'why, you might as well put a mole to talk about an eagle'.[10]

Fortunately, Wilberforce had an infinitely worthier memorial in the fact that where there had been a slave trade previously, there was not one anymore. The year the biography was published, 1838, the apprentice system ended, two years prematurely, after slave strikes and the familiar agitation in Britain. Jamaican chapels were decorated with flowers, and trees were planted. The next year, leading abolitionists regrouped once again, replacing the Anti-Slavery Society with the British and Foreign Anti-Slavery Society, their focus now on international emancipation – although they still had to deal with a Victorian revival of forced labour in the form of the coolie system. The society is still in business today, as Anti-Slavery International, and it still publishes *The Reporter*, working on behalf of an estimated 12.3 million people in some form of forced labour, including debt bondage, serfdom, sexual trafficking, child warfare, state work farms and caste labour. This fact has drawn pessimistic reflections from some about the irresistible continuance of slavery, but it is worth noticing one fact. When Wilberforce first stood before parliament to propose the abolition of the slave trade – when Clarkson sat down on the roadside at Wade's Mill, when Sharp started learning law to take on the lord chief justice, when Equiano began his memoirs of the Middle Passage, when Ramsay first invited the wrath of planters by teaching their labour force Christianity, and Benezet and the Quakers formed the first abolition society – the number of people in comparable forms of forced labour throughout the world was something like 75 per cent. Today it is one-fifth of 1 per cent.

How exactly you get there, from those half-dozen individuals and their friends, is hard to say. The relative importance of any one of them, with their diverse and interdependent gifts, experiences and circumstances, is an even more fruitless question. It is enough to say, of Wilberforce, as of any of them, that he fought the greatest evil in the world of his day, and played his part in its defeat. Who could ever claim more?

Note on quotations

Spelling and punctuation have not changed a great deal in 200 years. The one big difference is that we use fewer capitals. I have modified quotations in this respect and in a few other insignificant ways too.

More unusually, I have taken the liberty of changing the tense and person of secondary quotations, when they have obviously been changed from the original. In Wilberforce's time it was normal to reword a speech from your point of view when you quoted it. If an MP said: 'The consequences of this bill will be disastrous and I am full of apprehensions for my constituents', the newspapers, more often than not, would quote him as saying: 'The consequences of this bill would be disastrous and he was full of apprehensions for his constituents.' This would go for whole speeches.

It is usual today to record such quotations verbatim, despite the fact that they do not repeat the original verbatim. What I have done is to reverse the rewording process, restoring as closely as possible the original, putting speeches back into the present tense and first person. The sense is unchanged; it is arguably a more accurate quotation; and it reads a lot more easily.

Members of the Clapham Sect

The names of the Clapham Sect get hideously complicated towards the end of this book, as the friends intermarried and named their sons after each other. So here is a glossary of the Clapham Sect.

Predecessors

John Thornton – Wealthy evangelical, director of the Bank of England.

Hannah Wilberforce – John Thornton's sister and Wilberforce's aunt. Lived with John in Clapham in later life.

First generation

Thomas Babington – Wilberforce's contemporary at Cambridge, and campaigner from the early days of the abolition campaign. Married Zachary Macaulay's sister.

Edward Eliot – MP and tenant of Henry Thornton. Brother-in-law and close friend of Pitt.

Thomas Gisborne – Wilberforce's contemporary at Cambridge, and campaigner from the early days of the abolition campaign. Married Thomas Babington's sister.

Charles Grant – MP and chairman of the East India Company's Court of Directors. Tenant of Henry Thornton.

Zachary Macaulay – Governor of the Sierra Leone Colony, founder of the Anti-Slavery Society and the *Anti-Slavery Monthly Reporter*. Married Hannah More's pupil Selina Mills.

James Stephen – Maritime lawyer and MP. Married Wilberforce's sister Sarah.

Henry Thornton – Son of John Thornton, MP and banker. Owner of Battersea Rise in Clapham. The architect of the Clapham Sect.

John Venn – Rector of Clapham, appointed by Henry Thornton.

Second generation

Thomas Gisborne Babington – Called just 'Tom' Babington in this book. Thomas Babington's son. A partner in the Sierra Leone Company with Zachary Macaulay.

Tom Babington – see above.

Thomas Babington Macaulay – Zachary Macaulay's son. Abolitionist MP, later a historian.

George Stephen – James Stephen's son. Founder of the Agency Committee and author of *Anti-Slavery Recollections*.

Marianne Thornton – Daughter of Henry Thornton.

Endnotes

Chapter 1 – The Journey

1 Equiano, Olaudah, *The Interesting Narrative of the Life of Olaudah Equiano, or Gustavus Vasa, the African*, London, 1789. Page 79
2 *The Interesting Narrative*. Page 82.
3 Wilberforce, Robert Isaac and Samuel William, *The Life of William Wilberforce*, John Murray, 1838. 5 vols series; Vol I, page 4.
4 Furneaux, Robert, *William Wilberforce*, Hamish Hamilton, 1974. Page 8. Also, *The Life of*. Vol I, page 5.
5 Walvin, James, *Black Ivory: A History of British Slavery*, Fontana, 1993. Page 39.
6 Turner, Steve, *Amazing Grace: John Newton, Slavery and the World's Most Enduring Song*, Lion, 2002. Page 93.
7 Tomkins, Stephen, *John Wesley: A Biography*, Lion, 2003. Page 176.
8 *John Wesley*. Page 176.
9 Benezet, Anthony, *Some Historical Account of Guinea… With an Inquiry into the Rise and Progress of the Slave Trade*, Philadelphia, 1771.
10 *The Life of*. Vol I, page 7. Also Harford, John S., *Recollections of William Wilberforce*, Longman, 1864. Page 198.
11 *The Life of*. Vol I, page 8.
12 *The Life of*. Vol I, page 7.
13 *The Life of*. Vol I, page 7.
14 *The Life of*. Vol I, page 9.
15 Letter 18 July 1834, printed in Clarkson, Thomas, *Strictures on a Life of William Wilberforce*, London, 1838. Page 7.
16 Cowper, William, *The Task*, Indypublish.com, 2002. Book 2.
17 Wesley, John, *Thoughts Upon Slavery*, London, 1774. Page 5§5.

Chapter 2 – Cambridge

1 *Some Historical Account of Guinea*. Appendix.
2 Stephen, George, *Antislavery Recollections*, London, 1854. Page 81.
3 *The Life of*. Vol I, pages 10–11. Also *Recollections of William Wilberforce*. Page 199.
4 *The Life of*. Vol I, page 11.
5 *Hansard: The Parliamentary History of England, from the Earliest Period to 1803*, T C Hansard, 1814. Vol 8, page 719.
6 *The Life of*. Vol I, pages 14, 16.
7 *The Life of*. Vol I, page 16.

Chapter 3 – Gambling and Government

1 Raphael, Ray, *The American Revolution: A People's History*, Profile Books. Pages 276–77.
2 Murray, Venetia, *High Society: A Social History of the Regency period, 1788–1830*, Viking, 1998. Page 163.

3 *The Life of*. Vol I, page 11. Also *Amazing Grace*. Page 127.
4 Wilberforce, Anna Maria (ed.), *Private Papers of William Wilberforce*, Unwin, 1897.
5 *The Life of*. Vol I, page 22.
6 Roscoe, E.S. and Clergue, Helen (eds.), *George Selwyn: His Letters and His Life*, London, 1899. Pages 224–25.
7 *The Life of*. Vol I, page 19.
8 Buxton, Travers, *William Wilberforce: The Story of a Great Crusade*, Religious Tract Society, 1933. Page 19. Also *The Life of*. Vol I, page 26.
9 *The Life of*, Vol I. pages 28–29.
10 *The Life of*. Vol I, page 23, 33.
11 *Black Ivory*. Page 16.
12 *The Life of*. Vol I, pages 43, 45.

Chapter 4 – True Christianity

1 Hochschild, Adam, *Bury the Chains*, Macmillan, 2005. Page 158.
2 *The Life of*. Vol I, page 48.
3 *The Life of*. Vol I, pages 48, 50.
4 *The Life of*. Vol I, page 30.
5 *The Life of*. Vol I, page 51.
6 *The Life of*. Vol I, page 54.
7 *The Life of*. Vol I, pages 48, 50. Also *Recollections of William Wilberforce*, page 203.
8 *The Life of*. Vol I, page 59.
9 *The Life of*. Vol I, page 57.
10 *The Life of*. Vol I, page 64.
11 Some gentlemen of St Christopher, *An Answer to the Reverend James Ramsay's Essay, on the Treatment and Conversion of Slaves, in the British Sugar Colonies*, St Christopher, 1784. Page 19.
12 *Recollections of William Wilberforce*. Pages 209–210.
13 Milner, Mary, *The Life of Isaac Milner*, London, 1842. Page 23. Also *The Life of*, Vol I, page 75.
14 Doddridge, Philip, *The Rise and Progress of Religion in the Soul*, London, 1745. Pages 2§5.
15 *Gentleman's Magazine*. Vols 55, 619–20. Also *The Life of*. Vol I, pages 78–79.
16 *The Life of*. Vol I, pages 79–80.
17 Sypher, Wylie, *Guinea's Captive Kings: British Anti-Slavery Literature in the XVIIIth Century*, Octagon, 1969. Page 16.
18 Clarkson, Thomas, *The History of the Rise, Progress, and Accomplishment of the Abolition of the African Slave-Trade*, London, 1808. Pages 1 and 210.

Chapter 5 – 'Oh God, Deliver Me From Myself!'

1 Cugoano, Ottobah, *Thoughts and Sentiments on the Evil and Wicked Traffic of the Slavery and Commerce of the Human Species*, London, 1787. Pages 9–10.

2 *The Life of*. Vol I, page 84.
3 *The Life of*. Vol I, page 88.
4 Hague, William, *William Pitt the Younger*, Harper Collins, 2004. Page 217.
5 *The Life of*. Vol I, page 95.
6 *The Life of*. Vol I, page 93..
7 *The Life of*. Vol I, page 96.
8 *The Life of*. Vol I, pages 100–01.
9 Wilberforce, William, *A Practical View of the Prevailing Religious System of Professed Christians, in the Higher and Middle Classes in this Country, Contrasted with Real Christianity*, London, 1811. Page 18.
10 *Letters of John Newton*, The Banner of Truth Trust, 1960. Page 60.
11 *A Practical View of the Prevailing Religious System*. Pages 205–206.
12 Jeffrey, David Lyle (ed.), *English Spirituality in the Age of Wesley*, Eerdmans, 1987. Pages 354–55.
13 *The Life of*. Vol I, page 107.
14 *The Life of*. Vol I, page 105.
15 *The Life of*. Vol I, pages 110, 119.

Chapter 6 – Mannacles and Manners
1 Ramsay, James, *An Essay on the Treatment and Conversion of Slaves*, 1784. Pages 59–61.
2 *The Life of*. Vol I, page 131.
3 *The Life of*. Vol I, page 145.
4 Letter 15 January 1787, quoted in *The Life of*. Vol I, page 149.
5 *Strictures on a Life of William Wilberforce*. Page 46.
6 *The Life of*. Vol I, page 141n.
7 *The Life of*. Vol I, page 151.
8 *The History of the Rise, Progress, and Accomplishment of the Abolition of the African Slave-Trade*. Pages 1, 251.
9 *The History of the Rise, Progress, and Accomplishment of the Abolition of the African Slave-Trade*. Page 252.
10 *The Life of*. Vol I, page 146.
11 *The Life of*. Vol I, page 136.
12 *The Life of*. Vol I, page 149.
13 *Gentleman's Magazine*. Vols 58, 62.
14 Wedgwood, Josiah, *Correspondance of Josiah Wedgwood*, Women's Printing Society, 1906. Page 56.
15 *The History of the Rise, Progress, and Accomplishment of the Abolition of the African Slave-Trade*. Pages 1, 472.
16 *The Life of*. Vol I, pages 160–61.

Chapter 7 – The Valley of the Shadow
1 Lambert, Sheila (ed.), *House of Commons Sessional Papers of the Eighteenth Century*, Scholarly Resources, 1975. Page 28.
2 *The Life of*. Vol I, page 170.
3 *Gentleman's Magazine*. Vols 58, 211, 311.

4 *Private Papers of William Wilberforce*. 20.
5 *Hansard*. Vol 27, page 598.
6 *The History of the Rise, Progress, and Accomplishment of the Abolition of the African Slave-Trade*. Pages 1, 553. Also *Hansard*. Vol 27, pages 643–64, 648.
7 *Gentleman's Magazine*. Vols 58, 407–49.
8 *Gentleman's Magazine*. Vol 408.
9 Beckford, William, *Remarks upon the Situation of Negroes in Jamaica*, London, 1788. Pages 52–53.
10 Norris, Robert, *A Short Account of the African Slave Trade*, Liverpool, 1788. Page 9.
11 Thorkelin, G.J., *An Essay on the Slave Trade*, London, 1788. Pages 28, 30.
12 Thicknesse, Philip, *Memoirs and Anecdotes of Philip Thicknesse, late Lieutenant Governor of Land Guard Fort and unfortunately father to George Touchet, Baron Audley*, London, 1788. 2 vols. Pages 279, 281.
13 *Gentleman's Magazine*. Vol 858.
14 *The Life of*. Vol I, page 191.

Chapter 8 – The Greatest Speech in History
1 *The American Revolution: A People's History*. Page 298.
2 *Eighteenth Century Literature: An Oxford Miscellany*, Oxford University Press, 1909. Page 130.
3 *The Life of*. Vol I, page 218.
4 *Hansard*. Vols 28, 45.
5 *Hansard*. Vol 45.
6 *Hansard*. Vol 55.
7 *Hansard*. Vol 49.
8 *Hansard*. Vol 60.
9 *Hansard*. Vol 63.
10 *Hansard*. Vol 68.
11 *The Life of*. Vol I, page 220.
12 Taken from www.brycchancarey.com
13 Stephen, Sir James, in *William Wilberforce*. Page 284.
14 *Hansard*. Vols 28, 78, 98.
15 *Bury the Chains*. Pages 161–62.

Chapter 9 – The Vote
1 *House of Commons Sessional Papers*. Page 297.
2 *Some Historical Account of Guinea*. Page 63.
3 *The Life of*. Vol I, pages 256–57.
4 *The Life of*. Vol I, page 228.
5 *The Life of*. Vol I, page 229.
6 *The Life of*. Vol I, page 240.
7 *The Life of*. Vol I, pages 238–40.
8 *The Life of*. Vol I, page 241.
9 *Hansard*. Vols 29, page 258.
10 *The History of the Rise, Progress, and Accomplishment of the Abolition of the African Slave-Trade*. Pages 2, 200.

11 *The Life of.* Vol I, page 282. Also
*The History of the Rise, Progress, and
Accomplishment of the Abolition of the African
Slave-Trade.* Pages 2, 198–99.
12 *The Life of.* Vol I, pages 296–97.
13 *The History of the Rise, Progress, and
Accomplishment of the Abolition of the African
Slave-Trade.* Pages 2, 209–10.
14 *The Life of.* Vol I, page 298.
15 *London Chronicle*, April 16–19 1791.
Page 373.
16 *Hansard*. Vol 29, page 278.
17 *Hansard*. Vol 29, page 281.
18 *Hansard*. Vol 29, pages 295, 303.
19 *Hansard*. Vol 29, page 354.

Chapter 10 – Fighting Back
1 *Black Ivory*. Page 160.
2 *The Life of.* Vol I, page 333.
3 *The Life of.* Vol I, page 333.
4 *Hansard*. Vol 29, page 1093.
5 *Bury the Chains*. Page 264.
6 *Gentleman's Magazine*. Vols 64, 1169.
7 *The Life of.* Vol I, page 341.
8 *Hansard*. Vols 30, 1070–71.
9 *Hansard*. Vols 1133–58
10 *The Life of.* Vol I, page 345.
11 *Hansard*. Vol 30, page 1236.
12 *Hansard*. Vol 30, pages 1284–86.

Chapter 11 – Collapse
1 *Some Historical Account of Guinea*.
2 *The Life of.* Vol I, pages 357–59.
3 *Hansard*. Vol 30, page 654.
4 *The Life of.* Vol II, page 11.
5 *Hansard*. Vol 30, pages 657–59.
6 *The Life of.* Vol II, page17.
7 *The Life of.* Vol II, pages 26–27.
8 *The Life of.* Vol II, page 40.
9 *Hansard*. Vol 30, page 1444.

Chapter 12 – In Opposition
1 *Thoughts and Sentiments on the Evil and
Wicked Traffic of the Slavery and Commerce of
the Human Species*. Page 11.
2 *The Life of.* Vol II, page 67.
3 *The Life of.* Vol II, pages 71–72.
4 *Hansard*. Vols 31, page 1328.
5 *The Life of.* Vol II, page 114.
6 *Hansard*. Vols 32, 737–40.
7 *Hansard*. Vol 844.
8 *The Life of.* Vol II, page 142.

Chapter 13 – The Doldrums
1 *Christian Observer*. Pages 3, 344.
2 *Hansard*. Vol 33, pages 252–53.
3 Edwards, Bryan, *An Historical Survey of the
French Colony in the Island of St Domingo*,

London, 1797. Pages 83–84.
4 *William Wilberforce*. Pages 42–43.
5 *Hansard*. Vol 33, page 574.
6 *William Wilberforce*. Page 165.
7 Coleridge, Samuel Taylor, *Poems*, edited by
John Beer, Dent, 1974.
8 *William Wilberforce*. Page 85.
9 *The Life of.* Vol II, pages 265–66.
10 *Hansard*. Vol 33, pages 1378, 1384.
11 *Hansard*. Vol 33, pages 1387–92.
12 *Hansard*. Vol 33, page 1404.

Chapter 14 – Quiet Time
1 Stedman, John, *Narrative of Five Years
Expedition Against the Revolted Negroes of
Surinam*. London, 1798. Vol II, Page 116.
2 *The Life of.* Vol II, page 312.
3 *Hansard*. Vol 34, page 529.
4 *Hansard*. Vol 34, page 529.
5 *Hansard*. Vol 34, page 540.
6 *Hansard*. Vol 34, pages 1101, 1110; Also *The
Life of.* Vol II. Page 340.
7 *Hansard*. Vol 35, page 116.
8 *Bury the Chains*. Page 316.
9 *The Life of.* Vol II, page 369.
10 *The Life of.* Vol III, page 33.
11 Stephen, James, *The Crisis of the Sugar
Colonies*, London, 1802. Page 165.
12 *The Life of.* Vol III, page 88.
13 *The Life of.* Vol III, page 165.
14 *The Life of.* Vol III, pages 168, 170.
15 *The Life of.* Vol III, page 181.
16 *Hansard*. Vol 3, page 673.
17 *The Life of.* Vol III, pages 212–15.
18 *The Life of.* Vol III, page 245.

Chapter 15 – Abolition
1 Falconbridge, Alexander, *An Account of the
Slave Trade on the Coast of Africa*, London,
1788. Page 27.
2 *The Life of.* Vol III, page 267–68.
3 *Hansard*. Vol 8, pages 665–69.
4 *The Life of.* Vol III, pages 293–94.
5 *Hansard*. Vol 8, pages 951, 954.
6 *Hansard*. Vol 8, pages 978–79.

**Chapter 16 – 'What Shall We Abolish
Next?'**
1 *Black Ivory*. Page 194.
2 *Hansard*. Vol 9, page 133.
3 *Amazing Grace*. Page 139.
4 *Hansard*. Vol 10, pages 125–28.
5 *Hansard*. Vol 10, pages 627–28
6 *The Life of.* Vol III, page 362.
7 *The Life of.* Vol III, page 470.
8 Forster, E.M., *Marianne Thornton*, Edward
Arnold, 1956. Pages 137–38.
9 *The Life of.* Vol III, page 406.

Chapter 17 – Bramber and Bengal
1 Bontemps, Arna (ed.), *Five Black Lives: The Autobiographies of Venture Smith, James Mars, William Grimes, The Rev. G.W. Offley and James L. Smith*, Wesleyan University Press, 1971. Page 5.
2 Mathieson, William L., *British Slavery and its Abolition 1823–1838*, Longmans, Green & Co., 1926. Page 21.
3 *The Life of*. Vol III, page 487.
4 Wilberforce, Robert Isaac and Samuel William, *The Correspondence of William Wilberforce*, John Murray, 1840. 2 vols series; vol II, page 209.
5 *William Wilberforce*. Page 316.
6 *The Life of*. Vol IV, page 106.
7 Howse, Ernest Marshall, *Saints in Politics: The 'Clapham Sect' and the Growth of Freedom*, George Allen & Unwin, 1953. Page 144.
8 *Bury the Chains*. Page 317.
9 *The Life of*. Vol IV, page 187.
10 *The Life of*. Vol IV, page 224.

Chapter 18 – The Enemy Within
1 *House of Commons Sessional Papers*. Pages 69, 134.
2 *Bury the Chains*. Page 320.
3 *The Correspondence of William Wilberforce*. Vol I, page 358.
4 Briggs, Asa, *William Cobbett*, OUP, 1967. Page 31. Also Derry, John (ed.), *Cobbett's England*, Folio Society, London, 1968. Page 100.
5 *Hansard*. Vol 36, pages 1246–247.
6 *The Life of*. Vol IV, page 307.
7 *Saints in Politics*.
8 *Cobbett's England*. Page 97.
9 *William Wilberforce*. Page 385.

Chapter 19 – The Last Crusade
1 *Anti-Slavery Monthly Reporter*. Vol II, page 388–89.
2 *British Slavery and its Abolition*. Page 23.
3 *Antislavery Recollections*. Page 54.
4 *Marianne Thornton*. Page 136.
5 *Antislavery Recollections*. Page 76.
6 *Hansard*. Vol 8, page 712.
7 *Bury the Chains*. Page 324.
8 *Hansard*. Vol 9, page 265.
9 *British Slavery and its Abolition*. Page 134.
10 *British Slavery and its Abolition*. Page 147.
11 *William Wilberforce*. Page 419.
12 Heyrick, Elizabeth, *Immediate, not Gradual Emancipation*, Leicester, 1824. Pages 17, 20, 23.
13 *Marianne Thornton*. Page 130.
14 *Anti-Slavery Monthly Reporter*. Vol II, page 153.
15 *Antislavery Recollections*. Page 53.
16 *The Life of*. Vol V, page 276.
17 *Antislavery Recollections*. Page 120.

Chapter 20 – The Chimes of Freedom
1 Bleby, Henry, *Death Struggles of Slavery*, London, 1853. Page 114.
2 *Death Struggles*. Page 105.
3 *The Times*, quoted in *Strictures on a Life of William Wilberforce*. Page 50.
4 *Strictures on a Life of William Wilberforce*. Pages 121–22; *Anti-Slavery Monthly Reporter*. Vol II, page 241.
5 *The Life of*. Vol V, page 318; Also *William Wilberforce*. Page 443.
6 *Marianne Thornton*. Page 130. Also *The Life of*. Vol V, page 326.
7 *Hansard*. Vol 31.
8 *Private Papers of William Wilberforce*. 268.
9 *Private Papers of William Wilberforce*. 264.
10 *Recollections of William Wilberforce*. Page 23
11 *Death Struggles*. Page 291.
12 *Private Papers of William Wilberforce*. 265.
13 *Private Papers of William Wilberforce*. 281; Also *William Wilberforce*. Page 440; Also *The Life of*. Vol V, page 328.
14 *The Life of*. Vol V, page 328.
15 *The Life of*. Vol V, page 373.

Chapter 21 – The Long Run
1 *The Interesting Narrative*. Pages 2, 13–16
2 Hazlitt, William, *The Spirit of the Age*, London, 1825.
3 Williams, Eric, *Capitalism and Slavery*, University of North Carolina Press, 1944. Pages 181–182.
4 *Cobbett's England*. Page 103.
5 *Bury the Chains*. Page 248
6 Holland, Margaret Jean, Viscountess Knutsford, *The Life and Letters of Zachary Macaulay*, Edward Arnold, 1900. Page 202.
7 Trevelyan, G.M., *The History of England*, Longmans, 1945. Page 599.
8 *British Slavery and its Abolition*. Page 23.
9 *The Life of*. Vol V, page 376.
10 *Marianne Thornton*. Page 139.

Bibliography of works cited in this book

Bontemps, Arna (ed.), *Five Black Lives: The Autobiographies of Venture Smith, James Mars, William Grimes, The Rev. G. W. Offley, and James L. Smith*, Wesleyan University Press, 1971.

Beckford, William, *Remarks upon the Situation of Negroes in Jamaica*, London, 1788.

Benezet, Anthony, *Some Historical Account of Guinea... With an Inquiry into the Rise and Progress of the Slave Trade*, Philadelphia, 1771.

Bleby, Henry, *Death Struggles of Slavery*, London, 1853.

Briggs, Asa, *William Cobbett*, OUP, 1967.

Buxton, Travers, *William Wilberforce: The Story of a Great Crusade*, Religious Tract Society, 1933.

Clarkson, Thomas, *An Essay on the Slavery and Commerce of the Human Species*, London, 1786.

Clarkson, Thomas, *The History of the Rise, Progress, and Accomplishment of the Abolition of the African Slave-Trade*, London, 1808.

Clarkson, Thomas, *Strictures on a Life of William Wilberforce*, London, 1838.

Coleridge, Samuel Taylor, *Poems*, edited by John Beer, Dent, 1974.

Coupland, R., *The British Anti-Slavery Movement*, 1933.

Cowper, William, *The Task*, Indypublish.com, 2002.

Cugoano, Ottobah, *Thoughts and Sentiments on the Evil and Wicked Traffic of the Slavery and Commerce of the Human Species*, London, 1787.

Derry, John (ed.), *Cobbett's England*, Folio Society, 1968.

Doddridge, Philip, *The Rise and Progress of Religion in the Soul*, London, 1745.

Edwards, Bryan, *An Historical Survey of the French Colony in the Island of St Domingo*, London, 1797.

Equiano, Olaudah, *The Interesting Narrative of the Life of Olaudah Equiano, or Gustavus Vasa, the African*, London, 1789.

Falconbridge, Alexander, *An Account of the Slave Trade on the Coast of Africa*, London, 1788.

Forster, E. M., *Marianne Thornton*, Edward Arnold, 1956.

Furneaux, Robert, *William Wilberforce*, Hamish Hamilton, 1974.

Hague, William, *William Pitt the Younger*, Harper Collins, 2004.

Hansard: *The Parliamentary History of England, from the Earliest Period to 1803*, T. C. Hansard, 1814.

Harford, John S., *Recollections of William Wilberforce*, Longman, 1864.

Hazlitt, William, *The Spirit of the Age*, London, 1825.

Heyrick, Elizabeth, *Immediate, not Gradual Emancipation*, Leicester, 1824.

Hochschild, Adam, *Bury the Chains*, Macmillan, 2005.

Holland, Margaret Jean, Viscountess Knutsford, *The Life and Letters of Zachary Macaulay*, Edwin Arnold, 1900.

Howse, Ernest Marshall, *Saints in Politics: The 'Clapham Sect' and the Growth of Freedom*, George Allen & Unwin, 1953.

Jeffrey, David Lyle (ed.), *English Spirituality in the Age of Wesley*, Eerdmans, 1987.

Lambert, Sheila (ed.), *House of Commons Sessional Papers of the Eighteenth Century*, Scholarly Resources, 1975.

Mathieson, William L., *British Slavery and its Abolition 1823–1838*, Longmans, Green & Co., 1926.

Milner, Mary, *The Life of Isaac Milner*, London, 1842.

Murray, Venetia, *High Society: A Social History of the Regency Period, 1788–1830*, Viking, 1998.

Newton, John, *Letters of John Newton*, The Banner of Truth Trust, 1960.

Norris, Robert, *A Short Account of the African Slave Trade*, Liverpool, 1788.

Ramsay, James, *An Essay on the Treatment and Conversion of Slaves*, St Christopher, 1784.

Raphael, Ray, *The American Revolution: A People's History*, Profile Books, 2001.

Roscoe, E.S. and Clergue, Helen (ed.), *George Selwyn: His Letters and His Life*, London, 1899.

Some gentlemen of St Christopher, *An Answer to the Reverend James Ramsay's Essay, on the Treatment and Conversion of Slaves, in the British Sugar Colonies*, St Christopher, 1784.

Stedman, John, *Narrative of Five Years Expedition Against the Revolted Negroes of Surinam*, London, 1798.

Stephen, George, *Antislavery Recollections*, London, 1854.

Stephen, James, *The Crisis of the Sugar Colonies*, London, 1802.

Stoughton, John, *William Wilberforce*, Hodder and Stoughton, 1880.

Sypher, Wylie, *Guinea's Captive Kings: British Anti-Slavery Literature in the XVIIIth Century*, Octagon, 1969.

Thicknesse, Philip, *Memoirs and Anecdotes of Philip Thicknesse, late Lieutenant Governor of Land Guard Fort and unfortunately father to George Touchet, Baron Audley*, London, 1788.

Thorkelin, G. J., *An Essay on the Slave Trade*, London, 1788.

Tomkins, Stephen, *John Wesley: A Biography*, Lion, 2003.

Trevelyan, G. M., *The History of England*, Longmans, 1945.

Turner, Steve, *Amazing Grace: John Newton, Slavery and the World's Most Enduring Song*, Lion, 2002.

Walvin, James, *Black Ivory: A History of British Slavery*, Fontana, 1993.

Wedgwood, Josiah, *Correspondance of Josiah Wedgwood*, Women's Printing Society, 1906.

Wesley, John, *Thoughts Upon Slavery*, London, 1774.

Wilberforce, Anna Maria (ed.), *Private Papers of William Wilberforce*, T. Fisher Unwin, 1897.

Wilberforce, Robert Isaac and Samuel Wilberforce, *The Correspondence of William Wilberforce*, 2 vols, John Murray, 1840.

Wilberforce, Robert Isaac and Samuel William, *The Life of William Wilberforce*, 5 vols, John Murray, 1838.

Wilberforce, William, *A Practical View of the Prevailing Religious System of Professed Christians, in the Higher and Middle Classes in this Country, Contrasted with Real Christianity*, London, 1797.

Williams, Eric, *Capitalism and Slavery*, University of North Carolina Press, 1944.

Eighteenth Century Literature: An Oxford miscellany, Oxford University Press, 1909.

Letters of John Newton, The Banner of Truth Trust, 1960.

Newspapers etc.

Anti-Slavery Monthly Reporter

Barbados Gazette

Christian Observer

Cobbett's Annual Political Register

Gentleman's Magazine

London Evening Post

Public Advertiser

Index